THE STORY

OF

THE ILIAD

E.T. OWEN

Published by
BRISTOL CLASSICAL PRESS (U.K.)
General Editor: John H. Betts

and

BOLCHAZY-CARDUCCI PUBLISHERS (U.S.A.)
By Arrangement with Irwin Publishing

1989

Cover by Thom Kapheim
Achilles, Priam, Corpse of Hector

1989

U.K.

BRISTOL CLASSICAL PRESS
226 North Street
Bedminster
Bristol BS3 1JD

ISBN 1-85399-056-6

U.S.A.

BOLCHAZY-CARDUCCI
PUBLISHERS
1000 Brown Street, Unit 101
Wauconda, IL 60084

ISBN 0-86516-235-2

British Library Cataloguing in Publication Data

Owen, T.E.
    The story of the Iliad — 2nd ed.
    1. Epic poetry in Greek. Homer. Iliad—Critical studies
    I. Title
    883'.01

ὣς ἔφαθ’, οἱ δ’ἄρα πάντες ἀκὴν ἐγένοντο σιωπῇ,
κηληθμῷ δ’ἔσχοντο κατὰ μέγαρα σκιόεντα.

INTRODUCTION

THE clumsy-sounding title I have given this book defines its purpose with fair exactness. I am shutting out all questions about the Iliad except one—what makes it, just as it stands, a well-told story. That it is so there can be no reasonable doubt. The Iliad as an artistic success does not abide our question; for centuries its story, as the poem tells it, has held its listeners spell-bound. I wish, by following the way it is told, to see, if I can, how it works its spell.

With the Homeric controversy, then, this book has nothing to do. No one denies that the Iliad we possess, in whatever circumstances and from whatever sources it was put together, was designed to be taken as a single poem, as a continuous story. It is this poem only that I am talking about, not its history nor its authorship, but itself, and with a view, not to establishing, but to accounting for, its artistic integrity. In doing so I am not presuming to criticize the critics; I do not imagine I am disproving or discrediting any theories about the origin and growth of the poem; I am simply taking a position further along the line, so to speak, at the point, whenever it was, that the Iliad attained its present form. For, after all, this is the poem that chiefly concerns the student of literature. Historically we have in our Iliad the acknowledged master piece of masterpieces, the poem that first taught the world how to tell a story greatly; and when the Homeric question is settled once for all and the poem finally disintegrated into its original component parts by mutual agreement of the separatist critics, we shall be faced with exactly the same literary question as we now are—on what artistic principles has it all been put together to produce this astonishing result? There is no poem, therefore, more worthy to be studied as a work of art, and no one need have misgivings that he is somehow cheating himself if he treats it for this purpose as one and indivisible. Here, and nowhere else—not in any of the "originals" that have been disentangled from it—is the story that has some claim to be regarded as the most famous story in the world.

The book has grown out of lectures delivered to students of University College and Trinity College in Toronto, and it is largely their interest that has emboldened me to seek a wider audience. But it is still a student audience I am addressing, and my aim is limited to illustrating by an object lesson how to study the poem as a poem. It must not be thought that I regard all this explanation as necessary to enable a reader to *enjoy* the Iliad. It is for those who are studying it as a work of literary art and therefore want to find out why they enjoy it. "In studying a work of art, we should proceed as in studying a work of nature: after delighting in the effect, we should try to ascertain what are the *means* by which the effect is produced," says George Henry Lewes. That is exactly what I am trying to do; I am examining the under-side of the tapestry in an endeavour to detect by what workmanship such a lastingly impressive picture has been wrought. Needless to say, my findings must often be wrong; to unravel the inner secrets of great artistry is doubtless too delicate a task for anyone's fingers. But to attempt it is the proper business of a student of literature; for until he is studying the artistry of the poem—by what means it produces its effect—he is not studying the poem; all else that he does is, so far as the poem is concerned, preparation for studying it.

This sounds an ambitious undertaking, but indeed all I have done is to make a running commentary on the poem, going through it in order, book by book, picking up the contribution of each part or incident to the emotional effect of the whole. For what marks the born story-teller is that he knows how to write his story in the hearts of his auditors; he knows that it is their feelings that are the real events of his plot, and he invents and arranges what his *dramatis personae* say and do with a view to creating those events. It is emotional continuity and progress he aims at more than logical and factual. And that is, I believe, why the Iliad, for all our critical objections and denials, still leaves on us the impression of unity, of artistic integrity. The story wanders and pauses and digresses, but its emotional march never falters; it makes its way through and by the very obstacles that would seem to interrupt its course. We are swept forward, willy-nilly, in the wake of a great imagination.

I may be taken to task for seeming to ascribe so much conscious planning to the constructor of the Iliad. Robert Bridges has a good word on the subject: "All this explanation", he says concerning his own analysis of the story of Priam's journey in Bk. XXIV, "seems to imply more elaboration and ingenuity than Homer is usually credited with; but logical explanations are necessarily more elaborate than the instinctive rightnesses which they explain." Attempts at analysing literary workmanship always provoke such questioning. Did the author do these things intentionally? Did he think them out like this? It is difficult to draw a hard and fast line between deliberation and instinct on the part of a poet; for much of his deliberation is instinctive. His imagination is kindled by the tale he is telling, and his technical mastery responds instinctively to the demands his imagination makes on it. He perhaps may be said to feel his way through his story rather than deliberately think his way, but his trained artistic instinct falls naturally into the appropriate expression of his feelings, appropriate, that is, to the medium he is using. Practised in the methods of contemporary story-telling, Homer deliberately, no doubt, used its artifices to string his poem along with sufficient skill for his simple purpose of holding the immediate interest of his auditors and sustaining their continuous interest, but in the process his own profound imaginative response shaped them to express and satisfy it. But, however that may be, I am not concerned to probe into the poet's intentions; I am simply recording effects, and trying to determine by what means they are obtained.

THE STORY OF THE ILIAD

BOOK I

THE first verse announces the title and subject of the poem and also makes a claim. By calling upon the goddess (*i.e.* the Muse) to sing the wrath the poet is saying in effect "This is the true story of the Wrath of Achilles." The Muse is, as it were, the personification of all past poetry, of all the songs that preserve the record of the past, and in presenting himself as her mouthpiece he is asserting his claim to knowledge of the traditions and assuring his hearers that his account is the true one. "The *aoidos*, Homer or Hesiod, does not claim that he is the sole author of his poetry. He is only telling over again an old tale of 'true things' taught him by the Muses, the daughters of Memory."[1]

How far this claim is to be taken literally—whether the poem is the elaboration of a well-known story or a new story worked into the legend of the Trojan War—it is impossible to say, nor does it matter. A heroic story is always about famous men in connection with famous events; that is, it is part of what is already known; it is taken from, or put into, history or legend, and always purports to be true. So here, while Homer's audience may conceivably not have heard of the wrath of Achilles, his name would at once set the story announced in its proper environment, and they would instinctively supply the required background. At any rate, the magnification of the theme, we may be sure, was new, the

[1] J. A. K. Thomson: *Studies in the Odyssey*, p. 185.

3

big scale on which the figures and events were presented, and the consequent psychological elaboration this necessarily involved.

Those who are eagerly looking for traces of an older poem inadvertently left behind in the present Iliad point out that the verses immediately succeeding (2-5) give an inadequate account of the story that is actually told. This objection, quite apart from its questionable validity, is irrelevant. For the purpose of the description is not so much to summarize the contents of the poem as to advertise the kind of story to which the audience are invited to listen. They are promised a tale full of fighting and slayings, assured it is "a brave and noble song" of the sort they like. The value of the statement otherwise is mainly emotional. As the first word Μῆνιν ("Wrath"), besides focusing our thoughts, coloured the imagination at once with the appropriate hue, the impression is immediately deepened by the vague images of death which follow. The verses give a far view, glimpsed for an instant, and therefore indistinct, of dreadful things to come; the curtain is lifted momentarily upon the future, and this sight of the field with birds and dogs about the heaps of slain supplies the emotional background against which, accordingly, we watch the story rise.

For at once the story begins to move. The quarrel is to be the starting-point, and to the quarrel the poet immediately turns. Without more ado he concentrates the attention on the incident from which his story is to issue. The occasion of the quarrel is set forth in three brief scenes—the rejection by Agamemnon of Chryses' supplication, Chryses praying to Apollo beside the sea, and the god moving in his might down from the mountain against the Achaean camp. The most interesting feature here, besides the speed with which the poet gets down to business, is the immediate introduction of the dramatic method in narrative. We are not so much hearing the story told as seeing it happen. Aristotle says[1]: "Homer is the only poet who understands the narrator's place in a poem. He tells as little as possible in his own person. Other poets keep themselves on the scene throughout, and briefly and seldom represent the action as taking place. Homer, with little prelude, leaves the stage to his men and women, all with characters of their own." That is exactly what is done here. Homer merely sets the scene, puts his persons into it, and leaves it to them, being what they are, to carry the action forward; and we get to know them from what they do and say. Agamemnon comes before us with a characterizing gesture, which, to start with, prejudices us against him: in defiance of the unanimous feeling of the whole army, he rejects with rough threats Chryses' supplication, and so brings immediate calamity upon his people. Achilles, on the other hand, makes his entrance as the champion of the welfare of the army; with no personal motive, but simply from a disinterested anxiety for the common good, he initiates the action which, as we know, is somehow to bring trouble on himself. Thus we enter upon the quarrel scene with our sympathies so far in favour of Achilles and against Agamemnon.

The chief purpose of the very full development of this scene, we may judge, was to establish firmly the character of these men, and especially of Achilles. We are not to see Achilles again till the ninth book; therefore, since his wrath

---

[1] Poetics 1460a.

is the formative motive of the poem, a deep and lasting impression must be made. The poet does not describe Achilles' character, nor indeed say anything about him. We know him merely by what he does and says here and now, and it is the poet's business so to shape the progress of the quarrel that his words and his acts will reveal him as the poet wishes us to see him. It is the dramatist's method of projecting a personality inadvertently as it were in the course of creating an exciting incident. His first speech (59-67) is as impersonal as his motive, which is dramatically right as impressing the point that his forwardness in summoning the fateful assembly is entirely disinterested. The motive is, the poet tells us, a divine prompting, Hera's pity for the Danaans working in the mind of Achilles. The first personal touch comes in his reply to Calchas's appeal for protection—the ready self-confidence of his assurance:

οὔ τις ἐμεῦ ζῶντος καὶ ἐπὶ χθονὶ δερκομένοιο
σοὶ κοίλης παρὰ νηυσὶ βαρείας χεῖρας ἐποίσει
συμπάντων Δαναῶν, οὐδ᾽ ἢν Ἀγαμέμνονα εἴπῃς.

(88-90)

("No one while I live and see the light shall lay violent hands upon you, of all the Danaans, not even if you name Agamemnon.")

Nor was there any call for Achilles to put himself forward after Agamemnon's reply to Calchas (106-120). Agamemnon had not addressed himself to him, nor made any comment on his support of Calchas, nor, for all his fury against the prophet, had he threatened him. Achilles might at least have waited, one feels, to see if any of the others would reply to Agamemnon's unreasonable demand for immediate reparation. But Achilles waits for no man to act for him. It becomes abundantly clear that he regards himself as the most important man in the army. Headlong and tactless, he takes on himself the full responsibility of what he has started. He does not see that the diplomatic thing for the moment is to save Agamemnon's face, as no doubt Nestor or Odysseus would have done, but bluntly tells him that what he demands is impossible, and the sudden gratuitous insult—φιλοκτεανώτατε πάντων (122), "greediest of all men"—flashes his temperament upon us and prepares for the outburst that follows Agamemnon's deliberately provocative reply.

The crucial point in the quarrel is Agamemnon's decision to take the *geras* of Achilles himself, and to account for his coming to this decision is the artistic motive that shapes these speeches. A long history of mutual exasperation is skilfully touched in to support for the imagination the bitterness of the present quarrel. For Achilles' φιλοκτεανώτατε πάντων, we learn, is based partly upon a store of old grievances (163-168), and Agamemnon's words (176-177) equally reveal a long resentment against his arrogant vassal, and suggest that Achilles has not borne those past grievances as patiently as he himself made out. At any rate, the two men plainly dislike each other, and it only needed such an occasion as this to bring their antipathy to a head.

Agamemnon speaks with cold deliberation, declaring that he sees through Achilles' clumsy attempt to exalt himself at his expense. He announces that, if the Achaeans do not choose to acquiesce in his demand, he will simply use his authority and take the *geras* of one of his subordinates— "yours or Ajax's or that of Odysseus" (138), he says with elaborate carelessness. The cool superior tone is obvious even to a reader. Then, postponing this minor matter for future consideration, as if the principle were settled, he turns to the business of getting Chryseis off.

The man who could not hold back that angry exclamation at Agamemnon's simple demand for compensation will certainly not sit down under this. We turn our eyes eagerly toward Achilles, expecting now some violent retort; and we are not disappointed. He is all on fire in an instant at the bare suggestion of such an outrage on his rights, and the passionate side of his nature is at once and fully established. We see that in anger he is absolutely unrestrained and that, when he hates, all other considerations are thrown to the winds. Before the whole army he declares that Agamemnon is a leader unworthy of confidence, and all but calls upon the Achaeans to renounce his authority. He ends by announcing his determination to go home at once.

And so Agamemnon is goaded to take the fatal step. The thing has come to a head between him and Achilles. His authority is challenged, and he resolves to show who is master.

> ὡς ἔμ' ἀφαιρεῖται Χρυσηΐδα Φοῖβος Ἀπόλλων,
> τὴν μὲν ἐγὼ σὺν νηΐ τ' ἐμῇ καὶ ἐμοῖς ἑτάροισι
> πέμψω, ἐγὼ δέ κ' ἄγω Βρισηΐδα καλλιπάρῃον
> αὐτὸς ἰὼν κλισίηνδε, τὸ σὸν γέρας, ὄφρ' ἐῢ εἰδῇς
> ὅσσον φέρτερός εἰμι σέθεν, στυγέῃ δὲ καὶ ἄλλος
> ἶσον ἐμοὶ φάσθαι καὶ ὁμοιωθήμεναι ἄντην.

(182-187)

("Since from me Phoebus Apollo takes away Chryseis, her will I send with my ship and my comrades, but I will go myself to your tent and take Briseis, your *geras*, that you may understand how much stronger I am than you, and that another also may fear to match words with me and face me as an equal.")

Now what will Achilles do? Expectation is breathless, and the poet holds it in suspense for a few lines:

> Ὡς φάτο· Πηλεΐωνι δ' ἄχος γένετ', ἐν δέ οἱ ἦτορ
> στήθεσσιν λασίοισι διάνδιχα μερμήριξεν,
> ἢ ὅ γε φάσγανον ὀξὺ ἐρυσσάμενος παρὰ μηροῦ
> τοὺς μὲν ἀναστήσειεν, ὁ δ' Ἀτρεΐδην ἐναρίζοι,
> ἠε χόλον παύσειεν ἐρητύσειέ τε θυμόν.

(188-192)

("Thus he spoke, and grief struck the heart of Achilles, and he stood a moment pondering whether to break up the assembly and slay the son of Atreus or to stop his wrath and restrain his feelings.")

And as he is in act of drawing his sword, Athena appears to him and bids him desist.

One need look no further than the exigencies of the story for an explanation of this divine intervention. The taking of Briseis is the cause of the Wrath; therefore Achilles must suffer her to be taken. But that he should do so imperils at the outset the impression of the fierce and overmastering pride which the story requires him to possess and which he has already so forcibly displayed. Imagine the scene without the intrusion of the goddess: Agamemnon announces that he will do the incredible thing and take Achilles' prize; we see Achilles' hand fly to his sword; it is almost out of the scabbard, and then, after a moment's pause, he thrusts it back, and does nothing more than pour out further abuse on Agamemnon and declare his intention to withdraw from the fighting. By shifting the responsibility to the goddess the poet seeks to avoid, or at least diminish, this forcible-feeble effect, and allows us to retain our original impression of Achilles in the face of a submissiveness that is in itself out of character. His own scorn of his apparent pusillanimity, as expressed later (231-232), helps too to preserve the impression.

We are perhaps inclined to interpret Achilles' conduct in terms of disciplined armies and fighting for one's country, and so condemn it too much and too soon. It is not till Bk. IX that he puts himself entirely in the wrong. Whatever may have been the exact position of Agamemnon in regard to the other chieftains, Achilles' right to withdraw never seems to be questioned, even by Agamemnon, and there is no suggestion that he is liable to any penalty for his defection. On the contrary, it is taken for granted that he is the injured party and that it is Agamemnon who must make amends. His action apparently goes beyond his rights, and releases Achilles from further obligation. Nestor, eager only to calm them down, puts the case mildly, it is true, but he presses with more urgency upon Agamemnon than upon Achilles to yield (275-284).

It is interesting to observe that Nestor, unlike Agamemnon and Achilles, is formally introduced (247-252). The poet does not expect his audience to know about him, which suggests that the prominent part he plays in the story was an invention of the poet's. Homer needed as an agent in his story a man of reputed wisdom, to whose advice the leaders are inclined to listen, and took the opportunity to enrich his poem with this comico-pathetic figure of experienced old age. "The humour of story-telling," says Pope, "so natural in old men is always marked by Homer in the speeches of Nestor; the apprehension that their age makes them contemptible puts them upon repeating the brave deeds of their youth." Thus

he is a handy device in a poem which aims at gathering
together as many incidental stories as possible. They are told
not just for their own sakes, but have a dramatic function as
revealing a personality; the telling of them gives the additional
pleasure of amusement at the portraiture.

The poet promised at the beginning that in the tale of
the dire consequences of Achilles' wrath the end was to be
in accordance with the purpose of Zeus—Διὸς δ'ἐτελείετο βουλή
(5)—and so having pictured the quarrel and the cause of
the wrath, he next contrives a means of making clear what
the purpose of Zeus was in regard to the matter. So far as
the machinery of the poem is concerned, Thetis comes to
Achilles in order that she may carry the story to Olympus
and thus put us in a position to learn the plan that governs
the poem. But, as always, the poet covers up his mechanical
purpose by making it serve also dramatic ends. The scene
of her coming brings out a new fact about Achilles: he is
fated to die young, and he knows it, 'and for this fate his
unquestioned supremacy in glory was to be the compensation.
In the loss of his *geras* he sees himself bereft of the honour
for which he has devoted his life. This thought brings a note
of pathos, if not yet of tragedy, into his plight, which is
surely strengthened by associating it with his goddess mother.
The shortness of his life seems accentuated through being
mourned by an immortal mother; her feeling toward him is
dominated by this one dreadful realization, as a human
mother's would be if she knew her child had but a few days
to live. In fact, that is Thetis's artistic role in the poem—to
bring with her when she comes the thought of Achilles'
approaching death. Three times the point is stressed in this
book, so that even an audience at first hearing could hardly

fail to mark it—first by Achilles' complaint (352-356), then in Thetis's reply to his appeal (414-418), and again by Thetis when she makes her supplication to Zeus (505).

Her mission to Olympus is postponed to allow of an interruption in the narrative while the poet describes the restoration of Chryseis and so winds up the business of the pestilence.[1] The pestilence was invented just to create the occasion for the quarrel and now that it has done its work he formally dismisses the subject. Thus what may be called the first movement of the book is rounded off and completed. We have seen the pestilence come, we have seen its repercussions in the assembly scene, and now we see the deed that caused it being undone, marked by Chryses unpraying his former prayer (451-456). The account closes (467) with festivity and singing, the coming of night, and sleep, as does the second movement of the book (595-611). These little formal points are worth noting because it is such technical niceties that give a poem the cadence and finish which distinguish great writing. They are the large scale counter-

---

[1] But why it should be postponed for as much as twelve days it is hard to see. It may be that the poet simply wished to lengthen the time of Achilles' absence beyond the four days covered by the events of Bks. II-XXII, and certainly the picture of Achilles beside his ships (488-492) "fretting his heart out and longing for the battle-cry and the fighting" must refer to the whole time of waiting, not just to that required for the voyage to Chrysa and back which seems to have been no more than an overnight journey. It may be noted that again in Bk. XXIV twelve days are jumped by a similar simple *fiat* before the gods intervene on behalf of Hector's body, and again all that we know of the twelve days is what Achilles is doing and feeling. It is one of the many parallels between the last book and the first. But it looks as if in this instance Bk. I had been made to conform with Bk. XXIV, and not *vice versa*, for what Achilles did in the twelve-day interval there is a vital link in the action, whereas here it is not: which is interesting.

parts of the subtle harmonies of vowel and consonant sounds which without obtruding themselves upon the attention make great words live for ever in the memory.

Returning from this excursion, we pick up again the new interest to which the poet set us looking forward before he turned aside, *viz.,* Thetis's promise to put Achilles' prayer before Zeus. The scene between Thetis and Zeus is, as I have said, the poet's dramatic way of revealing his main design to his audience. He does not reveal it fully but gives just enough to face the expectation in the right direction. He fixes our eyes on a point in the future so that with this in view we can watch events shaping towards it. The device is obviously very helpful in a poem that plans to include a great variety of incident. We see whatever he chooses to relate with that particular terminus in view, see all the intervening events as leading to the promised result. The shape which the poet is imposing on his diverse material he thus makes us progressively impose for ourselves; we place the incidents as they occur in relation to a certain known end, and follow the poet's plan by knowing in advance what it is. Here the goal of our expectations is set as far as the defeat of the Achaeans as a consequence of Achilles' withdrawal. We do not know how it will be worked out, but the general direction of our interest is focused on the coming defeat.

When Thetis makes her appeal, Zeus, reluctantly consenting, expresses his fear of trouble with Hera over the matter, which in a story means there is going to be trouble; and so when Zeus goes to join the other gods we have our cue of interest; and at once ·Hera begins to play her expected part. The scene is amusing and lifelike and lively, but it is also functional; for in showing that there is opposition on

Olympus to the βουλὴ Διός, he leads us to expect that something will come of it, that there will be attempts to thwart his purpose; that is, he makes room in his poem for digressions and interruptions in the story of Achilles' wrath. In the words of Bury[1], "One of the principal functions of the gods who play such a large part in the Iliad was to provide devices for delaying the movement which conducts from Agamemnon's repulse of Chryses to the deaths of Patroclus and Hector." Also by the entrances and exits of the gods he can warn his hearers what the poem is doing, label one portion as a digression, or announce a return to the main theme.

But no one, while reading this wrangle on Olympus, thinks of its practical purpose; the scene carries itself, justifies itself, by its own inherent liveliness. It is the strength of the Iliad that the poet never forgets that he must amuse and interest always. Information is disguised as an event to be enjoyed for its own sake. The scene is pleasing, too, as providing variation of interest and variation of tone. It is clear throughout the Iliad that Homer knew by experience that constant variety of topic was necessary to keep the attention of his audience alive and fresh. The very shifting of the scene wakens the interest and rests the attention by diverting it to new objects. Variation in tone is still more necessary, and undoubtedly part of the function of the gods in the Iliad is to supply some measure of comic relief. It is remarkable that the first note of comedy in the poem comes in the first words spoken by Zeus (518 ff.). Thus, besides leading us to expect the next incident, and therefore making it imaginatively necessary, his speech sets the tone for it, prepares us to listen to

[1] *Cambridge Ancient History*, Vol. II, c. XVIII, p. 499.

what follows in the right spirit, brings us down, as we may say, from earth to heaven.

"The theme is an Olympian quarrel," says Sheppard, "the heavenly counterpart of the tragic quarrel between Achilles and Agamemnon. Like most scenes in Olympus it is amusing, graceful, irreverent, and of infinitely less importance than the tragedies of mortal heroes. Zeus and Hera are the disputants. The lame and famous blacksmith is the Nestor, who in this affair succeeds in restoring every one to good humour."[1]

The correspondence imparts to this light-hearted scene a touch of parody, which underlines its want of seriousness. Zeus, threatening Hera, borrows the form of Agamemnon's threat to Chryses, and, for all the added weight he gives it, there is no question which sounds the more dangerous. Hephaestus begins his appeal for amity in terms similar to those with which Nestor began his.[2] But the return of motif has also a structural value; it signals to the ear the close of a canto by completing musically a pattern of events. It helps too that this quarrel comes to nothing, has no consequences; it brings itself to an end, dissolving harmlessly in a burst of laughter, and, like the previous set of events, after feasting and music, is rounded with sleep. Here again, then, is the art that conceals art; what is functional pleases, and what

---

[1] *Pattern of the Iliad*, p. 22.

[2] *Cf.* l. 28, μή νύ τοι οὐ χραίσμῃ σκῆπτρον καὶ στέμμα θεοῖο.
with l. 566, μή νύ τοι οὐ χραίσμωσιν ὅσοι θεοί εἰσ᾽ ἐν Ὀλύμπῳ.
And ll. 254-7, ὢ πόποι, ἦ μέγα πένθος Ἀχαΐδα γαῖαν ἱκανει·
ἦ κεν γηθήσαι Πρίαμος Πριάμοιό τε παῖδες
ἄλλοι τε Τρῶες μέγα κεν κεχαροίατο θυμῷ,
εἰ σφῶϊν τάδε πάντα πυθοίατο μαρναμένοιϊν,
with ll. 573-4, ἦ δὴ λοίγια ἔργα τάδ᾽ ἔσσεται οὐδ᾽ ἔτ᾽ ἀνεκτά,
εἰ δὴ σφὼ ἕνεκα θνητῶν ἐριδαίνετον ὧδε.

pleases is functional. Whatever may be thought of the divisions elsewhere, Bk. I marks itself off by its structure, as well as by its subject matter, as the first chapter of the story.

BOOK II

AT the end of Bk. I what would the audience be looking for? We have heard Zeus's promise to Thetis that the Achaeans will suffer defeat on the battlefield as a consequence of Achilles' withdrawal. At the beginning of Bk. II Zeus sends, in the night following the interview with Thetis, a dream to Agamemnon to fill him with the mad hope of carrying Troy on the next day. Awaking, Agamemnon orders heralds to summon the army to an assembly, and holds a preliminary council of the chiefs, to whom he relates his dream, and announces his intention of acting upon it. This is a perfectly plain development of the expectation set up in Bk. I; the occasion for the promised defeat is being prepared; we can see the path of the poem running clear ahead to the fulfilment of the promise to Thetis. Then the poet suddenly calls a halt and deliberately obstructs his own progress: Agamemnon, out of his own head and without reference to the promise in his dream, closes his address to the council by the unexpected announcement that he will first test the feeling of the army by suggesting that they should give up the siege and go home, which proposal the other chiefs are instructed to oppose (75). The consequences of this action make up the bulk of Bk. II. Within itself the incident is consistent and completely intelligible. Agamemnon makes a mistaken move for a perfectly understandable motive, his plan miscarries, his army almost bolts for home; at the end

17

order is restored, and it is marching out to battle. But what is it all for? Does it make any difference in the sequel? Does it lead to anything? Would, for example, Bk. III necessarily have been any different if the testing of the army had not occurred? The answer to these questions is plainly, No; the events which follow could have been just the same without all this to-do.

The explanation is important for the understanding of the Homeric narrative method. That method probably grew directly out of the conditions the poet had to meet, and the conditions are indicated by the method. In his opening chapter he aimed at seizing the immediate attention of his hearers and so plunged straight into the first scene of his story and laid the train for the action that is to hold it to the end. What he has to do now is what every story-teller who begins in a similar way has to do, *i.e.* to explain the setting of his story. For even if his audience may be presumed to have known the circumstances that led up to the siege of Troy, he has to 'place' his opening incident within these circumstances, and, all the more if they are familiar, to select from among them those which are pertinent in his handling of the legend. He has to explain, for example, at what point in the war the quarrel took place, what in a general way has been happening up to this time, the ingredients of the situation on both sides in the matter of circumstance and the character of the persons concerned—sufficiently to make clear and complete the exact situation that is being developed. This, among other things, is what he is doing in Bks. II-VII. But in doing this he must still seem to be going ahead. For a narrator to switch back into the past for explanations is tolerable when he is dealing with readers, but it is apt to confuse a listening audience. It breaks the thread of their interest, and it is hard for them to pick it up again when the story is resumed. An audience, once they have got going, want to keep going, not feel that they have to stop and listen to explanations. So Homer, having begun his action with the quarrel, goes steadily forward from that point, and the next incident, no matter what it is, is depicted as occurring next. The past is brought before us through incidents that carry us forward in time. The illusion is thereby created that the story is progressing even when it is not.

Also, he must proceed by a series of episodes. He aimed at making a very long poem; I assume that from its existence, and do not stop to ask why. Being so long, it would have to be delivered in instalments, and each instalment therefore must be interesting not just as part of a whole, but in itself; each part must be to some extent a whole. Always the poet is thinking of the interest of the hour as well as the growing interest in the whole poem. Thus his poem is deliberately made into a collection of stories. The many episodes are clearly as much a part of his plan as the one story which he designs to hold them together. He must proceed largely by digressions, and out of patchwork form a growing pattern. He is actually looking for opportunities to insert as many stories as he can bring within the range of the main story that is to carry them; so every necessary turn in that story, every bit of information that is required, he expands into an incident or builds an incident round it. For the more he can include, the better for his obvious purpose of making his poem last.

Bk. II then has an expository purpose. It shows more
fully the situation in the Greek camp, and explains where-
abouts in the war we are supposed to be; we hear the prophecy
of Calchas at Aulis nine years before; we see in the Catalogue
the ships assembling there; we learn of the coming of the
allies to the assistance of Troy and watch them gathering in
the Trojan catalogue. But it is all done dramatically through
or in connection with the episode of the panic, which is his
first little plot to hold the attention of the audience while he
is setting the stage. He tells it both for its own sake and for
the sake of the poem. It follows in temporal and logical
sequence upon the events of Bk. I, showing the immediate
effects of the quarrel on Agamemnon and the army at large.

The point might be put in either of two ways: The
episode contained in Bk. II is the story the poet contrived
to engage the attention of the audience while he was slipping
in some of the necessary antecedents; or, better, wishing to
work in the episode, he bound it into the story of his poem
by using it as a vehicle for this necessary information.

The Homeric critics who seek only to disentangle an
"original" poem from the present Iliad, and are therefore
always looking for reasons to justify a "cut", sometimes
perform the useful service of raising questions that call atten-
tion to the artistic purpose of a suspected passage. Thus Leaf
says of Agamemnon's proposed test of the army: "The great
difficulty is to see why Agamemnon should wish to test the
army at all. We can understand why Zeus should send the
dream promising victory; that is the first step to the fulfilment
of his promise to Thetis; for it will bring the two armies face
to face, and thus lead to the defeat of the Greeks. But why,
after the explicit promise of the dream that final victory is

now within his power, does Agamemnon, instead of marching out to win it, run the perfectly gratuitous risk of the proposition to the army to flee back to Greece?"[1] It *is* surprising, and that is why the poet makes him do it; he wishes to surprise his audience, to give them something to wonder at, and want to hear the outcome of. At once the attention is directed to an immediate interest, *viz.*, What is to be the result of Agamemnon's test of the army? And so an episode that demands its own solution has been launched; with a jerk perhaps; Agamemnon, we may complain, has been forced to say this in order to drag the episode in. Which of course is quite true, but all the same this second thought of his serves the larger purpose of the poem as marking the uncertain, wavering temper of Agamemnon, which the course of the main story requires him to possess. It brings vividly before us the man with whom Achilles has to deal, Achilles to whom "hateful as the gates of hell is he who hides one thing in his heart and speaks another."

Certainly Agamemnon in this book acts very foolishly, but he acts from an intelligible motive. Before attacking without the aid of Achilles, as he is resolved to do, he wishes to ensure his own position; his plan is to represent himself as willing to give up his own cherished purpose for the sake of his army, while the other chiefs are to speak against his proposal and prevent its acceptance. Thus, if the attack fails, the responsibility will be theirs.[2]

Agamemnon is halting between two opinions; he half trusts and half mistrusts his dream, and, preparing for either eventuality, characteristically seeks to shift the blame in case

[1] Leaf: *Companion to the Iliad*, pp. 66, 67.
[2] J. T. Sheppard: *Pattern*, p. 27.

of failure upon the army itself or upon his subordinates—characteristically as we feel from the action that establishes the characteristic. Rationally speaking, *i.e.* leaving Zeus out of account, the dream is a natural one for him to have at this juncture; for it represents the height of his desire, just what above all things he would love to happen; to march out now and capture the city, immediately after the defection of Achilles, would be the perfect answer to him and the shocked army, and he dreams that it is so to happen. Thus the dream is his sense of the folly of his conduct expressing itself in terms of his desire, and the plan to test the army is the misgiving that is at the bottom of his rash resolve coming to the surface. Between these two feelings Agamemnon has lost his head, and by a kind of fatality, as we should put it, persistently does the wrong thing—in Homeric phrase, he is in the grip of Ate. Thus does the poem seize on the little internal requirements of an episode as footholds for its own progression. Agamemnon's tendency to shift from extreme depression to overwhelming confidence, and *vice versa*, is an essential element, or appears to be, in determining the future course of the action.

His address to the assembly (110-141) is well contrived both by Agamemnon and by the poet; it is good oratory and it is good drama. First, he is apologetic as having something unwelcome to say; he follows up that impression by emphasizing the shame of giving up the struggle. Having thus suggested the line they are expected to take, he then (as justifying to them his proposal and to himself the coming defeat which he really expects) speaks of the great numbers of the Trojan allies.

He has summed up the situation for us; he has revealed the secret misgiving of his own heart which is at the bottom of his proposal and prepares the ground for his repentance. The speech is well constructed to serve his plan and to serve the poet's plan: that is, it has its place in the episode, and it has its place in the poem.

The wild rush to the ships confirms and justifies the impression created by the picture of the army's excited and disorderly gathering in the assembly-place (87-100). Demoralized by the plague, expectant of some important announcement as a consequence of Achilles' withdrawal, it is swept away by Agamemnon's words and gives no opportunity for the projected speeches of the other chiefs; Agamemnon's plan is ruined. In its simple way it is a good situation to which the poet has brought us. He has made us feel more and more the precariousness of Agamemnon's plan: "How can he succeed with obviously reluctant subordinates and a demoralized army? And yet plainly he must succeed, for Troy, we know, was captured." Now, instead of being content with the excitement of uncertainty in which he has held us, he creates a situation that renews and sharpens the suspense. The crisis which excited us in the prospect but which we judged must somehow be averted has been reached; the story is dissolving before our eyes.

This trick (so to call it) is perhaps as far as Homer could go in the direction of mystification. Taking advantage of his audience's knowledge of the legend, he gives his story a turn that apparently leads to the opposite of the known end, that his audience may wonder how he is going to bring it back into harmony with the requirements of tradition. For of course he must; having created this situation, he has now

to undo it. The difficulty will be, the audience see, for
Agamemnon to explain away his words; what will he say to
the army now? But that course would be simply to retrace
one's steps, to hear explained what we already know. And
that, however natural and probable in real life, would in a
story be dull; realizing that the closing of the incident is
necessary in the interests of completeness we should give it
but perfunctory attention. But Homer makes a new incident
out of his resolution of the difficulty. Agamemnon does not
explain at all; he does not have to; the army's attention too is
turned in a new direction, when on their return to the
assembly-place Thersites, a common soldier, taking a leaf
from Achilles' book, hurls abuse at Agamemnon, urging his
fellows to go home and desert him, and Odysseus crushes him
by word and deed, making him an object of ridicule. Thus,
instead of what we were expecting, we have the amusement
of witnessing Odysseus' adroitness in turning accidents to
account. He promptly re-interprets the whole occurrence in
terms of Thersites' action, and before they know where they
are the soldiers find themselves being forgiven for their
shameful, but natural, loss of heart even at the moment when
their goal is in sight. He reminds them of the omen at
Aulis nine years ago, and of Calchas's prophecy therefrom
that Troy was to fall in the tenth year. Agamemnon has
already (134) informed us that nine years have passed since
the Achaeans came, and now Odysseus notes that Homer is
accepting or adopting the tenth as the final year of the siege.
The reference comes not as information to us but arises
directly out of the situation and bears upon it. These re-
minders are given to encourage the soldiers, not for our
benefit. The poet slips in the information incidentally,

dramatically, making its communication an effective element in the action.

Nestor takes up the tale, and the episode draws to its close, but before it ends new interests are promised and old ones restored. Nestor reinforces Odysseus' exploitation of the Thersites incident by definitely ascribing the flight to one or two malcontents in the camp, and then advises a rather obscure reorganization of the army, which seems to have no other excuse than to make room for the Catalogue of Ships.

Their skilful covering up of his folly is recognized by Agamemnon, sufficiently for dramatic purposes, by the warmth of the approval he lavishes upon Nestor's suggestion. He acknowledges his fault in quarrelling with Achilles and creates at least the public impression that he is going to move towards reconciliation. But it is plain that he is resolved to try first, on the strength of his dream, what he can do without the humiliation of approaching Achilles. For that was a promised interest on the part of the poet, and, now that he has successfully established certain aspects of the situation, he holds it out before us again, that in the strength of that hope we may be tempted to pass further. We know what the result will be, for we have been told Zeus's purpose, but we do want to see it happen and observe the repercussions on the relations between Agamemnon and Achilles. Out of this expectation and desire the poet develops the series of incidents through which he completes his exposition—though it is not done at all as we are expecting. The poem opens up from within itself; it unfolds and expands as a range of mountains does to an advancing traveller, drawing him on by distant prospects and disclosing unexpected peaks.

Signalling clearly the dismissal of the present incident in the words:

> τοῖσι δ' ἄφαρ πόλεμος γλυκίων γένετ' ἠὲ νέεσθαι
> ἐν νηυσὶ γλαφυρῇσι φίλην ἐς πατρίδα γαῖαν,

(453-454)

("Straightway war became sweeter to them than to return in their hollow ships to their native land.")

Homer (after a burst of descriptive similes, to dazzle us, perhaps, into investing with splendour the host of names that follow) calls the roll of all the Achaeans who fought at Troy. Whether the Catalogue of Ships was originally composed for this place in the Iliad, of course no one can say. "It seems rather", according to Leaf, "to describe the gathering of the ships at Aulis, and has only been adapted to the Iliad."[1] Very likely so, but I cannot agree with him that it is not suited to its place here. Assuming (as we must on any supposition of its origin) that the Homeric audience found an uncompromising list like this interesting, this is just the place for it. We are at the beginning of the poem, and the poet is building up the background of his story. Whether or not the Catalogue was originally a description of the gathering of the ships at Aulis, the poet so uses it. He wishes to recall that long past event, and so he takes this account and translates it into an event of the day we have reached in the narrative. It is presented as the march past of the Achaean host as they went forth to the first battle of the poem. Then he carries us to Troy that we may hear a corresponding roll of the Trojans and their allies. The two forces are now before us.

[1] *Companion*, p. 79.

BOOK III

Next comes what it is all about. For this, the cause of the war, is the subject round which Bk. III is built. It is the story of the abduction of Helen told in an action that took place ten years after. The poem marches on, taking in what it needs in its stride and gathering impetus from what it takes in.

Homer is engaged in laying, broad and deep, the foundations of his story. Having through the panic-scene made us in various ways more fully acquainted with the situation on the Achaean side, he now turns to Troy and expounds the situation there. "We could not understand," says Miss Stawell,[1] "what the loss of Hector will mean to Troy unless we were shown the relation between him and his city. We could not conceive in its fulness what the fall of that city itself will mean unless we had learnt both to love the citizens and their King and to despise the adulterer who brought the war upon his country. The poet needs for his own effect to let us know all this, and as soon as may be. He does not tell us *before* the quarrel, partly in order 'to secure a hearing' by a vivid scene at the outset, a scene that holds in itself the kernel of what is to come . . . but also, I believe, the poet adopted this scheme because he wanted to give the impression of a sudden fierce and hasty action, which we feel is bound to have momentous consequences, but what consequences we cannot yet discern:

[1] F. Melian Stawell: *Homer and the Iliad*, p. 50.

consequences which do not manifest themselves at once, and which we can only fully appreciate when we look, and look deeply, into the sea of character and circumstance that surrounds the initial deed. Slowly, as in actual life, we come to see what it all leads to." This statement, I think, describes truly the effect of the poet's procedure, but the points noted also show how a great artist turns his necessities to artistic profit. It is because he must seize the attention at once that he begins with the sudden momentous action; it is because he must explain the circumstances of this opening scene that these expository books follow; but he has used this necessity to serve not only the purpose of explanation but also the purpose of the development of his poem. These books are retrogressive and progressive at the same time. They contain reminders of past events; they contain the immediate interest of present events; but they also contain the shadows of coming events. We are not *just* standing still while the world of the poem is catching up, getting into line with the moment of the initial scene. We are doing that, but we are none the less moving forward; and not only superficially in time; we are progressing emotionally towards the crisis. The poem and the situation are getting set and developing at the same time.

The single combat between Paris and Menelaus is here the episode that explains the past, advances the present, and motivates the future. It has a beginning, a middle, and an end of its own and therefore holds the immediate interest of the audience to itself. Instead of merely waiting for it to be over so that we can get on with the story, we are engrossed with it for its own sake. The fact that it is a duel ensures this immediate interest, the simple desire to know how the thing will end, and the fact that it is a duel between Paris and

Menelaus brings out naturally the whole story of Helen and
the shameful cause for which Troy is fighting. And this is
told not by comments of the poet, but dramatically by the
actions of the persons concerned, and in relation to present
events. Consequently, as we listen, we are never thinking
firstly about the past; we see the past incidentally by seeing
its present consequences. It is by what Menelaus and Paris
and Helen feel about those past events now that we are
informed about them. The action is sweeping forward; the
poet cannot pause to explain; there is no time, too many things
are happening. That is the effect.

The book opens with a picture of the two forces, which we
have heard described, marching out to battle. The whole
scene is shown as from a distance with no separate figures or
interests distinguished. Then the poet suddenly shifts his
perspective: the figure of Paris fills the field of vision—Paris,
with his leopard skin and his bow and his sword, swaggering
in the van, hurling out challenges at the Argive leaders (15-20)
—and at the sight there swings into the memory the origin
of the war, the background of broken faith on which the
cause of Troy rests. This reference is confirmed by the
immediate mention of Menelaus (21), and the episode is
fairly launched in our expectations; something exciting is
going to happen—the seducer and the wronged husband are
going to meet. Then, as Aristotle puts it, the poet retires and
leaves the stage to the actors. He has set the scene, he hands
over the rest to them. Paris shrinks back in guilty terror, so
that this glimpse of that ancient wrong might seem to be all
the poet meant to show us. By this act Paris is further
characterized and the audience held in suspense—is it after all

to end there? Hector steps in and by his bitter taunts goads Paris to make his foolhardy challenge.

There is real artistic economy; one stroke serves two purposes. The episode in getting under way begins to bear the weight of the whole poem. The poet has so ordered his introduction to the duel episode that the intervention of Hector is required for its continuance, and that so Hector may make his effective entrance on this note. Paris is depicted as the sort of person to need a reproach to rouse him in order that Hector may utter it, and so stand cleared, on his first appearance, of any participation in the guilt of Paris (which in denouncing he explains). Hector is the pure patriot, who is fighting to save his city, not to defend his brother's guilt; he feels the sin of Paris as a stain upon his city's name, a fatal weakness in the Trojan cause. Thus he enters the poem with his nobility and purity of motive thrown into sharp relief against the background of guilt which spells Troy's inevitable destruction. These two strains are developed in the scenes that follow and together make up the theme of Troy's doom so far as it is required for the full harmony of the poem; they constitute the warp on which the varied woof of Bks. II-VI is woven. Paris symbolizes (*i.e.* conveys directly to the imagination) the certainty of Troy's fall; in a world of poetic justice a cause so based must fail; he and his guilt are the shadow of the coming doom, which we see deepening and drawing nearer in the immediately following books. Hector, we might say, in contrast embodies the tragedy of her fall, the thought of the noble, innocent, and happy lives involved in her destruction. But it is for the sake of Hector, not for the sake of Troy, that we are made to sympathize with the doomed city. Homer's thought is put absolutely at the service of his art, and the tragic implications of the fall of Troy have no concern for him except in so far as they serve the artistic purpose of his poem. Such thoughts are to form the context of Hector's death because a full realization of the tragedy of his fate is vital to the emotional balance of the poem.

Paris, roused by his brother's rebuke, impulsively offers to put his cause to the test of a meeting with Menelaus. Paris is in a sense, I suppose, the given villain of the piece, but he himself fully accounts for himself; he does not just play the part assigned him by the legend, but in his own way and out of his own character fills adequately his role in the poem. Superficially an attractive figure, good-natured, lighthearted, irresponsible—out of place and hence something of a relief among the grimly earnest warriors about him—he shows in his actions the underlying nature of which such engaging qualities are often the index. He feels only what touches himself, and that only while it touches him; incapable of sustained resentment through the same lack of imagination which permits him to watch his city suffer for his sake without a genuine qualm of remorse, he lives from moment to moment as a child does, taking the good the gods provide him and dodging the momentary evil, himself and his immediate mood the boundary of his world.

His challenge is proclaimed, and accepted by Menelaus, and preparations at once made for a formal "signing" of the terms. Then Helen enters the story, and we are off on a delaying episode which by its complete change of tone serves among other things to diversify the interest—"the principal preoccupation of a narrative poet".[1] The mind, as well as the

[1] T. W. Allen: Homer, *Origins and Transmission.*

ear, demands variety. Also, coming in where it does, it
heightens the expectation by prolonging it. But in this case
it is more than a mere interruption to vary and tantalize the
interest; for Helen's entrance completes the reference begun
in the meeting of Menelaus and Paris, and if she is going to
come into the story at all, this is the place to introduce her;
we are thinking of her and subconsciously expecting her. Her
coming is therefore welcome to the ear of the imagination.
No tale of Troy could leave her out or, without disappoint-
ment, scamp her part; her beauty is the cause of the war. The
first sight of Helen, therefore, must be made an event adequate
to her imaginative importance; her entrance must satisfy the
expectation of the audience. Even to Homer's original hearers
the beauty of Helen must have been already famous; the tale
of the siege of Troy involves that among its implications.
And so admirably has the poet performed his delicate task
that even we who are looking on "the face that launched a
thousand ships", on her whom countless allusions in later
literature have enthroned as the very symbol of feminine
beauty, are satisfied. The passage has become a *locus classicus*
of the right way to describe beauty, *i.e.* by its effect. "What,"
says Lessing, "can convey to us a more lively idea of beauty
than that cold old age should think it justified the woe which
had cost so much blood and so many tears?"[1] It has not so
often been noted that the poet supports this effect by deliber-

---

[1] *Laocoon*, c. XXI. See also Murray, *Rise of the Greek Epic*, 1st ed.,
p. 224: "Not one of all the Homeric bards fell into the yawning trap of
describing Helen and making a catalogue of her features. She was veiled;
she was weeping; and she was strangely like in face to some immortal
spirit. And the old men, who strove for peace, could feel no anger at the
war."

ately making us regard her with sympathy.[1] She is guilty
and shameful *ex hypothesi*, but she disarms our hostility by
her own attitude to her guilt and shame. Mr. Sheppard's harsh
comment[2]—"she is the perfect type of the vanities for which
men are content to live and die"—while it may be true in
fact, is, I think, untrue to our feelings here. As she enters,
the sense of her guilt, of which the occasion has so forcibly
reminded us, is at once softened by the sight of her tears:

> Ὣς εἰποῦσα θεὰ γλυκὺν ἵμερον ἔμβαλε θυμῷ
> ἀνδρός τε προτέρου καὶ ἄστεος ἠδὲ τοκήων·
> αὐτίκα δ' ἀργεννῇσι καλυψαμένη ὀθόνῃσιν
> ὡρμᾶτ' ἐκ θαλάμοιο τέρεν κατὰ δάκρυ χέουσα.

(139-142)

("Thus speaking the goddess put into her heart sweet longing
for her former husband and her city and parents. And
straightway veiling herself in shining linen she hurried from
her chamber, with tears rolling down her face.")

---

[1] But see note on the passage in Pope's Translation of the Iliad:
"The reader has naturally an aversion to this pernicious beauty, and is apt
to wonder at the Greeks for endeavouring to recover her at such an
expense. But her amiable behaviour here, the secret wishes that rise in
favour of her rightful lord, her tenderness for her parents and relations,
the relentings of her soul for the mischiefs her beauty has been the cause
of, the confusion she appears in, the veiling her face, and dropping a
tear, are particulars so beautifully natural, as to make every reader no
less than Menelaus himself inclined to forgive her at least, if not to
love her. We are afterwards confirmed in this partiality by the sentiment
of the old counsellors at the sight of her, which one would think Homer
put in their mouths with that very view; we excuse her no more than
Priam does himself, and all those do who felt the calamities she
occasioned; and this regard for her is heightened by all she says herself,
in which there is scarce a word that is not big with repentance and
good-nature."

[2] *Pattern*, p. 37.

And this impression is strengthened by her own words, as she sits humbly beside Priam, gazing wistfully into the past, which the poet thus artfully spreads before us.

Also, as the time has come for Priam's entrance into the poem (they are sending for him to represent Troy in the ratification of the oaths), Homer devises a scene, in direct connection with the duel, which serves to introduce both Priam and Helen, and from their attitude towards each other gives a definite direction to our feelings about them. As if by chance it is in relation to Helen that we first meet Priam, and his gracious, generous courtesy to her establishes him as a sympathetic figure.

But having arranged the scene of their meeting he must fill it out, give it an apparent purpose. This he does by means of the τειχοσκοπία, in which, while strengthening the impression of regretfulness in Helen's mood, he lets us see in the flesh some of the important Greek figures. It is the interest of the audience Homer has in mind. The scene is actualized, and the persons, by thus being observed as it were from the outside. Of course for the literal-minded there is the obvious objection that it is absurd for Priam to be asking Helen to identify the foemen with whom he has been contending for so many years, and accordingly it has been said that this portion is an excerpt from an account of the beginning of the war. That may or may not be so, but the artistic justification for its insertion here has been accurately expressed by Leaf himself, who for once in a way shows himself impatient of this sort of fiddling criticism: "To the hearer or reader of the Iliad this is the opening of the war, and no further justification of the book, as an introduction to the long tale of battles, is needed from a poetical point of view than the book itself. All the principal characters whom

we have not learnt to know in the first two books are set
before us in the most artistic and natural manner; the frequent
mention of earlier events, by allusion or narration, clears the
ground for the continuous action upon which we are gradually
launched."[1] That is it; the scene broadens and deepens; the
stage fills; the characters grow clearer and more familiar;
and always there is, superficially, an apparent movement
forward in time, to satisfy the desire for progression, and,
underneath, the growing emotional sweep which is carrying
us imperceptibly into the full stream of the tragedy.

   For episodic as this sight of Helen is and logically non-
essential to the story of Achilles, it has its effect in establishing
our feelings in regard to what is to come. It stresses, and
especially the scene between Helen and Paris at the end of
the book (383-447), the fundamental guilt of Troy. This
scene pictures, as it were, the original seduction of Helen with
the necessary adjustment to present circumstances. Helen's
thoughts have gone back into the past, and our thoughts have
gone there with her, and we see that past through her eyes,
and judge it and her accordingly. Thus in viewing her
weakness and shame, we remain sympathetic towards her,
that so our condemnation may be concentrated upon Paris.
We are made to feel the frivolity of his mind, his indifference
to the claims of honour or of other people's sufferings, not
for the sake of the moral lesson, but that, realizing the nature
of the Trojan cause, we may so far acquiesce in the condem-
nation of the city. This feeling is to be established before the
other aspect is developed; for the further effect of this scene
is felt in the contrasting one between Hector and Andromache
in Bk. VI, and Andromache's appeal to Hector there gets
immense additional force and significance from its resem-

[1] *Commentary*, vol. I, p. 87.

blance to and difference from Helen's to Paris here (428-436).
Thus the introduction of Helen is made integral in the poem
as part of the process of building up Hector's role therein.

This is the skill of the Iliad, and in part the secret of its
power as a story, despite its apparently ramshackle construc-
tion: The poet's whole interest seems concentrated on the
incident he is reciting, and consequently the hearer's or
reader's interest is so concentrated too. We need not look
beyond it nor think beyond it. With an audience's limitations
in view, he asks no more of us than that we should attend to
the business immediately in hand, and the incidents are put
in a simple logical and temporal sequence for the mind to
run easily along. It is, superficially, the least exacting of all
narrative constructions—a succession of incidents loosely
strung together. Such a method the conditions of publication
prescribed. But the order in which our interests are thus
engaged forms an emotional development that progresses
unerringly to its climax and solution. Homer roams freely,
no doubt, in search of topics of interest, but he never loses his
grip on the essential movement of his poem. The incident
may be logically unnecessary, but in its effect on the feelings
it turns out to be an event in the emotional plot that is
building in the hearer's mind. And that is the fundamental
test of artistry. To arrange his story in the most convincing
logical order is not a story-teller's main problem in construc-
tion; it is to manipulate the feelings of the reader in a way
that is imaginatively effective. He must arrange and insert
events in his story so as to guide the reader's response in the
direction intended. Thus in estimating the purpose of any
particular incident, the critic should consider not so much
its effect on the happenings of the story as its effect on the
feelings of the reader.

BOOK IV

THE end of the duel episode in Bk. III is artistically inconclusive; it leaves us wondering what is going to happen next, and so calls for a sequel. Paris has been defeated, and it looks as if, in accordance with the spirit of the agreement, Troy should surrender Helen, and the war end. The audience therefore, who certainly knew that the siege of Troy did not according to legend end like this, would be curious to see how the poet was going to retrieve the situation.

In Bk. IV the gods decree that the war shall be resumed and proceed to the fated destruction of Troy. This decision is put into effect through Pandarus, who shoots at and wounds Menelaus. Agamemnon, furious at the treachery, orders his army to attack, and the battle begins.

That is the substance of the book. It opens with a scene on Olympus, and Zeus puts into words the perplexity of the audience, asking in effect, "Shall the legend of the Fall of Troy be changed?" (14-19). But we are explicitly told that Zeus says this to annoy his wife (5), so that there is no real inconsistency between his suggestion and his promise to Thetis. He takes advantage of the issue of the duel to taunt Hera and Athena with Aphrodite's success in rescuing Paris, and then pretends to regard the immediate ending of the war as a possibility, knowing that this suggestion will annoy them more than anything. It is reasonable that he should not

37

mention his promise to Thetis, for the other gods are not supposed to know about it; it is also artistically right; in this way the poet tells the audience that the βουλὴ Διός (*i.e.* the story of Achilles) is still in abeyance, that he is still engaged with other matters.

This little squabble forms an introduction (light and would-be comic for the sake of variation of tone again) to an important scene. Homer wishes his hearers to have clear before their minds the fact that Troy is doomed, and so, true to his method of exposition, he shows the gods decreeing her fall as an event of the present day, an event that issues in another which solves the problem created by the preceding situation and pulls back the story into line with tradition. Also, he is preparing the ground both for the first battle of the poem and for the Hector-Andromache scene. He is making sure that we do not just know about the coming doom of Troy, but *feel* it coming, and also that our attitude towards it may be definitely biased. For this feeling is to be the setting of the Hector-Andromache scene; they are to meet in the unmistakable shadow of that doom.

The thought entered with Paris at the beginning of Bk. III. Paris represents for the imagination the certainty of Troy's fall, because he embodies, as we are there reminded, the treachery and broken faith that are the fatal weakness in her cause. The incident that follows forces attention upon the point, and its sequel confirms its significance. The ratification by Zeus of the decree of destiny is immediately succeeded by its visible ratification on earth in the act of Pandarus. The cause of Troy is again rested upon treachery and broken faith. That act, which is, artistically, a deepening of an essential line in the picture, is, dramatically, the publishing of the decree among men, and thereafter a general feeling that Troy is inevitably doomed pervades both camps. Agamemnon, beside the fallen Menelaus, so reads it:

εὖ γὰρ ἐγὼ τόδε οἶδα κατὰ φρένα καὶ κατὰ θυμόν·
ἔσσεται ἦμαρ ὅτ' ἄν ποτ' ὀλώλῃ Ἴλιος ἱρὴ
καὶ Πρίαμος καὶ λαὸς ἐϋμμελίω Πριάμοιο,
Ζεὺς δέ σφι Κρονίδης ὑψίζυγος, αἰθέρι ναίων,
αὐτὸς ἐπισσείῃσιν ἐρεμνὴν αἰγίδα πᾶσι
τῆσδ' ἀπάτης κοτέων.

(163-168)

("For I know this well in my mind and heart, the day will come when sacred Ilios shall perish and Priam and the people of Priam of the good ashen spear, and Zeus, the son of Cronos, throned on high, who dwells in the heavens, shall shake his dark aegis over them all in wrath for this treachery.")

So do Idomeneus (270) and, later on, Diomedes (VII, 401-402). Thus it is artistically right that this incident should be followed by a burst of confidence on the part of the Achaeans, which expresses itself in a series of victorious feats by them. It is the poet's way of underlining, of making us realize, with the Achaeans, the significance of the treachery of Pandarus. Similarly, the sense of defeat is strong upon the Trojans, and in Bk. VI, in the scene which is the culmination of this feeling, Hector echoes with "infinite pathos the triumphant cry of Agamemnon".[1] In a word, the treachery of Pandarus is a restatement of the Paris theme, dramatized into a new event, and completed by inclusion of the consequences.

The internal management of the incident illustrates several

---

[1] Stawell: *Homer and the Iliad*, p. 41.

interesting points in Homer's narrative method. Athena, coming down to the battlefield to stir up the war again, in the likeness of a Trojan urges Pandarus to win fame and gratitude by shooting Menelaus. And at this point, while the war and the poem are hanging in the balance, while we are watching, breathless, the shaping of these dire and far-reaching events, wondering whether he will do it, Homer proceeds as follows (104-126):

"So spoke Athena, and persuaded his fool's heart; he began to strip his polished bow, made of the horn of a wild goat, which he himself, with a shot in the chest, as it came forth from a rock, while he lay waiting in a lurking place, had struck in the breast, and it fell backwards upon the rock. It had horns of sixteen palms growing on its head. And a horn-polisher, having prepared these, had joined them together, and having smoothed it well, had fitted thereon a golden tip. Leaning this bow then with an end on the ground, he strung and laid it carefully down, while before him his comrades held their shields, lest the war-like sons of the Achaeans should first spring upon him before Menelaus was struck. Then he stripped off the covering of his quiver, took out a feathered arrow, never yet shot, and fitted it in the bowstring, and vowed to Apollo, son of light, glorious archer, to sacrifice a splendid hecatomb of firstling lambs when he returned home to the city of holy Zeleia. Then he drew, holding together the notch and the leathern bowstring—the string he brought to his breast, the iron head till it touched the bow. And when he had pulled the great bow into a circle, it rang, and the string sang loud, as the sharp-pointed arrow leapt, eager to wing its way through the throng."

That is what is called, in the language of the theatre, "holding a situation". It is partly for the sake of prolonging the suspense and partly to make the hearer realize the tenseness of the crisis, by forcing him to pause on it. As in the acting of a drama the actors pause in their dialogue, and by some stage "business" or by standing tense and silent allow the dramatic value of a situation to sink into the minds of the audience, so the reciting poet achieves the same effect in his own way: the stage business is made part of his poem.

Lessing uses this passage to illustrate the Homeric method of describing an object.[1] This is the true way, he says, for a poet to draw a picture. "Homer wishes to paint for us the bow of Pandarus: a bow of horn, of such-and-such a length, well-polished, and tipped at both ends with beaten gold. What does he do? Does he give us a dry enumeration of all its properties, one after the other? No such thing; that would be to give an account of a bow, to enumerate its qualities, but not to paint one. He begins with the chase of the wild goat, out of whose horns the bow is made. Pandarus had lain in wait for him in the rocks, and had slain him; the horns were of extraordinary size, and on this account he destined them as a bow. They were brought to the workshop; the craftsman unites, polishes, decorates them. . . . The poet disperses, as it were, the picture in a kind of history of the object, in order that the different parts of it, which in nature we see combined together, may in his picture as naturally seem to follow upon each other, and to keep true step with the flow of his narrative." Lessing means that Homer, understanding the capacities and limitations of his medium, does not try to

[1] *Laocoon*, c. XVI.

achieve in words the methods of a painter; as in poetry a picture can be given only in a succession of statements, *i.e.* a movement in *time*, he translates his picture into a series of events, which, being events, are necessarily a succession and therefore require a succession of statements to describe them.

There is another characteristic of Homer's style which this passage invites comment on, and that is the extraordinary prominence he habitually gives to such minute details. It has been likened to the absence of perspective in primitive pictures; figures that belong to background and foreground alike are all set out in a row.[1] Whatever the poet is speaking of seems to occupy his whole and enthusiastic attention; it fills for the time being the whole stage. The Homeric treatment of a simile is typical of this characteristic; beginning as an illustration it grows under the poet's hand into a picture that lives by its own right. A good example occurs here:

> Ὡς δ' ὅτε τίς τ' ἐλέφαντα γυνὴ φοίνικι μιήνῃ
> Μῃονὶς ἠὲ Κάειρα, παρήϊον ἔμμεναι ἵππων·
> κεῖται δ' ἐν θαλάμῳ, πολέες τέ μιν ἠρήσαντο
> ἱππῆες φορέειν· βασιλῆϊ δὲ κεῖται ἄγαλμα,
> ἀμφότερον κόσμος θ' ἵππῳ ἐλατῆρί τε κῦδος

(141-145)

("As when a Maeonian or Carian woman stains ivory with crimson, to be a cheekpiece for horses, and it lies in a treasure-chamber, and many horsemen crave to wear it; but it is laid up for a king's delight, alike an adornment for his horse, and for its driver a glory")

—an image peculiarly effective both for its resemblance and its contrast to white flesh stained with blood; but that ivory

---

[1] J. W. Mackail: *Lectures on Greek Poetry*, I, p. 62.

cheekpiece does for the moment blot out the sight of "the shapely thighs and legs and ankles" of the wounded Menelaus.

"The art of the epic poet", remarks Macneile Dixon[1], "is the art of deliberate amplification. To retain and heighten our interest without satisfying it, he will check his step, he will pause to describe the hero's sword or shield, or weave a simile, or turn aside into some Elysian meadow. He is skilled in delays, in the creation and management of suspense. He will take no count of time while he enriches and decorates his theme, sweeping, as into a treasure-house, all that lies within the wide horizons of human experience." This statement well describes how an artist adapts difficulties to the service of his art, for I suspect that this characteristic is in its origin the outgrowth of necessity. No doubt by Homer's time, it has, so to say, forgotten its origin and developed into an expected convention which in consequence has established and reflects a taste of the audience. A reciting poet must not lose the attention of his audience for a moment. Therefore everything that is for any reason considered worth saying at all must be said with the emphasis of complete conviction of its importance. The poet dare not drop his voice, for to do so would be to invite inattention.

So here, as he wishes to hold the attention by the description of the bow, he must make it as alive, as arresting as he can. Our attention must be held even while our expectation is being delayed. It is as if in watching the picture of the tempting of Pandarus, the eye had suddenly been caught by the detail of the bow, and for the moment had become engrossed with it to the exclusion of the rest of the picture.

[1] *English Epic and Heroic Poetry*, p. 23.

So it is to the poet himself, and so, he hopes, his assumption of intense interest will make it appear to his audience.[1]

The important thing in this incident is the treachery of Pandarus, but the target of that treachery cannot be passed over unnoticed. Menelaus has to be wounded and enough made of it to establish the seriousness of what Pandarus has done. The story otherwise does not need that Menelaus should be wounded, so, having wounded him, the poet has no other concern with the wound except to heal it and get Menelaus on his feet again. But he resourcefully finds an artistic use for it by making it the occasion for that outburst of indignant grief on the part of Agamemnon which voices, as I have noted, the real significance of the treachery, and also motivates Agamemnon's behaviour in the succeeding incident.

This, the *epipolesis* of Agamemnon (*i.e.* his inspection of his troops) (223-421), is the link that binds the Pandarus

---

[1] "The poet having held us through the foregoing book in expectation of peace makes the conditions to be here broken after such a manner as should oblige the Greeks to act through the war with that irreconcilable fury which affords him the opportunity of the full fire of his own genius. The shot of Pandarus being therefore of such consequence, it was thought fit not to pass it over in a few words, like the flight of a common arrow, but to give it a description some way corresponding to its importance. For this, he surrounds it with a train of circumstances; the history of the bow, the bending it, the covering Pandarus with shields, the choice of the arrow, the prayer, and posture of the shooter, the sound of the string, and flight of the shaft; all most beautifully and livelily painted. It may be observed too how proper a time it was to expatiate in these particulars, when the armies being unemployed, and only one man acting, the poet and his readers had leisure to be the spectators of a single and deliberate action. I think it will be allowed that the little circumstances, which are sometimes thought too redundant in Homer, have a wonderful beauty in this place."—Pope.

episode with the next. It expresses the natural sequel of the
one in dramatic pictures which are arranged to throw into
prominence the central figure of the second. The *aristeia* of
Diomedes (Bk. V) grows directly out of the treacherous
shooting of Menelaus. That is, the next incident the poet
set himself to contrive was the slaying of Pandarus, in order
to clinch for the imagination the truth of the conclusion
Agamemnon and Idomeneus drew from this breach of faith;
in the punishment of Pandarus we read the assurance of
Troy's fall. To carry out his intention, then, the poet has to
select one person to do the slaying, and casts Diomedes for
the part.

But why an *aristeia* of Diomedes? Why not have him
simply kill Pandarus? Because Homer wishes to register
firmly in the minds of his audience the new confidence the
Achaeans now feel in the triumph of their cause and to
confirm its significance by staging a successful battle for them.
And a successful battle in the Iliad means a series of individual
victorious feats; therefore, as Diomedes is already cast for one
such, the need of a series suggests an *aristeia*, and hence the
invention of other feats, for him. The poet gives this, the first
battle of the poem, a backbone of story by focusing the
interest on the one figure. Such an *aristeia* is not, then, some-
thing thrust arbitrarily into the poem just to swell its bulk;
it is an artistic device for describing a battle in an interesting
way.

There is also something else that all this business of
Pandarus accomplishes. It enables the poet to make the first
battle of the poem an Achaean victory by leading the audience
through it to expect one. Here was an obvious artistic diffi-
culty. The expectation set up in the first two books is of an

immediate Achaean defeat, and when in Bk. II we watch the
two armies marching out to battle, we know that the Achaeans
are headed for disaster. But is this the thought in our minds
at the moment when the battle actually begins at the end of
Bk. IV? Zeus is plainly hanging back and has not yet begun
seriously to fulfil his promise, and the business of the duel
and the treachery of Pandarus has supervened and not only
altered the nature of our expectations, but put heart and hot
anger into the discouraged Achaeans. I do not believe that
anyone, reading the events in the order presented, gets an
imaginative jolt when the battle develops as an *aristeia* of
Diomedes, *i.e.* as an Achaean triumph, that he is conscious of
the inconsistency. The poet has not just wrenched his poem
aside to make his first battle an Achaean success; he has
deliberately so shaped events since the close of Bk. II that
we are at the moment expecting it. And the momentary
expectancy is enough for him; he is composing for listeners,
not for readers, and has little care about an inconsistency that
reveals itself to after-reflection.

It is plainly right to give the first battle of the poem to the
Achaeans. In this way there is placed in our minds, before
the defeat comes, the conception of them as the stronger and
normally winning side. Otherwise we should lose much of
the effect of the Achaeans' dismay when the Trojans pen
them at their ships and hold the plain. The poet wants us
to feel for ourselves, and not merely to be told, that that is
a new and amazing occurrence, a complete reversal of the
normal order of things. And there is no doubt that our sense
of the meaning of the defeat is greatly enhanced by this
procedure, that we do enter imaginatively into the feelings

of the Achaeans more directly because we have started off with this clear picture of Achaean superiority in our minds.

Secondly, in that it is a battle that typifies and establishes the usual battle-relations of the two armies, it serves also as part of the exposition of antecedent events. It sums up in convenient dramatic form the previous history of the war; or to put it another way, it is the picture of a battle in the days before Achilles withdrew, dramatically transferred, by the necessity of the story, to the time after his withdrawal; and the role of Achilles is played by Diomedes. It is truly remarkable with how many threads of interest Homer weaves his episodes into the inner fabric of his poem. The *aristeia* of Diomedes is not only appropriate and effective in the place where it occurs for the reasons I have before given, *viz.*, as clinching and driving home the lesson of Pandarus's treachery and as the necessary emotional preparation for the effectiveness of the battle in Bk. VIII, but through the character here given to Diomedes, its influence is felt long after at the crisis of the poem. He shows us in Diomedes the perfect Homeric knight, to supply a background against which we view and measure the conduct of Achilles when he takes the field.

It is with this effect in view that Diomedes is characterized as he is, and the whole matter of the *epipolesis* is designed as a setting for Agamemnon's rebuke of him. The poet is preparing for his *aristeia*, and aims at centring attention upon him, motivating his special effort to distinguish himself (*i.e.* motivating an *aristeia* of Diomedes), and incidentally touches in his character as he wishes us to see him in what follows. Instead of an explicit description he makes an event of it, we see his character by his action. Agamemnon, thrown

off his balance (as he so easily is) by his anger and alarm
at the wounding of Menelaus, insults Diomedes gratuitously
as he had insulted Achilles:

$$τὸν \ δ' \ οὔ \ τι \ προσέφη \ κρατερὸς \ Διομήδης,$$
$$αἰδεσθεὶς \ βασιλῆος \ ἐνιπὴν \ αἰδοίοιο.$$

(401-402)

("And Diomedes answered never a word, for he reverenced
what should be reverenced, the rebuke of a king.")

To ensure our marking it as something distinctive of
Diomedes the poet makes his squire, Sthenelus, fire up and
protest angrily, so that we may hear Diomedes rebuke him
and expressly declare his respect for authority. And the pre-
ceding incidents of the *epipolesis* help to throw emphasis
upon the point. While the conduct of Diomedes is clear
enough so far as it goes, if it stood alone, it might be regarded
as typical of the subordinate chieftains, whereas we are to
feel that Diomedes is distinguished among them for his lack
of presumption, for what the Greeks called *sophrosyne*. So
the poet points his conduct by contrast, and before intro-
ducing Diomedes, shows us the attitude of another warrior
towards a similar, though lighter, rebuke, and chooses that
one whom we have already seen as the chief support and
bulwark of Agamemnon's authority in Bk. II, *viz.,* Odysseus
(350-355). Even this he judged not enough, for it might give
the impression that Agamemnon talks in this way to any and
every one; he must show that Diomedes is being singled out
for insult and therefore has good reason to be aggrieved;
hence the scene is enlarged to include the specific praise
Agamemnon bestows upon Idomeneus, the two Ajaxes, and
Nestor.

BOOK V

IN the preceding section I have indicated the place of
Bk. V in the essential forward movement of the whole poem.
But these purposes, are, as ever, achieved casually, incidentally,
in the course of concentrating the attention on the episode
for itself. It is first and foremost an account of a battle, and
is constructed to interest as such, and, though for that reason
modern readers may find it monotonous with its repeated
dwelling upon the details of the fighting, yet we can recog-
nize, critically, the care that has been taken to avoid monotony.
There is constant variation in the kind of incident related;
dialogue alternates with narrative; the scenes on Olympus
lighten and break the battle scenes. Also, the handling of the
battle here is typical of the poet's method in such cases. To
make the account of a battle interesting, obviously one should
represent its issue as at least a little uncertain, it must not go
all one way. So, though he is here depicting Achaean
superiority, he varies it with a temporary Trojan success.
First, led by Diomedes, the Achaeans push back the Trojans,
and we have a list of Trojans slain. From 460 to 590 the
battle wavers. Then Hector drives into action, and fortune
turns in the Trojans' favour; the Achaeans begin to fall back
(699-702), and there is a corresponding list of Hector's victims.
These two phases are clearly marked and announced, as it
were, by the gods. Ares, the supporter of the Trojans, is
ceremoniously conducted from the field (35), a signal to us

49

to look for Achaean success. He returns at 461 and attention is called to his return by the formal summons of Apollo. Similarly at 711 the much more elaborate and dramatic entrance of Hera and Athena preludes the swing back to the Achaeans. Thus does the poet do all he can to prevent any confusion in the expectations of his audience.

To my mind this bears all the marks of a made-up episode; I mean it does not sound like a legend of Diomedes worked into the poem; there is nothing here that stands out distinctly enough, nothing good enough, to have formed the basis of a legend. The deeds ascribed to him seem invented to suit the poet's immediate purpose. The most prominent person slain by Diomedes is, after all, only Pandarus: otherwise the poet creates the impression of great deeds by rolling up the list of his victims, by the wounding of Aphrodite and Ares, and by the talk of the Trojans. To carry out his intention of getting Pandarus promptly killed, he has selected Diomedes as the slayer, and since an *aristeia* of Diomedes is thereby suggested to represent the first battle, he contrives as a contrasting pendant to the slaying of the truce-breaker with its tragic implications the wounding of Aphrodite, a comparatively frivolous event.

He very properly draws out and holds the Pandarus incident so as to ensure its significance being felt, and he makes the second—the Aphrodite incident—grow out of it. First he shows Pandarus repeating against Diomedes the feat he had attempted against Menelaus. Although there is no treachery this time, the poet's purpose is plainly to recall that act to the minds of his hearers. Pandarus, in his talk with Aeneas, explicitly notes the similarity between the two events (206-208). Diomedes, being wounded, like Menelaus,

prays to Athena for strength to avenge the shot; and this calls
forth the special promise of the goddess (124-132), which is
the link between the two incidents, for it tells the audience
what they are to look forward to next. And how shall he
bring Aphrodite into the fighting? The winding up of the
first incident is made the occasion for the second. As Dio-
medes, revived by Athena, continues on his victorious way,
Aeneas, moved by the slaughter he is dealing, urges Pandarus
to take a long shot at him; and so a place is prepared for the
subsequent interference of his mother.

The reply of Pandarus to Aeneas's suggestion deserves
notice in itself as illustrating Homer's method of getting his
characters to do his necessary work for him. Pandarus is to
be killed; but as long as he stands at a distance and shoots at
his opponents, it will be hard to bring Diomedes within reach
of him. So the poet motivates a change in his method of
fighting by this delightful grumbling speech which seems to
come straight from the man's own heart—because his words
are characterizing him for us. There is the true dramatist's
touch. The man says what the poet wants him to say, but
he says it in a way that accounts for his saying it. Homer has
built up an individuality for him from the one circumstance
that he is to be represented as too discouraged to use his bow
again, and so his quaint despair at his want of luck leads to
his being taken up into Aeneas's chariot, and thus to his death
and to Aeneas being involved therein, and hence to the inter-
vention of Aphrodite.

The incident of her wounding, composed, one would say
for the sheer fun of the thing, yet fulfils a serious purpose also
It helps to establish the impression of Diomedes' *sophrosyne*
The point is emphasized by depicting him as almost carried

away by his success; after wounding Aphrodite, and sending her weeping from the field, he still continues to attack the wounded Aeneas, although he knew that Apollo himself had spread his arms over him; he reverenced not even that great god (433-434). Then, at Apollo's stern warning to remember that he is but a mortal (the essence of *sophrosyne*), Diomedes comes to his senses, and withdraws. So, later, he even retires from the field rather than meet Ares (596-606, and 822-824), and it is only by the express command of Athena that he subsequently attacks and wounds him.

But certainly both these incidents are designed as they are, chiefly, to lighten the narrative, to give the audience something to laugh at. (He pegs them in their place by making them useful also; that is his astonishing way; with all his exuberance and careless prodigality of material he wastes remarkably little space. He piles it all in with casual hand, anyhow, anywhere, and miraculously it does its work: every delay is a step forward. The reader has only to note his own emotional progress, and he will see wherein lies the soundness of the structure of the Iliad.) I remark on the obvious comic tone of the Aphrodite and Ares incidents, not because any reader in a natural state of interest is likely to miss it, but because there are commentators who choose to take them solemnly as an excuse for casting suspicion on the whole episode of Diomedes' *aristeia*. Such deeds as these, they say, would put Diomedes above Achilles in our regard. But as a matter of fact they don't; the rightness of the poet's judgment is proved by the result. Who does place Diomedes imaginatively above Achilles? "The critics, if they could believe that Homer has a sense of humour," says Sheppard, "would perceive that Diomedes, with all his bravery and nobility of gesture, is in fact engaged upon a series of adventures in which the element of comedy, not tragedy, prevails. It is indeed an exploit to wound Aphrodite and Ares. But is it tragically great? Can it compare for tragic greatness with the killing of Patroclus by Hector and the revenge of Achilles for his friend? It is precisely because he must not overshadow Achilles that Diomedes is pitted against gods. Because the gods in Homer, magnificent as they are, are less serious, less important morally, than men. Where the gods intervene, except when the main tragedy of Achilles is concerned, they generally bring a touch of comedy."[1]

One would think that the reception of the Aphrodite exploit in Olympus makes plain enough the comic intention and corrects any disposition to be too much impressed with the seriousness of what Diomedes has done (421-425). Athena, after watching Aphrodite being fondled and comforted by her mother, remarks to Zeus: "The fact is she was urging some Achaean woman to follow her beloved Trojans, and in stroking her scratched her soft hand on a golden brooch." At least the father of men and gods had the grace to smile (426).

In the course of developing the action in which Diomedes is engaged, Homer calls attention to the minor figure of Sarpedon the Lycian. As we have seen, it is part of his plan for the variation of this episode that Diomedes should be momentarily checked, and he uses the occasion to bring Sarpedon to the fore. The supernatural urgings of Ares to the Trojans (464) take a human voice in Sarpedon's rebuke to Hector (471-492), and this is shortly followed by the fully elaborated incident of his slaying of Tlepolemus (628-698).

---

[1] *Journal of Hellenic Studies*, 1920, p. 49.

We are to see Sarpedon again, and he is being impressed upon our memories. Homer has to furnish his heroes with worthy opponents without killing off his main characters, and Sarpedon is being thus decked out to be a notable victim for Patroclus on his great day. Twice he crosses the stage before his final appearance, and so effectively on each occasion that, when he goes to his death, it is as a well-known and remarkable figure.

BOOK VI

THE *aristeia* of Diomedes is wound up in this book by the incident of his meeting with Glaucus, but, before it comes, the preparation for the next episode has begun. The poet winds up the *aristeia* of Diomedes for the simple reason that it has served its turn; he wishes now, for the sake of his poem and for the sake of the audience, to pass on to something different. Oddly enough, it seems necessary to remind modern readers that the Iliad is literature, not life, poetry, not history; and a poem is always full of artificialities by which it is kept to its business as a poem. Homer's first concern is to amuse by a succession of dramatic episodes, and, when Diomedes has played the role for which at the moment he required him, attention is simply withdrawn from him. As the audience forget him in their absorption in the new episode, the poem also forgets him.[1]

[1] Monro's note on the structure of the poem here is excellent (vol. I, p. 309): "It has been maintained that the Aristeia of Diomede is in fact a separate poem incorporated into the Iliad. Such a view may seem to be confirmed by the circumstance that the points at which the prominence of Diomede begins and ends can be so clearly traced. These points, however, cannot be regarded as preserving for us the limits of an originally independent poem. The first half of the sixth book (1-311) concludes nothing, and is an integral part of a new episode, the visit of Hector to Troy. The real question is, how are we to account for the fact that of the three scenes which make up this new episode the first—the meeting with Hecuba—recognizes and indeed turns upon the exceptional prowess of Diomede, while the other two ignore it? The explanation seems to be that the poet was obliged in the sixth book to

The battlefield being now left to the mortal combatants, the normal superiority of the Achaeans is indicated by a list of victims that fall before various Achaean warriors. The rout of the Trojans seems imminent (73-75). It is out of this situation that the poet creates a motive for the return of Hector to Troy and so allows for the staging of the Hector-Andromache scene. Now why should he be at pains to work in Hector's farewell just at this point? Is it not too early? Would not a more fitting place be just before he goes out to his final battle? So far as the actual progress of events is concerned, this scene is not needed at all; its value is purely emotional, and it is put here because this is where it belongs in the emotional march of the poem. It is the doom of Troy we are contemplating, and we contemplate it from two aspects. That is why the *aristeia* of Diomedes is followed by the Hector-Andromache scene and runs into it. The theme of Troy's doom, which has been set forth in the act of Pandarus and its retribution, is now restated in a different key, which repeats and expands the notes struck at its introduction in Bk. III, and thus marks the completion of the statement of the subject, and makes it touch and pass into the main theme of the poem. We have read Troy's condemnation in the act of Pandarus; we have seen it foreshadowed in the spirit of confidence that fills the Achaeans and displays itself in

---

disguise the want of any definite result, such as could bring the career of Diomede to a fitting close. He had also to take up the narrative of the third book, and put an end to the situation created by the defeat and consequent inaction of Paris. Both these dramatic requirements are met by Hector's visit. At first Diomede is kept in mind, both by his meeting with Glaucus and by the terror which he excites in Troy. But with Hector's progress he is forgotten. The sound of his exploits is allowed to die away, as it were, in the distance: and the main thread of the story is resumed with the return of Hector and Paris."

Diomedes' *aristeia*. Now we are to see something of what is involved in her doom; having shown the justice of it, the poet is now going to make us feel the pity of it. But not just for the sake of the emotion itself; its pitifulness is with a view to our attitude towards Hector, and therefore towards Achilles.

The two episodes are interlocked. Before the series of events that constitute the *aristeia* of Diomedes dies away in the incident of his meeting with Glaucus, a new series has begun, a new expectation has been awakened, and not only during the first subject, but out of it. It is because Diomedes is continuing his victorious career that Hector goes to Troy.

But before starting this new interest the poet pauses to note the death of one of the minor victims by making an extended incident of it (37-65). Adrestus, while fleeing before the Achaeans, is upset from his chariot, and throws himself on the mercy of his pursuer, Menelaus. Agamemnon, seeing that his brother is preparing to send him a captive to the camp, hurries forward and bids him give no quarter to any Trojan: "Let not one of them escape death, not even the child in his mother's womb." (57) A nice example of the poet's sureness of touch in filling in the random details of his picture. For this little incident throws into relief, and is itself thrown into relief by, the scene of friendship that follows between Diomedes and Glaukus, each thus emphasizing the other. Also it has its influence in increasing the pathos of the final scene, where there is brought home to us the sort of thing that the savage command of Agamemnon really involves.

At this point (77) comes the advice of Helenus and the consequent departure of Hector. Of course Helenus's suggestion is merely an excuse to get Hector to Troy, and I do not

think that we are intended to reflect upon the strangeness of
Hector's conduct in withdrawing from the field at such a
moment of crisis. It is the poet who sends him to Troy, and
the full and sufficient artistic reason is that he wishes to insert
just here the parting scene. If the effect is adequate, a reader
readily forgets and forgives, in a story, a logical sin. The
trouble is that we have lost our innocence in reading Homer;
we read him suspiciously, unconsciously judging his artistry
by the canons of historical enquiry instead of the canons of
art. We should take what the poet has given us in the spirit
in which it is offered, and not pause to read into a particular
act all the implications it would have in real life. His audience
had no time so to reflect and judge: they felt the emotional
impact of each incident as it occurred, and accepted on the
authority of the Muse events as they came; so as a matter of
fact it happened next, and there was no more to be said. The
poet's concern with the *rationale* of the thing is to preserve it
enough not to disturb assent at the moment.

With Hector, then, started on his way and the Trojans
holding the battle (106), Homer closes the Diomedes episode
with the scene of his meeting with Glaucus. The incident is
a lovely and pleasant thing in itself. It lights up the field with
a sudden gleam of kindliness and the high chivalry that can
beautify war. There are still other feelings, we are shown,
stronger than the hate that war engenders, than the implacable
desire for revenge that Agamemnon has just given expression
to; the sanctity of other relationships can overrule the bitter
relationship of foe with foe. The point is established in our
minds without perhaps our particularly noticing it, but who
shall say it has not its soothing effect in the bitter developments

that are to come? There is, as it were, a promise, the sug-
gestion of a hope, stored in the mind, waiting for fulfilment.
But, besides this long-range value, the tone of the passage is
adjusted to fit it in its place between the two episodes. Being
what it is, it forms a perfect transition from the scenes of
battle to that tender picture of the love and sorrow of Hector
and Andromache. The poet is, as musicians say, modulating
into another key to fit his new subject. The battle interest is
fading; we are still on the fighting line, but the scene is one
of friendship and reconciliation instead of combat and death.
For the simple reason that the one follows upon the other,
the hearer cannot help entering upon the Hector-Andromache
scene with the feelings aroused by the preceding, and the
poet, composing with the projected scene in mind, delicately
harmonizes them. The same feelings are roused, but with
the emphasis interchanged. In the Diomedes-Glaucus inci-
dent the main theme is a happy one, full of kindness and
friendship, and ending on a note of laughter (234-236). The
tale of Bellerophon (150-211) stiffens this pleasant theme,
deepens it with a note of solemnity, almost of tragedy. The
sorrow is remote, concerned with old, unhappy, far-off things,
but, with its strange preface (146-149)—perhaps the saddest
and least exaggerated of all sad commentaries on human life
—, the story sets up a dark background to the cheerful scene.
The Hector-Andromache scene takes over the same double
strain of laughter and tears, but blends them differently. In
it the sorrow fills the foreground; it concerns those we see and
hear. That distant note of menace has come near and grown
into the dominant strain; that sad generalization is exemplified
and realized in and by the individuals before us. But through
it there sounds a reminiscence of the lighter note which pre-

dominated in the former scene—I refer, of course, to the baby frightened by his father's helmet, Andromache smiling through her tears. In each case the two tones are perfectly blended, so as not to disturb the main effect of the whole; the deeper tone of sorrow in the first is so generalized, referred so far back, that it just invests the happy scene with a solemn beauty, that points its significance; the lighter tone in the second, far from jarring, adds infinitely to its pathos.

As for the so-called inconsistency involved in Diomedes' doubt whether Glaucus is a god or man, and his declaration that he would not fight with gods, in view of the fact that Athena bestowed on him the gift of seeing the gods and that he has already fought with Aphrodite and Ares, the sufficient explanation is probably that suggested at the beginning of this section. The gift has served the poet's turn; we have seen an adequate result of Athena's special favour, and so that interest is satisfied; neither Diomedes nor the poet is to be hampered any longer with the burden of the gift. But the change is acceptable enough to reason, and various considerations may be put forward to justify it. Diomedes' idea of the advantage of Athena's gift was that he might *avoid* attacking a god in the disguise of a man (V, 604-606), and he attacked Aphrodite and Ares only because Athena commanded it. As to his doubt about Glaucus, it is one thing, we may readily believe, to know Aphrodite when you see her, or Ares, and quite another to be confronted by a splendid warrior whom you have never seen before, and whom you don't recognize either as man or god. "As a rule", notes Andrew Lang,[1] "any stranger may be a god", and Athena has left the field; who knows whether she has taken her gift with her? Diomedes has to discover that for himself; and true to his nature he

[1] *Homer and the Epic*, p. 108.

does not presume on the favours of the gods. His question—
not necessarily required at all, observe, by the incident and
perhaps on the poet's part merely an excuse for working in
the allusion to the Lycurgus story—incidentally serves to
strengthen the impression of Diomedes' *sophrosyne*.

The rest of the book is the poet's full-length portrait of
Hector. Hector is, after Achilles, the chief person of the poem,
so that we must know him and realize him more fully than
the others; he must fill a place in our minds commensurate
to his place in the poem—and the proper place for the purpose
of the poem. It is not the way of a dramatic poet to describe
his characters, but to show them. We see them and estimate
them by what they do, by their relations to other persons.
And here we are shown Hector in his relations with, and
therefore to some extent through the eyes of, his mother, Paris
and Helen, and Andromache. That in itself is significant of
the poet's purpose in regard to him; for in such a method of
presenting a character, it clearly makes all the difference to
the readers' view of him what persons he is shown with. By
thus drawing Hector in his relations with those who love and
admire him most, the poet has deliberately chosen to make
him a sympathetic figure, a figure of splendid nobility and of
deep pathos.

This apparently plain fact has indeed been denied either
explicitly or implicitly, and we are asked to believe that our
sympathy with Hector and the Trojans is a misreading of the
poem, due to our altered standards of value. For instance
H. V. Routh says[1]: "It is nearly always the Trojans or their
allies who excite the compassion of the modern reader.

[1] *God, Man, and Epic Poetry*, p. 51. Mr. Routh seems a little
inconsistent in thus stressing the modernity of the feeling. For he does
not deny the intentional pathos of such passages.

Neither the fate of Patroklos nor the destiny of Achilles brings with it that sense of irony and regret which we recognise, from our modern point of view, in the deaths of Lykaon, Sarpedon, and Hektor." Well, Zeus at least, it may be pointed out, shares our modern point of view:

> καὶ γὰρ ἐγὼ σοὶ δῶκα ἑκὼν ἀέκοντί γε θυμῷ·
> αἳ γὰρ ὑπ' ἠελίῳ τε καὶ οὐρανῷ ἀστερόεντι
> ναιετάουσι πόληες ἐπιχθονίων ἀνθρώπων,
> τάων μοι περὶ κῆρι τιέσκετο Ἴλιος ἱρὴ
> καὶ Πρίαμος καὶ λαὸς ἐυμμελίω Πριάμοιο.
> οὐ γάρ μοί ποτε βωμὸς ἐδεύετο δαιτὸς ἐΐσης,
> λοιβῆς τε κνίσης τε.

(IV, 43-49)

("For verily I grant it to you", *i.e.* the destruction of Troy, "of my own free will, though with reluctant heart. For of all cities of men that lie beneath the sun and the starry sky, of these most honoured in my heart was sacred Ilios, and Priam and the people of Priam of the good ashen spear. For never did my altar lack fair feast, libation and burnt offering.")

Thus Zeus, like us, mourns over the fate of Troy; and he mourns, too, over that of Sarpedon and of Hector, and from his own limited moral standard expressly recognizes the sense of the pathetic irony of their fate (*cf.* XXII, 169-171, with ll. 48-49 of the above passage). And here in Bk. VI the sorrow of Zeus over the destruction of Troy for all its beauty and righteousness is dramatically communicated to us the readers or listeners; the regret of Zeus is here expressed in terms of our concern with the fall of Troy, in terms, that is, of the poem's concern with it. Indeed it may be said that the meeting of Hector and Andromache is the goal to which the poem has been travelling since the beginning of Bk. III. It comes about naturally enough through the events that followed the shot

of Pandarus, but, when it occurs, it gathers up and interprets
in terms of the main subject the imaginative significance of
what we have been seeing. The poet, building up and
enlarging, as opportunity offered, digressions suggested in
the course of developing and establishing the realization of
Troy's doom, suddenly centres them on the thought of Hector
and Hector's death. Having served their other purposes,
they become also the frame for the poet's portrait of Hector,
the background against which we view him. With the
true economy of a dramatic poet, as approved afterwards
by Aristotle, Homer has drawn Hector's character just in so
far as it is needed for the requirements of his plot. He lives
to die, and to die at the hands of Achilles. And it is clearly the
poet's purpose to make his death as pathetic, as regrettable as
possible. In these scenes in Troy we are shown what his
death involves. It is Hector, the sole hope of Troy, Hector
surrounded by the love and admiration of his kinsmen,
Hector bound to life by such dear ties, whose death involves
the destruction of innocent and happy lives—this is the Hector
we are made to see. And it is expressed not by comments of
the poet, but chiefly through his own intense realization of
it. We feel through his own words all that life means to him,
so that when at last he stands face to face with Achilles we
know that he is fighting for something more, something
infinitely more to him than his own life, for when we come
to that later scene we cannot fail to see behind him, defence-
less but for him, utterly dependent upon his protection,
Andromache and her little son. It is for the sake of that later
scene that this exists and is what it is.

Hector has gone to the city ostensibly to carry out the
instructions given him by Helenus. This purpose, though

merely a shift to get him to Troy, is not slurred over; in true
epic fashion the poet reproduces the scene in full, telling us all
that Hector said to his mother and all that Hecuba did. And
yet the full attention given to this minor point becomes
effective by its very fullness:

Ὣς ἔφατ᾽ εὐχομένη, ἀνένευε δὲ Παλλὰς Ἀθήνη.

(311)

("Thus she spoke in prayer, and Athena shook her head.")

The rude shock of this abrupt dismissal of what has been so
elaborately described gives us a sharp realization of the hope-
lessness of Troy's cause, and thus helps to establish the mood
for the meeting of Hector and Andromache.

So, too, in a different way, does the visit of Hector to
Paris's house. Because of it, we enter upon the scene with the
attitude of Helen to Paris throwing into still stronger promi-
nence the relations between Hector and Andromache. It
serves also another purpose. The long day that began in
Bk. II is drawing to its close, and the pattern of its events is
rounded off by a recurrence of motifs. The husband and wife
theme of Bk. VI balances the husband and wife theme at the
end of Bk. III, and our memory of the earlier scene is refreshed
by thus showing us Paris and Helen again and confirming
the impression there made of their characters and their
relation to each other. So, it may be noted now, this is to be
followed by the second single combat, which, whether
'historically' absurd or not, deliberately continues the rhythmic
pattern, and the debates at the close of Bk. VII balance those
in the opening of Bk. II. For this day carries the exposition
of the whole situation, and the poem thus signifies to the ear
the winding up of the exposition.

It should be noticed that there is no hint in the poem that the poet intends to stage a meeting with Andromache before Hector's final words to Helen (365-368):

καὶ γὰρ ἐγὼν οἶκόνδε ἐλεύσομαι, ὄφρα ἴδωμαι
οἰκῆας ἄλοχόν τε φίλην καὶ νήπιον υἱόν.
οὐ γὰρ οἶδ' εἰ ἔτι σφιν ὑπότροπος ἵξομαι αὖτις,
ἢ ἤδη μ' ὑπὸ χερσὶ θεοὶ δαμόωσιν Ἀχαιῶν.

("For I will go to my home, to see my household and my wife and my infant son, for I do not know whether I shall ever come back to them again or whether now the gods will subdue me beneath the hands of the Achaeans.")

That accordingly gives the note for the scene; it comes to us coloured by the feeling which Hector expresses here, it comes to us, that is, as a parting scene. This feeling is both Hector's reason for seeking Andromache and the poet's reason for introducing her. Their meeting is the culminating expression of the thought of Troy's doom which has been gathering through these four books, and it is the point and purpose of the whole development.

Having roused our expectation, the poet tantalizes us by seeming to drop his intention. Andromache is not at home (371), and Hector sets himself to return forthwith to the battlefield. We can amuse ourselves with speculating why Homer changed the natural setting of the scene. There is, in the first place, the effectiveness of the apparent disappointment. Her absence shows too Andromache's anxiety (note the words of the servant—μαινομένη εἰκυῖα—"like a mad woman"), and so far motivates her passionate plea. The symmetry with the Helen episode of Bk. III is sustained; Andromache, like Helen there, has gone to the tower to watch the battle. And it does, to some extent at least, give

66 THE STORY OF THE ILIAD

the impression of haste on Hector's part; he is doing what
he came to do with as little delay as possible. Thus by remov-
ing the scene from his home to the city-gate the poet helps to
lessen the resemblance between the conduct of Hector and
that of Paris, which an ill-natured critic might like to point
out, and which, perhaps, Paris himself jestingly notes when
he unexpectedly catches his brother up—(518) "I'm sorry to
have kept you waiting, old man, when you are in such a
hurry, too!" (ἠθεῖ', ἦ μάλα δή σε καὶ ἐσσύμενον κατερύκω).

The description of Andromache's entrance is as instantly
revealing of her relations with Hector as the actual occurrence
would be on the stage:

ἔνθ' ἄλοχος πολύδωρος ἐναντίη ἦλθε θέουσα.

(394)

("There his wife came running to meet him.")

We see in the action her relief and delighted surprise after
her anxious search of the battlefield, and are therefore keyed
to hear her hopeless attempt to forestall a repetition of the
suspense she has borne. Then, holding the moment of her
entrance, that we may look at her, the poet formally intro-
duces her:

Ἀνδρομάχη, θυγάτηρ μεγαλήτορος Ἠετίωνος,
Ἠετίων, ὃς ἔναιεν ὑπὸ Πλάκῳ ὑληέσσῃ,
Θήβῃ Ὑποπλακίῃ, Κιλίκεσσ' ἄνδρεσσιν ἀνάσσων·
τοῦ περ δὴ θυγάτηρ ἔχεθ' Ἕκτορι χαλκοκορυστῇ.

(395-398)

("Andromache, daughter of greathearted Eetion, Eetion who
dwelt beneath wooded Plakus, in Thebe under Plakus, ruling
over Cilician men; it was his daughter that was the wife of
bronze-clad Hector.")

So much he tells us here of Andromache's father. The sack of Thebe has already been casually mentioned (I, 366-369); it was there that Chryseis was captured. But the poet makes no reference as yet to its destruction, nor to the fate of Eetion. He is keeping that for the appeal of Andromache, because he can there make a dramatic point of it. Now, what is the dramatic point? Everyone can see that the account is developed beyond the natural requirements of her rhetoric, as Dryden has, with stupid smartness, pointed out.[1] It cannot be supposed that Hector did not know these facts, nor have the details she gives any bearing on the main point she is making —that she has no one in the world but Hector. So what is clear is that the drama of it lies in Andromache's reference to Achilles. We see him here, as so often, spreading destruction and terror through the land; by the skill of the poet, Achilles, though he remains sullenly in his tent doing nothing till nearly the end, also stalks through the poem as the unequalled warrior, the sword-point of the Achaean war.

[1] "Andromache, in the midst of her concernment and fright for Hector, runs off her bias to tell him a story of her pedigree and of the lamentable death of her father, her mother and her seven brothers. The devil was in Hector if he knew not all this matter as well as she who told it him; for she had been his bedfellow for many years together; and if he knew it, then it must be confessed that Homer in this long digression has rather given us his own character than that of the fair lady whom he paints. His dear friends the commentators, who never fail him at a pinch, will needs excuse him by making the present sorrow of Andromache to occasion the remembrance of all the past: but others think that she had enough to do with that grief which now oppressed her, without running for assistance to her family. Virgil, I am confident, would have omitted such a work of supererogation."—*Dedication to Examen Poeticum.*

ἤτοι γὰρ πατέρ' ἀμὸν ἀπέκτανε δῖος 'Αχιλλεύς,
ἐκ δὲ πόλιν πέρσεν Κιλίκων εὖ ναιετάουσαν.

(414-415)

("My father glorious Achilles slew, and destroyed the city of the Cilicians.")

That is Achilles; but so, strikingly, arrestingly, is this:

κατὰ δ' ἔκτανεν 'Ηετίωνα,
οὐδέ μιν ἐξενάριξε, σεβάσσατο γὰρ τό γε θυμῷ,
ἀλλ' ἄρα μιν κατέκηε σὺν ἔντεσι δαιδαλέοισιν
ἠδ' ἐπὶ σῆμ' ἔχεεν.

(416-419)

("Yes, he slew Eetion, but he did not despoil him—the reverence in his heart kept him from that—but he burnt his body clothed in his splendid armour, and heaped a mound over him.")

This conduct may not greatly impress us moderns. But it impressed Andromache. As the Indian coveted his enemy's scalp, so the Homeric warrior prized the armour of his opponent. Without it victory was not complete; the attainment of it, rather than the death of its wearer, marked the end of the combat. So that Achilles here in the moment of victory gave up his triumph, left the spoils of victory with his vanquished enemy. And why? For no reason at all—just a generous impulse, as we should say; σεβάσσατο γὰρ τό γε θυμῷ is Andromache's profounder appreciation of its implications.[1] Through her eyes we catch a momentary glimpse into the hidden places of the hero's heart. And how could it be more impressively, more violently, given us? What stuck in Andromache's memory about the man who had made desolate her home was his respect for the dead body of his foe. "Such",

[1] See the fine comment in Murray's *Rise of the Greek Epic*, pp. 80-1.

says Sheppard,[1] "are Andromache's memories of the man who is to kill her husband. The poet means Achilles not only to kill Hector, but to drag his body in the dust; and he means it to be tragic that Achilles of all people should thus treat him." That is the point; the poet is building towards the effect of Bk. XXII; and this is the seed cast into the imagination that will come to its promised blossom in the beauty of Bk. XXIV. Could there be finer or more compelling artistry than thus to bring in the thought of Achilles' *aidôs* in direct association with those whom it is to concern most both in its tragic violation and in its final triumph, and related immediately to Andromache's fear of Hector's approaching death? The thought of his death is set in apparently accidental juxtaposition with thoughts that will be foremost in our minds when it occurs. And is not the conduct of Achilles the more noticeable because we have just witnessed Agamemnon's mercilessness to Adrestus? And does it not give a deeper relevance to the Diomedes-Glaucus episode by hinting already that in Achilles as in Diomedes there are feelings that overrule and soften the pitilessness of war? This is not to claim that those passages were put in with a view to this, but records the fact that when it comes they fall also into pattern with it. The emotional pattern of the poem grows by an infinity of little patterns that weave and interweave into each other, ever discovering new centres, new pertinences.

In Hector's reply to her appeal (441-465) we hear the authentic voice of the heroic age. Through these words so simply and naturally spoken the sorrow of Hector and Andromache becomes more than their own sorrow, more than the sorrow of Troy; it is the universal sorrow of man

[1] *Pattern*, p. 58.

facing the destiny on which he must build his conduct and
within which he must make a value for human life. Hector
knows that fighting is useless, that, whatever he does or does
not do, Ilios will fall, and his family and his people be de-
stroyed. His position is an extreme and bitter instance of the
common lot of human kind, as these heroes saw it. They are
all fighting in a hopeless cause, for they and their generation
will pass away and be of no more account than the leaves of
the forest. What men do in the long run comes to nothing.
They simply live and die, and there is no point or purpose in
it all. And Hector, faced with the fact as an immediate
pressing reality, gives the answer of them all. He confronts his
destiny without fear or resignation or revolt. This knowledge
can make no difference to his conduct, though of course it
does to his happiness. There is no hope, but there is no
despair.

$$\dot{a}\lambda\lambda\dot{a} \ \mu\dot{a}\lambda' \ a\dot{\iota}\nu\hat{\omega}s$$
$$a\dot{\iota}\delta\acute{\epsilon}o\mu a\iota \ T\rho\hat{\omega}as \ \kappa a\grave{\iota} \ T\rho\omega\acute{a}\delta as \ '\epsilon\lambda\kappa\epsilon\sigma\iota\pi\acute{\epsilon}\pi\lambda ous,$$
$$a\ddot{\iota} \ \kappa\epsilon \ \kappa a\kappa\grave{o}s \ \dot{\omega}s \ \nu\acute{o}\sigma\phi\iota\nu \ \dot{a}\lambda\upsilon\sigma\kappa\acute{a}\zeta\omega \ \pi o\lambda\acute{\epsilon}\mu o\iota o.$$
$$o\dot{\upsilon}\delta\acute{\epsilon} \ \mu\epsilon \ \theta\upsilon\mu\grave{o}s \ \ddot{a}\nu\omega\gamma\epsilon\nu, \ \dot{\epsilon}\pi\epsilon\grave{\iota} \ \mu\acute{a}\theta o\nu \ \ddot{\epsilon}\mu\mu\epsilon\nu a\iota \ \dot{\epsilon}\sigma\theta\lambda\grave{o}s$$
$$a\dot{\iota}\epsilon\grave{\iota} \ \kappa a\grave{\iota} \ \pi\rho\acute{\omega}\tau o\iota\sigma\iota \ \mu\epsilon\tau\grave{a} \ T\rho\acute{\omega}\epsilon\sigma\sigma\iota \ \mu\acute{a}\chi\epsilon\sigma\theta a\iota,$$
$$\dot{a}\rho\nu\acute{\upsilon}\mu\epsilon\nu os \ \pi a\tau\rho\acute{o}s \ \tau\epsilon \ \mu\acute{\epsilon}\gamma a \ \kappa\lambda\acute{\epsilon}os \ \dot{\eta}\delta' \ \dot{\epsilon}\mu\grave{o}\nu \ a\dot{\upsilon}\tau o\hat{\upsilon}.$$

(441-446)

("I honour too much the respect of the men and women of
Troy to shrink away from the battle like a coward. My own
feelings too forbid it, seeing that I have been taught to be
valorous always and that my place is in the forefront of the
Trojans, to add to my father's great fame and my own.")

That is the simple creed of the heroic age. The hero is very
far from being the master of his fate, but one thing there is
that is his—the power to make his life glorious. Because it is
all that a man has and is, because it is brief and uncertain

and death ends all, man has the opportunity to transform his life into a splendid thing by his courage in risking it. Thus man himself imposes a value upon life, and he creates it out of the very thing that robs it of value. He cheats death of its victory by making it the servant of his glory.

The lines 447-449 are a repetition of Agamemnon's words in Bk. IV (164-166) and, being so, bring back to the memory that former scene to reinforce the effect of this one. There, spoken by Agamemnon beside the wounded Menelaus, struck down by treachery, they came to us as the utterance of righteous wrath; the fate foreseen was the just retribution for a dastardly act. Here their repetition in the new context brings the fact home to us in a new light. We see what the fulfilment of that just sentence really means. Troy is no longer just the treacherous enemy, whose destruction is altogether virtuous and desirable; it is Hector and Andromache and their little son. Also, that former scene rising before us in his words makes us think the thought that is troubling Hector's mind— the broken truce and the consequent curse upon his country's cause; and thus this scene becomes the culminating expression of the significance of Pandarus's act in Trojan despondency, and focuses to the dramatic purpose of the poem the thought of Troy's certain fall.

The deliberate tenderness of the picture the poet has drawn in the passage 466-484 can hardly be denied, and warnings against sentimentalizing Homer by ascribing to him the feeling he happens to arouse in our modern hearts surely stultify themselves here at least. Andromache's smiles and tears express exactly the emotion the passage arouses in us, and it is absurd to say that the poet who recorded them was unaware of the exquisite tenderness we find in his description.

It is, I suppose, the perfect and unaffected simplicity with which he describes the scene that enables him to strike so obvious a note of pathos without sentimentality and without loss of grandeur. There is no straining to be pathetic, and no straining to be restrained. He just tells what we might have seen, had we been there. And what is it for? For one thing, I think, to give to us, as the actual occurrence did to Andromache, relief from the painfulness of the scene, and in the same way. Also, paradoxically, with the relief, a deeper pang of pity, from the glimpse it gives us of another aspect of Hector. It is his father's helmet the baby is frightened of; once it is laid aside he recognizes and goes to him willingly; Hector the *warrior* the baby has never seen, but Hector he knows well. A little touch that goes straight home to the heart, and, more than that, plays an integral part in shaping the eternal significance of the farewell scene.[1]

The poet formally dismisses the episode with the same thought with which he introduced it. Andromache returns to her house, ἐντροπαλιζομένη,—"looking back again and again", and sets her handmaids lamenting for Hector;

> οὐ γάρ μιν ἔτ' ἔφαντο ὑπότροπον ἐκ πολέμοιο
> ἵξεσθαι, προφυγόντα μένος καὶ χεῖρας Ἀχαιῶν.

(501-502)

("For they did not think that he would come back any more from the battle, escaping the fury and hands of the Achaeans.")

The curtain is thus rung down on this inner scene, and we, like Hector, must return to the battlefield.

---

[1] Lascelles Abercrombie (*Idea of Great Poetry*, pp. 46 and 47) in his *résumé* of this scene notes the point, and ends "Homer has there sublimed and compacted into a single living moment the whole lamentable, infinite splendour of man's courage."

BOOK VII

Hector must return to the battlefield (the fare-well scene requires it) and therefore the description of the battle must be in some way resumed. The poet might have dismissed this necessary battle in a few lines and brought it to an end by the coming of night. But to do so would have too obviously flattened the effect of the parting; emotionally we are expecting to see Hector do something notable on his return to the field, and it was a right artistic instinct to build some sort of incident around him. For his own good reasons Homer has put the farewell logically too early, and endeavours thus to satisfy for the moment the expectation set up by it. He is, as so often, covering up con-structural difficulties. The character of the incident chosen has been much criticized, principally on the grounds of its historical credibility; would the Achaeans, in view of what had happened in connection with the first duel, have con-sented to a second on the same day? Probably not, and therefore, if the improbability is very striking, its insertion is so far a weakness; at its worst it is no more than that; it is certainly not an incredible and ruinous flaw that must be got rid of to save the sanity of the poem, as Leaf pretends to believe.[1]

And one can see that, apart from the question of historical

[1] *Commentary*, Introduction to Book VII.

73

probability, this incident of the second duel fits admirably in
its place, and serves exactly the poet's evident purpose of
winding up the events of the day and his exposition. As the
account of the battle must be resumed, he describes it by
means of an event which enriches and enlarges his poem
with another story; this story makes a sharp and telling
contrast to the immediately preceding incident in that it
shows Hector as warrior and pitted against a first-class
opponent, and thus also satisfies sufficiently the expectation
set up by the farewell scene. In that it has no effect on the
sequel, concludes with itself and does not leave us waiting for
the consequences, it forms a natural termination, marks a
pause in the movement of the poem. Also, as I have noted,
it continues the rhythmic pattern; the drawing in of the
events of the day is formally indicated by a return of the
motifs with which it began.

Homer's art, of course, is accommodated to the require-
ments of his own audience, and therefore cannot be expected
to satisfy in all respects our more sophisticated standards. We
must at least be ready to allow for the fact that, as Andrew
Lang says,[1] "Homer was composing for an audience of eager
warriors, not for a public of professors poring over his work
with spectacles." That audience wanted stories, and especially
stories of fights, and would not, we may surmise, be as
exactingly critical as ourselves of the way they were brought
in.

The subject is announced through the conversation of
Athena and Apollo (24-42). Here, as so often, the poet uses

[1] See his sensible comment on the whole point in *Homer and the
Epic*, pp. 117-19.

gods to tell his audience what he is going to do, and explains what the episode is for.

νῦν μὲν παύσωμεν πόλεμον καὶ δηϊοτῆτα
σήμερον.

(29-30)

("Now let us stop the fighting for today.")

The incident is just to fill in the rest of the day without changing the situation. And he shows excellent judgment in not telling us this time how the fight is going to end; the gods merely plan to get Hector to make the challenge (38-42); the issue is left in doubt (except indeed for the assurance that Hector is going to survive). Elsewhere his practice is different; the gods announce what is to be the upshot of the various moves. That is clearly because the interest on those occasions lies in seeing the destined end approaching. But this, having no significance beyond itself, is contrived to provoke interest just as an incident. The poet bends his efforts to making it exciting within its own limits. For the hearer, who has no inscribed titles before him, the name of Hector's opponent is not revealed until line 183, and all that precedes it is an excellent example, on the small compass suited to the story, of the poet's adroitness in prolonging suspense. The silent consternation that falls on the Achaeans on hearing the challenge (92), besides directing the interest in the projected channel, conveys briefly, dramatically, the impression of Hector's prestige. Then we are offered the suggestion of Menelaus as his opponent, which is rather disappointing as we have already seen him in just such a combat. Agamemnon intervenes—a happy intervention, so natural, so pleasing as recalling that deep affection for his brother which he has shown before[1]—but the purpose of it is just to hold off what we want to know. Nestor, indignant at their hesitation, rises, and it is with some humour, surely, that Homer makes us now listen to him telling the story he had not time for earlier in the day (IV, 319). Then, what an array of names he gives us to guess from! (162-168) Nine of them; these are practically narrowed down to three, by the prayers of the onlookers, to sharpen the interest (179-180); and in the sentence that announces the result of the lottery the name is withheld till the last word:

ἐκ δ' ἔθορε κλῆρος κυνέης, ὃν ἄρ' ἤθελον αὐτοί,
Αἴαντος.

(182-183)

("But leapt the lot from the helmet which they themselves wished, that of Ajax.")

The termination of the fight by mutual consent, with honours even, makes a good contrast with the earlier duel, and is in itself entirely satisfying—we have had a good fight between two of the greatest warriors, and have lost neither. The courtesy of the exchange of gifts recalls the pleasant scene between Diomedes and Glaucus; the glow of that chivalrous episode is still lighting up the battlefield; the tone is right for the coming armistice. And certainly a reader

---

[1] Pope's note *ad loc.*: "The poet everywhere takes occasion to set the brotherly love of Agamemnon towards Menelaus in the most agreeable light: when Menelaus is wounded, Agamemnon is more concerned than he; and here dissuades him from a danger which he offers immediately after to undertake himself. He makes use of Hector's superior courage to bring him to a compliance; and tells him that even Achilles dares not engage with Hector. This is not true, but only the affection for his brother thus breaks out in a kind of extravagance. Agamemnon likewise consults the honour of Menelaus; for it will be no disgrace to him to decline encountering a man whom Achilles himself is afraid of. Thus he artfully provides for his safety and honour at the same time."

who knows the poem feels the contrast with the next single combat in which Hector engages another and greater warrior while, as here, both the hosts look on.

The poet now announces explicitly, though dramatically, a pause in the movement of his poem by a pause in the action: Achaeans and Trojans agree to a temporary cessation of hostilities to bury the dead. The clearing of the field expresses in terms of the story the poet's clearing of the stage for the next act. Nestor proposes to the Achaeans (327 *ff.*) the request for an armistice and the building of the wall. The simultaneous decision of the Trojans to ask for an armistice grows out of Antenor's proposal to restore Helen in accordance with the terms of the morning's duel (345-353). The poet thus in the course of arranging the truce which signalizes the artistic pause in his poem reminds us in express terms of the ultimate rights of the quarrel. Without marring the emotional effect of the Hector-Andromache scene he is correcting (or trying to) the possible consequential bias in our judgment of the main issue. We are to be against Troy to the extent of acquiescing in the justice of her doom, but with Hector. So the guilt of Troy is here emphatically restated, and, so to speak, re-enacted without Hector. He takes no part in the debate nor indeed is mentioned in connection with it. Thus we launch out into the development of the story with the sympathy deliberately aroused for Hector unimpaired and with our judgment (so far as the poet can make it) unwarped by this sympathy. At the first introduction of this theme Hector dissociated himself from the guilt of Paris; at its close Paris's guilt and Troy's complicity in it (as represented by Priam's tacit support of Paris) are sharply separated from our feelings for Hector.

As he has now a breathing-space from the forward sweep of the action, the poet seizes the opportunity to run up hastily the necessary wall before the Achaean camp. No doubt, historically, so to speak, the Achaeans built their defences years before, but Homer is telescoping events of these years to bring them within the range of the presentation, and this is just the place to call attention to the wall. It is soon to figure prominently in the fighting, and its presence is required in the next incident. He is setting the scene, arranging the properties. Like a good dramatist, he does not heap together his preliminaries at the beginning and expect his audience to remember and sort them out as required, but explains a past event when a knowledge of it is going to be needed. And anywhere else an account of the building of the wall would be an interruption. Here, since the action pauses, there is an interval, and he fills it up by describing this necessary preliminary event. Because he needs the wall, and has had no occasion to mention it before, he builds it here and now before our eyes just before he is going to make use of it, without caring much, perhaps, for fully motivating the building of it—though it does seem to me effective as a material symbol of the change of mood that is coming over the combatants.

It is contended that the wall is both present and absent in the fighting that follows. If that is so, it merely shows that Homer takes advantage of his audience's blindness to the scene, to suit his momentary convenience. Such a practice is not unknown even in Shakespearean drama, where the un-localized, unpropertied stage offered the same freedom to ignore obstructions built only in the imagination.[1]

[1] See H. Granville-Barker: *Prefaces to Shakespeare*, Second Series, pp. 9 and 10, on the wall outside the Capulets' orchard, *Romeo and Juliet*, Act II, Scenes 1 and 2.

Homer likes to describe, when opportunity offers, events subsequent to the action of the poem. In Bk. VI he told of the future captivity of Andromache by the natural and most dramatic expedient of making Hector's vivid vision of it the most disturbing thought in his mind. So here, Zeus, in reply to Poseidon's angry outburst (445 *ff.*), foretells the subsequent destruction of the Achaean wall. The poet includes his literary notes in his poem, perhaps with no further purpose than to enrich it with more anecdotes, but these glimpses into the future, like those into the past, do seem effective as widening the perspective of the action, enabling us to see beyond its bounds forward and back down the long vista of the years. As the similes increase the spaciousness of the poem by leading us out into the world beyond the battlefield, so the allusions to past and future place the action in a wider temporal environment. Life is felt to be going on round it and apart from it, after it and before, and this placing of the story in space and time, casual though it may be, does help to give it reality, and to deepen its import. Whatever may have been Homer's conscious motive, the device became an established feature of the epic tradition. Every reader of the Aeneid knows how magnificently Virgil used the device of prophecy to make explicit the larger significance of his poem. This little passage is perhaps the germ of that great development, and while no such profound artistic purpose can be ascribed to it, it is surely not without intention that it repeats the thought of the transitoriness of human effort, showing us in a vivid picture how the waves of oblivion overwhelm and wipe out each generation's eager achievement. Zeus says to Poseidon:

ὅτ' ἂν αὖτε κάρη κομόωντες 'Αχαιοὶ
οἴχωνται σὺν νηυσὶ φίλην ἐς πατρίδα γαῖαν,
τεῖχος ἀναρρήξας τὸ μὲν εἰς ἅλα πᾶν καταχεῦαι,
αὖτις δ' ἠϊόνα μεγάλην ψαμάθοισι καλύψαι,
ὥς κέν τοι μέγα τεῖχος ἀμαλδύνηται 'Αχαιῶν.

(459-463)

("When the long-haired Achaeans shall have gone again with
their ships to their native land, break up the wall and sweep
it all into the sea, and cover the wide shore again with sand,
that not a trace of the great Achaean wall shall remain for
you.")

Once more our thoughts are made to travel down the gener-
ations, and we see a time when not only Ilios shall have
perished, and Priam and the sons of Priam, but when every
trace of her conquerors' mighty effort shall be obliterated
and their glory as if it had never been. And this vision of the
coast restored to its original loneliness is immediately succeeded
by a reminder of what it looks like now, crowded with eager
life, and the sea beyond dotted with ships busily plying to and
fro (466-475). The short range of men's hopes and fears, the
essential momentariness of the present and its concerns, are
thus directly brought home to the imagination in a scene, by
setting the picture of the Achaean host, busy at their feasting
and with their thoughts intent upon the morrow, against the
background of the long view of the indifferent gods calmly
contemplating the time when all signs of this great event
shall be obliterated. Thus the incident of the building of the
wall, flung in as chance offered, briefly and hastily, to fill in,
apparently, the pause in the action, recalls the thought already
associated with Troy and its fate, and draws the whole of this
long development together, making it, besides the exposition

of the story's environment, the setting forth of the emotional environment in which the poet saw his story, and in which accordingly we too see it.

It is an effective trick to let the audience hear, as this part of the poem ends, the rumble of distant thunder (478-479); it is the sound of the next day's battle, and, as such, an enticement to the audience to come back and listen, a stirring of their curiosity to turn, as it were, the page.

I have called this part (that is, from Bks. II to VII) the exposition, and such it is, though it is exposition disguised. The story has in fact been waiting while the poet gives us information, but he has imparted it casually by amusing us with stories that seem to have carried us on in time. The listener has been beguiled into feeling that events have progressed; it is the critic, the reflective reader, who sees that the story of the wrath of Achilles has not moved from the situation in which it was left at the end of the first book.

So far as mere information is concerned, we have been told why the Achaeans are here, how long they have been here; the two forces have been paraded before us, and have shown too their relative fighting value; we have become familiar with the prominent Achaean heroes, both personally and as warriors, and on the Trojan side Hector, Andromache, Priam, Paris, and Helen are now, to say the least, distinct personalities. We have been shown the powerful gods at work behind the scenes and where their sympathies lie. Besides this, the stage is being prepared for the wrath of Achilles. We have watched Zeus decree the fall of Troy; we heard in the first book his promise to Thetis, and have now seen the man through whose agency, it is clear, that promise will find its fulfilment, and whose fall must prelude the fall of his city.

And Achilles himself—has he been forgotten? In one connection or another his name has kept appearing, so that we get the impression of a long absence from the field. In his absence the poet keeps him present in our minds by showing him present in the minds of the Achaeans and the Trojans, as a hope and a dread. And surely it is an effective bit of preparation for the next meeting with him (to look no further) that the last extended mention of him should call sharp attention to the queer incalculable mercifulness of the man.

In all this it is pure exposition. But what I have been trying to suggest is that, besides managing to impart necessary information in a skilfully unobtrusive way, besides using it as an excuse for including episodic stories, he has made it all integral to the development of the emotional plot. The events related here are not as events part of the story of Achilles' wrath. Plainly that story could be told without including the duel between Menelaus and Paris, the wounding of Menelaus by Pandarus, the exploits of Diomedes, Hector's farewell to Andromache. Nor is any one of these the cause of any event that takes place later. The story of Achilles has its own chain of causation, and these do not touch it. But they are vital in another and more important way. They constitute in the full sense the setting of the story, that is, they affect not what happens in the story but our feelings about what happens in it. The moods and thoughts stirred by this series of events are to meet and modify the moods and thoughts roused by the later events. The poet paints on the mind the preparatory colours which, when blended with those he plans to use, will produce exactly the desired effect. They supply ingredients essential in creating the emotional context in which we receive the events which follow.

BOOK VIII

THE new day begins with an assembly of the gods. Zeus announces, indirectly, that he is now going to take charge, and with threats forbids the other gods and goddesses to interfere in the battle. Though there is no mention of Thetis, no hearer could have a doubt that the poem is returning to Achilles and his story. Through the divine machinery the plan of the poem is kept clear. We know what the βουλὴ Διός is, so that his command here that the rest are to stand aside is the poet's announcement to his audience that for the time being digressions are over, and that the situation started in Bk. I is going to be developed.

This is one of the few occasions in the poem where it may be said that the poet hurries his action, and the reason is plain. The defeat described here is merely preparatory to the sending of the embassy. It is not the defeat promised in Book I. The events which the poet has designed as the fulfilling of Achilles' prayer, that terrible series of events so tragic to Achilles himself, cannot begin until he has committed the fatal blunder of refusing reconciliation, for they are to appear to flow from that. This is merely to bring about the appeal to Achilles, and in describing it the poet has in mind the effect of the real defeat to come. As Leaf expresses it:[1] "It is inserted here not for its own sake, but simply to form an introduction to Bk. IX. When it was decided to introduce the

[1] *Companion*, pp. 159-160.

poem of the Embassy to Achilles, it was clearly necessary to duplicate the defeat of the Greeks. It was only after a Greek defeat that the embassy could be sent to ask Achilles to relent. . . . As a whole it is clear and consistent. . . . The chief fault to be found with it is the want of sufficient explanation for the changes of the battle, which are brought about by repeated thunderings on the part of Zeus, not, as in the best parts of the Iliad, by the death or wounding of prominent Greek heroes. This means is in fact forbidden by the conditions under which the book was composed; for all the prominent Greeks have to be reserved for wounding in XI." Exactly; to motivate the embassy he must picture a defeat; but must not use up either the persons or the interests of the real defeat that is to follow. He therefore takes the quickest and most obvious course to bring it about; Zeus simply sends a panic upon the Achaeans. But, at the same time, he must not appear to scamp it; he must impress the fact of defeat upon the imagination of his audience firmly enough to make them ready for the embassy, and he must, as always, interest them by his method of impressing it upon them. Again, then, personal incidents must be invented, for the double purpose of providing the transient interest and of showing the state of mind that issues in the appeal to Achilles arising in the breasts of individuals. Accordingly we do not hear only

$$\theta\acute{a}\mu\beta\eta\sigma\alpha\nu, \kappa\alpha\grave{\iota} \pi\acute{a}\nu\tau\alpha\varsigma \acute{\upsilon}\pi\grave{o} \chi\lambda\omega\rho\grave{o}\nu \delta\acute{\epsilon}o\varsigma \epsilon\tilde{\iota}\lambda\epsilon\nu.$$

(77)

("They were dismayed, and pale fear seized them all.")

but we see Nestor and Diomedes and Odysseus in the midst of the panic, and realize that very literally the fear of God has been put into the hearts of these men, and of Agamemnon, and the rest, who are to face this night the prospect of the morrow.

The bullying tone Zeus assumes in issuing his command is clearly intended by him to crush debate and frighten off questions into his reason for this move. Only the favourite, Athena, dares to speak. She meekly expresses their acquiescence in his order, but diplomatically assumes that it does not exclude their helping the Achaeans with advice (31-37). Thus room is made for the brief rally of the Achaeans inspired by Hera (218), which, like that of the Trojans in Bk. V, gives the account of the battle a centre to pivot on; and, at the same time, in Zeus's bland reply, which in effect gives his assent to her suggestion, the poet reminds his hearers of Thetis, as plainly as the dramatic situation allows. οὐ νύ τι θυμῷ πρόφρονι μύθεομαι ("I don't really mean it"), Zeus says confidentially to Athena, only not telling her that the plan is not his own. The poet is at pains to prevent any possibility of misunderstanding without breaking his dramatic picture, reminding us that Zeus is acting on the promise to Thetis, and that therefore what he is now going to do does not represent his serious intention in regard to the outcome of the war.

Likewise, in the "golden scales" passage (68-74) he is indicating to his audience what is to be the immediate goal of their expectations: this battle is to go against the Achaeans. As before, he dramatizes his announcement, translates it into action. Zeus has driven down in state to Mt. Ida to direct the battle. We see him seated at his ease watching the unconscious combatants struggling in all good faith on the field, and we wait to see him strike. The moment of his entrance into the fight is thus effectively delayed, and then effectively signalized. The poet turns his prefatory note of explanation into a dramatic picture arresting in itself; that is all, and it is idle to worry the passage for Homer's belief about the relations between Zeus and destiny. It is merely expanding the statement that Zeus "tilted" the battle in favour of the Trojans into a literal picture of his doing it; a metaphor strays into the narrative and takes its place there as an event. Homer's use of the gods is, I think, purely poetical, *i.e.* his statements about them are dictated almost solely by the needs of the poem, and not the poem adapted to fit his religious beliefs.

The incidents of the battle are contrived, as always, for liveliness and variety, and are adroitly arranged to run into and lead to each other. First, Nestor is shown in difficulty with his chariot (80) as one of his horses has been shot, and by introducing Diomedes as his rescuer the poet manages to involve him in the panic without depicting him as panic-stricken. For Diomedes is refusing to play the poet's game and join in the required flight. However, the wisdom of Nestor saves the poet's plan, without besmirching in our eyes the gallantry of Diomedes. When Zeus's thunderbolt falls immediately in front of Diomedes' horses, Nestor takes the matter into his own hands, and simply drives Diomedes off the field, followed by shouts of derision from Hector whom he was about to attack (161-166).

Hector's tremendous excitement, as expressed in his two exhortations—to the Trojans and to his horses (173-197)—is the dramatic communication to the hearer of the *sensation* of what is occurring. We have not seen the two forces fighting often enough to realize fully for ourselves the startling nature of the Achaean panic, so that the poet tries to impart the "feeling" of it through the infection of Hector's excitement. He is drunk with a sense of power, the realization that the luck has suddenly, inexplicably, turned, and surely the exhilaration of his words carries us with him so that we too feel for the moment that he will, if he is quick, outstrip his poetic destiny and, before the story has time to stop him, indeed fire the ships and slay the Achaeans; and the boisterous gaiety of his address to his horses, by expressing his own exhilaration, catches and heightens the excitement in our minds as we cheer him on to his expected triumph. Surely only Andrew Lang's despised audience of professors would pause to worry about the probability or advisability of administering wine to horses; all others doubtless recognize in the humorous exaggeration of Hector's reference to Andromache a reminiscence of the affectionate, intimate tone of the farewell scene. It is by such light and apparently casual touches that Homer carries forward the effects he has gained, and ensures their not dying out of our minds. It shows us too how the thought of Andromache is constantly with Hector (as indeed it must now be with us in connection with him), so that, when the time comes and he waits alone outside the Scaean gate for Achilles, we are thinking the thought that he tries to smother.

His boisterous spirits and confident boastings are more than Hera can bear—

$$\sigma\epsilon\acute{\iota}\sigma\alpha\tau o \; \delta' \; \epsilon\acute{\iota}\nu\grave{\iota} \; \theta\rho\acute{o}\nu\omega, \; \grave{\epsilon}\lambda\acute{\epsilon}\lambda\iota\xi\epsilon \; \delta\grave{\epsilon} \; \mu\alpha\kappa\rho\grave{o}\nu \; "O\lambda\upsilon\mu\pi o\nu$$

(199)

("She rocked in her chair, and made great Olympus shake")

—and she tries to persuade Poseidon to head a revolt against Zeus's command. As nothing comes of her attempt, why was it introduced at all? Surely to stress the opposition of the other gods and so make us feel that it is going to be difficult for Zeus to prevent them from spoiling his plan, especially as they are so much in earnest, and he, as we are immediately reminded, is but half-hearted in the business. We see pleasant possibilities of clashes ahead, which of course are to be realized. This little incident foreshadows and prepares the mind for Poseidon's and Hera's almost successful attempt to overturn the destined course of the story in Bks. XIII and XIV.

Here, however, Poseidon curtly refuses Hera's proposal, and she for the moment dares do no more than avail herself of the concession won by Athena to stir Agamemnon to action (218). It is not much that he does—only reproaches for his army and a despairing prayer to Zeus—but it serves to introduce the rally of the Achaeans, which thus appears to issue out of the two preceding incidents. Nor is Zeus's complaisance left unaccounted for. Agamemnon's appeal touches his heart, and one feels that it is the shadow of his pity that passes over the field in the brief stand of the Achaeans. Of this rally a subordinate person, Teucer, is made the central figure, which thus scales it down imaginatively to the proportions proper to this whole series of events.

With the wounding of Teucer the effect of Zeus's half-relenting passes, and the rout of the Achaeans is renewed. The descent of Hera and Athena to their aid, being described in the same words as that in Bk. V, rouses the expectation that the sequel is going to be repeated, that they are again going to change the face of the battle; wherefore their hasty retreat, at the command of Zeus, is an effective surprise just because it is so feeble. But also it leads directly to and motivates the next incident: Zeus, returning to Olympus as the day ends, is amused to note the offended mien of the two goddesses whom he has just sent scurrying back from the field, and he cheerfully remarks that they were wise to get away so quickly. In reply to Hera's very moderate protest, he in order to taunt them further gives them a further glimpse of what they will yet have to put up with:

ἠοῦς δὴ καὶ μᾶλλον ὑπερμενέα Κρονίωνα
ὄψεαι, αἴ κ' ἐθέλησθα, βοῶπις πότν α Ἥρη,
ὀλλύντ' Ἀργείων πουλὺν στρατὸν αἰχμητάων·
οὐ γὰρ πρὶν πολέμου ἀποπαύσεται ὄβριμος Ἕκτωρ,
πρὶν ὄρθαι παρὰ ναῦφι ποδώκεα Πηλείωνα,
ἤματι τῷ ὅτ' ἂν οἱ μὲν ἐπὶ πρύμνῃσι μάχωνται
στείνει ἐν αἰνοτάτῳ περὶ Πατρόκλοιο θανόντος.

(470-476)

("At dawn you shall see, if you will, my lovely lady Hera, the mighty son of Cronos making still greater havoc of the host of Argive spearmen; for Hector shall not cease from battle until the swift-footed son of Peleus rise up beside the ships on that day when they shall be fighting at their sterns, in direst straits, around the dead Patroclus.")

That again is the poet telling his auditors what is to come. And spoiling the interest? By no means—increasing it. They know now that something decisive is at hand and can watch the events that follow shaping towards the destined end. Think what this knowledge means for the appreciation of Bk. IX. Unless the audience realized what Achilles was preparing for himself by his rejection of Agamemnon's offer, that scene would lose for them a great part of its tragic effect. And no more information is given here than is necessary to invest it with ironic significance.

The end of the book is designed to emphasize the novelty and importance of the present situation of the combatants. The great new fact is that the Trojans are encamped upon the plain, they hold the ground that they have won. We must not merely know the fact, but feel its significance. In a word, the poet has expressed the Achaeans' need of Achilles in a scene. And this scene he impresses on us in two ways: first, by the speech of Hector (497-541), which rings with the sense of impending triumph; all he is afraid of now is that the Achaeans will try to get away during the night; he is so convinced of the significance of their encamping on the plain that we cannot miss feeling it too; secondly, by that vividly drawn picture of their bivouac, which, whatever its effect on its first audience, has stamped the scene unforgettably on the memory of the world.

BOOK IX

AGAMEMNON hastily summons an assembly, and in all sincerity this time proposes immediate flight. "The despair of Agamemnon seems exaggerated and out of proportion to the check which his army has received", comments Leaf[1], apparently not noticing that he has been anticipated in his objection by Diomedes. For that is the point; the situation is not yet desperate, but Agamemnon is, which two facts account for what happens—Agamemnon's abject surrender and Achilles' uncompromising refusal. It is solely Agamemnon's mood that matters here, not our estimate of the danger, nor the army's; we must be convinced that his state of mind is such that he will go to any length to win back Achilles, so that we may realize that what Achilles rejects is not just reasonable atonement, but any atonement at all. And I do not think Agamemnon's conduct comes as a surprise. We have been prepared for it by what we have seen of him before, and those occasions are here deftly brought back to mind to support our expectation. He has already shown that he tends to lose his head in a crisis (this impression is steadily maintained in the sequel). There was his stupid handling of the situation at the beginning of Bk. II when, hesitating between his foolish hopes and his fears, he chose an obviously inopportune time to test the army by proposing flight. The recollection is enforced by the convenient epic device of

[1] *Companion*, p. 172.

repetition. The king harks back to his former words in making his present proposal (*cf.* 17-28 with II, 110-118 and 139-141. When spoken before, they were followed by the wild rush to the ships. This time οἱ δ' ἄρα πάντες ἀκὴν ἐγένοντο σιωπῇ (29) ("His words were received in silence"). The contrast brings out well the feeling of the army now. Then when Pandarus had broken the truce by shooting Menelaus (in Bk. IV), Agamemnon was pictured hurrying about, indiscriminately praising and blaming his subordinates, in a fluster of fear and anger. That occasion Diomedes explicitly recalls in his outspoken criticism of the king's pusillanimity (32 *ff.*).

Diomedes voices the feeling of the army—

Ὣς ἔφαθ', οἱ δ' ἄρα πάντες ἐπίαχον υἷες Ἀχαιῶν

(50)

("So he spoke, and all the sons of the Achaeans applauded") and thus corrects any false impression we might gather from Agamemnon's speech as to the poet's intention; we are not to consider the Achaeans' plight as desperate; it is just Agamemnon who is beaten in spirit. Nestor sees in the gravity of the situation and in Agamemnon's mood an opportunity to end the disastrous quarrel with Achilles, and begins to move cautiously towards proposing it. It is pleasing and dramatic that he should be much more diplomatic about it than, as the event shows, he need have been. He seeks to offset the effect of Diomedes' contemptuous tone by restoring to Agamemnon his priority of place both in his own estimation and that of the assembly (69-73), hinting at the same time that it would be better if he did not make decisions without consulting his council (74), and being careful, for the sake both of the king's honour and of his own purpose, not to lessen the gravity of the crisis (75-78).

Immediate steps are taken to ensure the camp against a surprise attack, and the council meets to hear what Nestor has to suggest. With a great display of tact and even what sounds like hesitation as he approaches the point (105-106), he proposes that they should seek to appease Achilles. There was no need of such caution; Agamemnon wallows in self-condemnation, and offers, besides gifts of atonement, the restoration of Briseis, as much of the wealth of Troy as he can carry away, marriage with one of his own daughters with an extraordinary dowry, and seven cities of Agamemnon's own domain to rule over. The deputation, selected by Nestor, sets out. Their excitement as they walk along the shore (183) transfers to the narrative the feeling of the reader. We have not seen Achilles since the first book, and somehow he has grown in stature by his absence. And though doubtless we know that the embassy is going to fail, yet we willingly suspend our knowledge, and for the moment share the uncertainty of the actors. And this is how we first see him:

τὸν δ' εὗρον φρένα τερπόμενον φόρμιγγι λιγείῃ,
καλῇ δαιδαλέῃ, ἐπὶ δ' ἀργύρεον ζυγὸν ἦεν,
τὴν ἄρετ' ἐξ ἐνάρων πόλιν 'Ηετίωνος ὀλέσσας.

(186-188)

("They found him delighting his heart with a sweet-toned lyre, a lyre of beautiful and curious workmanship, with a bar of silver, which he had taken from the spoils when he destroyed the city of Eetion.")

Is not the picture well drawn to rouse false hopes? This seems a gentler Achilles that we had known. The courtesy of his welcome helps to strengthen the impression of a possible yielding mood, and twice he asserts his especial affection for Odysseus and Ajax. Even the passing allusion to the destruction of Eetion's city surely has its effect as stirring an auspicious memory. The omens could not be more favourable.

The characterization at the end of the supper-party (223) is a charming little touch of humorous imagination, Ajax very willing to pass on the task to Phoenix, Odysseus confident that in any other hands than his own the thing will be bungled. And his speech is indeed very skilful. He shows considerable adroitness in introducing his subject. Knowing that the really dangerous thing he has to say is Agamemnon's name with its infuriating associations, he brings it in casually at the outset in the course of thanking Achilles for his hospitality—by not seeming to say so, breaking it gently that they have indeed come from Agamemnon. Then he passes to the peril of the army, making the extremity of the peril the occasion for a compliment to Achilles (231). He stresses the triumphant attitude of the Trojans, and particularly tries to prick his pride by dwelling on the insolence of Hector. Then his appeal begins, and in the forefront he puts the words of Peleus, so that Achilles may feel that in rejecting their appeal he is rejecting that of his father. Immediately thereupon comes Agamemnon's offer. It is artistically right and effective that it should thus be repeated at full length; it doubles its force for us and makes us feel that it has been all spread before the eyes of Achilles. He ends by repeating the appeal for the army—"if you cannot bear to think of him, think of us" (300-302)—, and by the challenge to the eagerness of the warrior in the chance offered him to get at Hector at last.

The speech that follows is by general admission one of the greater glories of the Iliad. For example, Leaf says:[1] "For passionate rhetoric the reply of Achilles to Odysseus is above

[1] *Companion*, p. 172, and *Commentary*, p. 286.

praise" and "perhaps no finer speech was ever written." Of
course Leaf means not as a model of oratory but as a dramatic
speech, a representation, within the limits of the artistic
convention, of a man's actual spontaneous words. Now I
take it that a good dramatic speech should, first, be vital in
the story, *i.e.* should make or seem to make a difference to
the course of events; secondly, it should reveal the character
of the speaker; and thirdly, convince us that it is just what
such a man would say in such circumstances.[1]

That this speech is vital to the story is obvious from the
fact that it comes just when we are waiting in breathless
excitement for it. Everything hinges on it; we know that
upon it depends not only the safety of the Achaean army, as
the ambassadors think, but the life of Patroclus and the
happiness of Achilles; it is in fact the keystone of the structure
of the whole poem. As I have said, the events which the poet
has designed as the fulfilling of Achilles' prayer in Bk. I,
cannot begin until he has committed his tragic blunder of
refusing reconciliation, for they are to appear to flow from this
act. This speech is, in short, the wrath of Achilles, and there-
fore the next step in his story after Bk. I. With it the
movement begun in that book is completed, the waiting
wrath theme fully developed. Bk. I described the cause of
the wrath of Achilles, this book exhibits his wrath, and what
follows is the result of it.

That it reveals the character of the speaker is, then, clear.
For it is Achilles explaining himself. What the scene with
Andromache did for Hector, this speech does for Achilles.

---

[1] See H. Granville-Barker: *Dramatic Method*: "Each sentence (*i.e.* in
a dramatic speech) must be made to do full service, double service indeed,
even treble: to advance the story, to reveal the character in the speaker,
and responsively in the listener too."

As there we were shown something of the inner personal life of Hector, the motives which constitute the mainspring of his actions, here we are given a glimpse into the fierce heart of Achilles. The difference in setting is very marked. Everything was done to surround Hector with our sympathy. He came before us clad in the beauty and sorrow of the doomed son and husband and father and patriot. Achilles for the moment is stripped bare of everything but the strength of his own personality. Boldly the poet has chosen to make Achilles state his case when he has been put hopelessly in the wrong by the complete surrender of Agamemnon. Thus our thoughts are concentrated on the intensity of his wrath, we realize how it has shaken the very foundations of his life, and so are prepared to watch it bring countless woes upon the Achaeans. It is indeed μῆνις οὐλομένη.

That this speech has the third requirement postulated of a dramatic speech (*viz.* that it should convince us that it is just what a man of such a character would say in such circumstances) is obvious from what I have just said—"stripped bare of everything but the strength of his own personality". Everyone must feel that this is no one but Achilles speaking. There is no character in literature that is more of a self-willed individual, a person in his own right, than Achilles. He always speaks and acts as of his own will, ἀπηλεγέως, as he says his intention is to speak now, *i.e.* without regard for consequences or persons (309). His declaration here,

> ἐχθρὸς γάρ μοι κεῖνος ὁμῶς Ἀΐδαο πύλῃσιν
> ὅς χ' ἕτερον μὲν κεύθῃ ἐνὶ φρεσίν, ἄλλο δὲ εἴπῃ,
>
> (312-313)

("For hateful to me as the gates of Hades is the man who hides one thing in his mind and speaks another") is not, as it has been taken[1], a comment on Odysseus' speech (which was a straightforward genuine appeal), but is, as the γάρ shows, his characteristically violent apology for his plain speaking. He wishes to state his case clearly and coolly, but his words are pulled hither and thither as his smouldering fury blazes up at the thought of his wrongs. That is the effect; he seems to be speaking not as the poet dictates but straight from his own heart with all the disorder of impromptu passionate speech, darting from thought to thought as this or that rises spontaneously in his mind. But of course it is really Achilles explaining himself under the guidance of the poet with the purpose of his poem before him; that is, it is the poet's preparatory explanation of the character of Achilles so far as it is needed to make clear his conduct now and later.

The cause of his wrath may seem to us trifling and out of all proportion to its intensity, as absurd, almost, as the cause of Lear's wrath with Cordelia. Whether it is or no, undoubtedly part of what makes tragic characters is that what moves them moves them wholly; there are no half-feelings with them. And Achilles is the first of the great roll of tragic heroes—those tremendous figures in which great imaginations

---

[1] *e.g.* Pope. But with this exception his comment on the character of the speech is excellent: "He begins with some degree of coolness, as in respect to the embassadours, whose persons he esteemed; yet even here his temper just shows itself in the insinuation that Ulysses has dealt artfully with him, which in two periods rises into an open detestation of all artifice. He then falls into a sullen declaration of his resolves, and a more sedate representation of his services; but warms as he goes on, and every minute he but names his wrongs, flies out into extravagance. His rage, awakened by that injury, is like a fire blown by a wind that sinks and rises by fits, but keeps continually burning, and blazes out the more for these intermissions."

have explored the heights and depths of human passion. Under the influence of some strong emotion, which they alone are capable of feeling with such intensity, they press on ruthlessly, indifferent to all prudent considerations, to the accomplishment of the object to which they are moved. It is their capacity for passion that lifts the circumstances in which they find themselves to the tragic level.

It is interesting to compare what Bradley says of the heroes of Shakespearean tragedy[1]: "His tragic characters are made of the stuff we find within ourselves and within the persons that surround them. But, by an intensification of the life that they share with others, they are raised above them; and the greatest are raised so far that, if we fully realize all that is implied in their words and actions, we become conscious that in real life we have known scarcely any one resembling them. Some, like Hamlet and Cleopatra, have genius. Others, like Othello, Lear, Macbeth, Coriolanus, are built on the grand scale; and desire, passion or will attain in them a terrible force. In almost all we observe a marked one-sidedness, a fatal tendency to identify the whole being with one interest, object, passion, or habit of mind. This, it would seem, is, for Shakespeare, the fundamental tragic trait. It is present in his early heroes, Romeo and Richard II, infatuated men who otherwise rise comparatively little above the ordinary level. It is a fatal gift, but it carries with it a touch of greatness; and when there is joined to it nobility of mind or genius or immense force, we realize the full power and reach of the soul, and the conflict in which it engages acquires that magnitude which stirs not only sympathy and pity, but admiration, terror, and awe. . . . In the circumstances in which we see the hero placed, his tragic

[1] *Shakespearean Tragedy*, pp. 20 and 21.

trait, which is also his greatness, is fatal to him. To meet these circumstances something is required which a smaller man might have given, but which the hero cannot give. He errs, by action or omission; and his error, joining with other causes, brings on him ruin."

Surely Achilles is the prototype of these. Here you have the essential tragic temperament, as there described, with its terrific force, its complete absorption in one interest, object, passion, and its consequent fatal blindness. Everyone can see how different it would have been if Agamemnon had decided to take—as he thought of doing (Bk. I, 138)—the *geras* of Ajax or of Odysseus. They would have known how to meet the situation, with dignity, no doubt, but with the necessary sense of proportion. It takes a tragic character to make a tragedy.

Achilles at first tries to set forth the reasonableness of his conduct (315-320). His point is that Agamemnon has confounded all distinctions. Glory cannot be won here, for the brave man is treated like the coward; all that he could win, therefore, by fighting under these conditions would be what he will get anyway—death. Line 320,

κάτθαν' ὁμῶς ὅ τ' ἀεργὸς ἀνὴρ ὅ τε πολλὰ ἐοργώς,

("Death comes alike to the shirker and to him whose deeds are many")

regarded by many as an inapt "gnomic" interpolation, is an essential part of his argument. The thought of death is ever present in Achilles' mind; one must remember this, and that he has, in consequence, the irritability of a man of great gifts who knows that his time is short; he has none to waste, and the precious days are going, and, worse than that, he has been

wasting it all along. There is certainly no wistful pathos in
the simile of the mother-bird's devotion (323-324); it is scorn
of himself and his foolish efforts—"Here have I been running
to and fro, picking up choice morsels for Agamemnon, like
some silly bird." And the man who has done so much
Agamemnon has actually singled out for especial disgrace
(335), and his voice rises to fury as he speaks of his wrongs.
Then he pulls himself up with the bitter τῇ παριαύων τερπέσθω
(336)—"Let him sleep with her and take his pleasure." But a
new argument strikes him as he pauses, suggested probably
by the scornful μαρνάμενος ὀάρων ἕνεκα σφετεράων of 327: his
quarrel with Agamemnon is the same as Agamemnon's with
Troy; he has collected a great armament to avenge just
such a wrong as he has himself inflicted on Achilles (337-
343). It is a weak argument, but very human; at the best
it justifies his anger, but not his persistence in the face of
Agamemnon's capitulation. "Well, anyway," he goes on,
"he will have to get on as best he can without me, and
with your assistance" (344-347), and he taunts them and
him with the glaring failure of their attempt so far to do
without him. He will return home immediately, he announces,
going into details to show how calm and indifferent he is.
Then, as his fury breaks out again when he recalls the absence
of the thing most precious to him (367-368), comes his message
to Agamemnon with its scorn of his offer of gifts. There is
but one thing which to his mind will restore his honour, and
that is the complete disgrace of Agamemnon as the plain
result of his treatment of Achilles (387). The patent fact
of his humiliation is the only thing that can proclaim Achilles'
glory undiminished to the world, that will show his disgrace
not as disgrace at all, but the means of greater glory. There

can be no atonement, and in offering him gifts Agamemnon
is daring to ask him to *sell* his life for wealth. For that is all
he can get out of it now; there is no chance of glory here,
the conduct of Agamemnon makes that impossible. And as
compared with wealth, life is infinitely more precious. He
knows he must perish if he stays; therefore he chooses life;
he will go home and give up his glorious destiny, which is now
impossible of attainment; there is no point or purpose in
fighting any more; Agamemnon has destroyed the meaning
of heroic endeavour.

While we may find it difficult to sympathize with the mood
of Achilles, we should at least recognize that the wrong as he
sees it is much greater and deeper than it appears to us, and if
we put it back into its heroic context of thought, his terrific
fury becomes more explicable, wrong-headed as it is. A man's
glory is the measure of what he has made of his life, the
goodness that Achilles, and men like Achilles, wrung from
the essential evil of human life. For this Achilles has bartered
his proper span. When, therefore, his *geras*, the symbol, the
concrete embodiment of the glory he has won, is taken from
him, he feels he has suffered the ultimate injustice:

μῆτερ, ἐπεί μ' ἔτεκές γε μινυνθάδιόν περ ἐόντα,
τιμήν πέρ μοι ὄφελλεν 'Ολύμπιος ἐγγυαλίξαι.

(I, 352-353)

("Mother, since you bore me to so short a life, honour verily
the Olympian was bound to give me.")

He has paid the price and been defrauded. Through the
action of Agamemnon, the glory which is the worth of life
to the hero, that good for which he has already given his life,
is turned to evil; his *geras* has been made an instrument of
shame, a means of disgracing him. His life has lost the great

and splendid meaning he himself had given it, and Achilles' occupation's gone.

That is the blow and disillusionment he is still suffering from, and under its influence he pretends to regard his bond with fate as cancelled, that he is now reversing his choice. I say 'pretends' because he does not go, nor make any preparations to go.

This speech is, as I say, the wrath of Achilles, and therefore in the artistic structure the central event, the turning point, of the poem, and the poet has done all he can to make clear the significance of what Achilles does here. Many critics have wished to cast out this whole episode, not only because of inconsistencies with it which they find in later parts of the poem, but to save the hero's reputation. "The question of the embassy," says Leaf[1], "fundamentally affects our whole conception of the character of Achilles. On the question whether or no he refused the humiliation of Agamemnon and spurned his gifts must turn our sympathy for him. If he did indeed refuse them, then he was beyond measure inexorable, and the loss of his friend was but a small punishment for his betrayal of his country. If, on the other hand, no such atonement had been offered him, and he was only waiting for Agamemnon to fall at his feet in order to relent, then we can feel for the passionate but high-hearted man." Certainly we could feel for him, but he would fall far short of being the tragic figure that he is. Up to this Achilles has been rather sinned against than sinning, except for the violence of his language; and if we were to omit this book, we should enter upon the final scenes with no other conception of him than as the sympathetic figure which Leaf pictures, and that is not enough to

[1] *Companion*, p. 23.

explain his conduct. Passionate and high-hearted he is, but there are depths in his nature which these epithets do not reach. The Achilles that slays Hector cannot be described as just a passionate but high-hearted man, and Leaf has to wrench the plain intention of the later book to make it square with his own truncated conception of Achilles' character. But the Achilles depicted there is the same that is revealed here, obsessed with one idea felt with a single-hearted intensity which we can marvel at, even if we cannot comprehend it. Also, it is the Achilles revealed here, his whole being absorbed with one interest, object, passion, that we see at the last surrendering with an effort that tears up his soul, the absolute fullness of his revenge.

No, here is the cause of the tragedy that follows, here is the tragic error, inherent in his nature, that wrecks his world; and the overwhelming effect of the sequel lies in the fact that Achilles brings it all on himself because he is what he is. Like Agamemnon in the first book, he commits the tragic blunder of rejecting the suppliant. Grote objects to the incident because "it carries the pride and egotism of Achilles beyond even the largest exigencies of insulted honour, and is shocking to that sense of Nemesis which was so deeply seated in the Grecian mind."[1] This is exactly the point which Homer has laboured to establish; he is building on that feeling, and the account of the rejection is told to the accompaniment of two reiterated themes—the fatal power of Ate and the sanctity of the suppliant. The conception of Ate as causing the tragic follies of men has been introduced in Agamemnon's words

[1] *History of Greece*, c. XXI. An odd statement, for it seems to imply that the Greeks could not have accepted the Iliad in its present form, or that they were shocked by it.

(115-120), and the burden of the long appeal of Phoenix is "the sanctity of suppliants, the wisdom and solemn duty of respect for a suppliant's appeal."[1]

Phoenix has been introduced suddenly and clumsily, and it has been thought that his whole part is a later insertion. This may be so, and the reason just precisely to make unmistakably clear how Achilles' act is to be judged. No doubt his appeal is unnecessarily long drawn out for our tastes, but yet we can recognize the skill with which the poet has managed once more to make his points by stories which are at least intended to interest and entertain his hearers. One is a story taken from life—that of Phoenix himself, how he came as a suppliant to Peleus, and, though stained with deep guilt, was received and well treated. The other—the story of Meleager —is taken from the great store of ancient legend. Thus Homer sets Achilles' conduct against the background of contemporary life and hallowed legend to show how both condemn it; and between the two he puts the apologue of the *Litai*, and Ate (502-512). Everyone who knows the end of the Iliad can see that this apologue is more than the warning to Achilles that Phoenix intended it to be; it is the reading of his doom.

$$\text{ὃς δέ κ' ἀνήνηται καί τε στερεῶς ἀποείπῃ,}$$
$$\text{λίσσονται δ' ἄρα ταί γε Δία Κρονίωνα κιοῦσαι}$$
$$\text{τῷ Ἄτην ἅμ' ἕπεσθαι, ἵνα βλαφθεὶς ἀποτείσῃ.}$$

(510-512)

("Whoever denies them and stubbornly refuses, they go and entreat Zeus, the son of Cronos, that Ate may now follow him, that he may fall and pay the price.")

[1] Sheppard: *Pattern*, p. 77.

Ajax, the greatest warrior in the Achaean army after
Achilles,[1] voices his feelings plainly (624-642). Agamemnon
has done all he could to make amends, and now Achilles is
definitely and expressly regarded as being in the wrong.
Through the words of Ajax he is condemned by his peers and
his friends. Achilles' wrath, he asserts, now rests on a trifle—
εἵνεκα κούρης οἴης, just for a girl; before, he was standing for a
principle which concerned them all; now he is simply in-
dulging his anger and is solely to blame.

Achilles, who is always surprising us, acknowledges the
justice of what Ajax says, but simply declares that he does not
and cannot forgive Agamemnon. Then he pronounces the
fatal words which are to hold him back when Patroclus makes
his appeal to him, and so lead him to send his friend to his
death:

> οὐ γὰρ πρὶν πολέμοιο μεδήσομαι αἱματόεντος,
> πρίν γ' υἱὸν Πριάμοιο δαΐφρονος, Ἕκτορα δῖον,
> Μυρμιδόνων ἐπί τε κλισίας καὶ νῆας ἱκέσθαι
> κτείνοντ' Ἀργείους, κατά τε σμῦξαι πυρὶ νῆας.

(650-653)

("I will not think of fighting until Hector, slaying Argives,
reaches the tents and ships of the Myrmidons and scorches
the ships with fire.")

---

[1] Now we see the value of our having got something of Ajax's
measure in Bk. VII.

BOOK X

THE first part of the poem being thus rounded off by the resumption and completion of the wrath theme of the first book, we are now ready to hear of its consequences. But before the second part begins, the poet inserts what there is some justification in regarding as an extraneous story—the raid by Odysseus and Diomedes on the Trojan camp. Leaf says of it that "it holds no essential place in the story of the Iliad. If it had accidentally been lost, we should have had no possible ground for supposing that it had ever existed. Not the slightest allusion to it is made in any subsequent book." Granted; but he also notes: "The Doloneia can never have been an independent lay; it is obviously adapted to its present place in the Iliad, for it assumes a moment when Achilles is absent from the field, and when the Greeks are in deep dejection from a recent defeat," (and, I may add, when the Trojans are encamped on the plain). "These conditions are exactly fulfilled by the situation at the end of IX."[1] It is clear then that in the poem as we have it, the insertion of this isolated episode was deliberate; it spaces off the second development from the first, marks a break between them, thus creating for a listening audience the sense that with the new day they are making a fresh start.

The Iliad, as Sheppard notes, and as is indeed obvious, falls into three great main divisions—movements he calls

---

[1] *Companion*, p. 190.

them: the first ending with the rejection by Achilles of
Agamemnon's offer, the second with the bringing to Achilles
of the tidings of Patroclus's death. These are the two chief
turning points in the poem. When the first critical point is
reached, we have this interlude of the night-raid inserted
before the next movement begins. So at the end of the next
movement, at the second critical point in the story of Achilles,
when the dead body of Patroclus is brought to him, there is
another interlude—the making of the new arms for Achilles
and the pictures on the shield. The symmetry shows deliberate
method. Whoever inserted Bk. X did so with a view to the
general design. He is marking off the completion of the first
series of events and separating it from the new series that is
about to begin.[1]

As to the nature of the episode chosen for this interlude,
the reason of the choice is clear if one glances from the end
of Bk. IX to the beginning of Bk. XI. In the former the
Achaeans are in deep dejection over the failure of the
embassy; Bk. XI shows them beginning the day's battle in
high spirits. The poet was here faced with a difficulty. To
motivate the embassy he had to stage a defeat of the Achaeans,
and so to weaken somewhat the effect of the great defeat
which leads to the sending of Patroclus and the tragedy that
ensues. The battle that begins in Bk. XI is the great battle
of the poem. The poet plans to develop it at length; and to

---

[1] See *Pattern*, p. 83: "He wants an episode, clearly designed as an
interlude, though not quite irrelevant to the main theme, marking the
point at which the introductory series is completed and the tragic sequel
is about to begin. Achilles has made his fatal choice. The knot is tied.
The development of the tragedy will begin when Agamemnon takes the
field. Between the two great movements the poet has set the Lay of
Dolon."

start with the Achaeans depressed and already beaten in spirit
would be beginning, emotionally, at the end. We are to go
back, so far as that is possible, to the feelings and expectations
we had before the defeat in Bk. VIII; and so, as a preliminary
to that—to make the transition from a mood of dejection to a
mood of renewed spirits—he feels he must insert some success-
ful exploit. Looking about for such among his material he
found this story of Dolon and adapted it to his purpose (if
so, it was certainly worth preserving, and the really note-
worthy thing about it is not its detachableness, but the skill
with which it has been incorporated so as to fit the general
scheme); or, not finding anything suitable, he invented it,
and, as his method always is, developed it for all it was worth
in itself. What chiefly makes it effective for this transition
purpose is not so much the incident itself (which would in
fact be too small a success to offset the effect of Achilles' now
definite desertion) as the spirited tone in which it is related.
For it is not what the Achaeans would as a matter of fact
feel that matters; it is what the poet can get his audience to
feel. If a story-teller wishes to convey the impression of rising
spirits in his characters, the best way to do it is not just to
present convincing evidence that they had good reason to be
cheered, but to communicate the feeling to his readers, to
make them feel excited and inspirited by the doings of these
characters. Thus the poem here indicates rising spirits by the
simple process of its own spirits rising. It obviously enjoys
itself as it plunges into the rush and excitement of the night-
raid. Homer plainly regarded the whole affair as great fun
and poor Dolon, I am afraid, as a comic figure; and the cold
brutality of his slaying and the massacre of the Thracians
are described as if it were all a great lark. After all, men take

their fun where they find it, and make it, if necessary, out of
the most unpromising stuff. This is war-time fun, and such
skylarking as the conditions of war offer to the adventurous
and high-spirited.

BOOK XI

THE poet opens this book by calling attention to the change of heart we are now to imagine in the Achaeans as a result of the cheering raid; that is, he confirms the effect Bk. X has had on us by transferring it to the persons of the story. Again his statement of the fact takes place within the narrative; the announcement that "the Achaeans arose all agog for battle" *occurs* in the camp as Eris calling them to battle and putting might into their hearts (3-14).

The day which now begins continues to the middle of Bk. XVIII. It is the day of the great battle for the Achaean ships, the battle in which Achilles' prayer is fulfilled. This, the second division of the poem, is ushered in with ceremony, and its place and purpose in the development of the subject are expressly stated (52-55):

$$\text{ἐν δὲ κυδοιμὸν}$$
ὦρσε κακὸν Κρονίδης, κατὰ δ' ὑψόθεν ἧκεν ἐέρσας
αἵματι μυδαλέας ἐξ αἰθέρος, οὕνεκ' ἔμελλε
πολλὰς ἰφθίμους κεφαλὰς Ἄϊδι προϊάψειν.

("And the son of Cronos roused an evil din among them, and down from the sky rained a bloody dew, because he was about to send many valiant heads to Hades.")

That is, this portion is to describe the result of the wrath of Achilles promised in the proem:

ἣ μυρί' Ἀχαιοῖς ἄλγε' ἔθηκε,
πολλὰς δ' ἰφθίμους ψυχὰς Ἄϊδι προϊάψεν.

(I, 2-3)

("The accursed wrath which sent many valiant souls to Hades.")

The first incident in the battle is an *aristeia* of Agamemnon. As the day has to begin well for the Achaeans, that we may feel the full shock of the defeat that follows and may not regard it as just the continuation of that of the previous day, the poet has to choose one of his heroes to lead off with a victorious career. His reasons for choosing Agamemnon are plain. For one thing, the turn in the battle could not be better signalized than by the wounding and retirement of the leader of the whole host. Again we have not yet seen Agamemnon as a warrior, except for casual glimpses; we must realize his prowess as a fighter in order that we may recognize the loss to the Achaeans in actual fighting strength when he withdraws wounded. Thus he accomplishes his two objects by one stroke: the day begins auspiciously in the victorious career of Agamemnon, and his prowess is impressed upon us, so that we are also impressed with the significance of his retirement.

The poet is endeavouring to wipe out for the moment the effect of Bk. VIII and take us back to the position at the beginning of that book. The defeat there was necessary to account for the sending of the embassy, and now that it has served its purpose its effect has to be cancelled to make room for the real defeat that is the answer to Achilles' prayer. Accordingly Agamemnon sweeps back the Trojans across the plain, and the situation is almost what it was before their success in Bk. VIII (153-180). And just when we are beginning to wonder what Zeus is doing, and what Hector, the poet explains in the passage 181-209, in which he gives us another forward glimpse of his intentions: Agamemnon is to be wounded, and then is to come Hector's time of triumph, which is to end when he reaches the ships, "when the sun sets and the sacred darkness comes on" (191-194).

αὐτὰρ ἐπεί κ' ἢ δουρὶ τυπεὶς ἢ βλήμενος ἰῷ
εἰς ἵππους ἅλεται, τότε οἱ κράτος ἐγγυαλίξω
κτείνειν, εἰς ὅ κε νῆας ἐϋσσέλμους ἀφίκηται
δύῃ τ' ἠέλιος καὶ ἐπὶ κνέφας ἱερὸν ἔλθῃ.

("But when, wounded with spear or arrow, he leaps into his chariot, then I will grant to Hector might to slay, until he reaches the ships, until the sun sets and the sacred darkness comes on.")

The retirement of Agamemnon is, then, to be the signal for the beginning of the Achaean defeat, and the occasion is marked by a preparatory appeal to the Muses (218-220), fitly introducing "what is really the turning point in the poem. For now begins, with the wounding of Agamemnon, the disastrous rout of the Greeks which prevails upon Achilles to relax his anger and send Patroclus to the rescue."[1]

This incident is quickly followed by the wounding of Diomedes and of Odysseus, and the retreat of Ajax, that thus by rapid successive blows the impression of a great disaster may be created. For, because we have learned to know these men in the earlier books, we do not need to be told that the cause of the Achaeans is tottering when Diomedes is wounded and Odysseus is wounded, and Ajax giving back. Each of these stages is developed at length, and with astonishing variety and vigour of imagination.

Hector, seeing Agamemnon driving off the field, orders a general advance of the Trojan chariots, and the Achaeans begin to break. Diomedes and Odysseus stem the Trojan advance, and give the Achaeans time to rally. Hector attacks them but is repulsed. Diomedes is wounded by a shot from

[1] Leaf: *Commentary*, ad. loc.

the bow of Paris, and, despite his scorn of the wound, finds
himself disabled and retires, leaving Odysseus alone well in
front of the other Achaeans, and we now watch him being
surrounded by the Trojans. He puts up a stout fight, slaying
five men before he himself is badly wounded by the spear of
Sokus, and though he revenges himself on him, the rest,
seeing that he is wounded, close round to finish him off.

αὐτὰρ ὅ γ᾽ ἐξοπίσω ἀνεχάζετο, αὖε δ᾽ ἑταίρους.
τρὶς μὲν ἔπειτ᾽ ἤϋσεν ὅσον κεφαλὴ χάδε φωτός,
τρὶς δ᾽ ἄϊεν ἰάχοντος ἀρηΐφιλος Μενέλαος.

(461-463)

("And he began to give back, and he shouted to his comrades;
three times he shouted, at the full pitch of his voice, and
three times Menelaus heard his cry.")

Menelaus thereupon calls Ajax, and they hurry to the rescue.
The interest now shifts to Ajax, the transition taking place in
the simile of the wounded deer, the jackals, and the lion, a
two-fronted simile which begins by illustrating what has gone
before and serves to introduce what follows (474-486). Odys-
seus is put into his chariot, and Ajax attacks the Trojans who
had scattered at his approach.

Then for a moment we pass to another part of the field,
to see Paris repeat his success, this time on Machaon (a small
but, as it turns out, vital incident), and Nestor drives off with
the wounded man. The Trojans, headed by Hector, concen-
trate their attack on Ajax, and we have the masterly scene of
the slow retreat of Ajax, which perhaps does more to distin-
guish him as a personality than all the previous occasions on
which he appears, and it may be that the "beef-witted" Ajax
of later story stems from the memorable simile of the recalci-
trant donkey. Eurypylus, seeing Ajax's plight, essays to go to
his help, but is wounded by an arrow from Paris's potent bow.

The poet has a use, too, for the wounding of this minor figure. The little links are carefully forged.

When Ajax has made good his escape, reaching the main body of his comrades, the scene shifts to the camp (596). In Bk. VIII Zeus saw, for our benefit, that the fulfilment of his promise to Thetis involved the death of Patroclus, and now we are shown that predestined event shaping through the characters of the actors. Achilles is eagerly watching the battle from his ship. He is burning to hear firsthand news and, seeing Nestor's chariot passing, bearing a wounded man, sends Patroclus to make inquiries, being too proud to go himself. Thus it is Achilles who takes the first step towards the death of Patroclus, as the poet expressly notes—κακοῦ δ' ἄρα οἱ πέλεν ἀρχή (604) ("and so evil began for him").

The words in l. 606 are actually the first words spoken by Patroclus in the poem. He has been kept in the background until he has to play his part, is not made important until he becomes important for the story. Now great care is taken to make his appearance at the tent of Nestor fully dramatic, to throw the spotlight on him. Nestor and Machaon have arrived at Nestor's tent and are settling down to comfort and refresh themselves (618-643). They are completely taken up with their own immediate needs, and in the fullness of his description of the scene the poet aims to carry our thoughts away from the approaching messenger, to reproduce in us, as it were, their ignorance of his coming and hence the startling effect of his sudden appearance. Patroclus holds the centre of the stage.

There follows a remarkable and vividly imagined scene, in which behind the words the movements and attitudes of the *dramatis personae* are plainly visible. "Seeing him the old man sprang from his chair, and, grasping his hand, brought him in, and bade him sit down" (645-646). Patroclus's reply is full of dramatic humour. One can feel that he sees with vague alarm the purposeful manner of the old man, and therefore makes us see it too: "No, I can't sit down, sir; it is no use asking me. I have too much respect for the anger of him who sent me. He wanted to find out who it was you had brought in wounded. But I can see for myself, it is Machaon. Now I will go back and tell Achilles. You know what I mean, sir, you know what he is like, a terrible man, and swift to find fault even where there is no fault" (648-654). This last appeal to let him off is almost pathetic and intensely dramatic, *i.e.* it makes one *see* the scene—Patroclus backing towards the door before the obvious intention in Nestor's eye. For Nestor instantly realizes that a great opportunity has been offered him of getting at Achilles, of getting perhaps some sort of help from him. The situation is becoming desperate, and this unlooked for chance has arisen out of it. He has got Patroclus away from Achilles. You can talk to Patroclus, he is gentle and polite. And so Nestor is going to talk to him. But he must not frighten him off by showing his purpose too soon; he must prepare the ground.

Therefore he begins with a very natural scoff at the genuineness of Achilles' concern, slipping in some information as to what has happened. He knows that, whatever Achilles may think of it, Patroclus will be startled at hearing that Diomedes and Odysseus and Agamemnon are wounded and out of the fight. Then he sets to work to talk, and his talk takes the usual form of reminiscences of his own youth— nothing could seem more guileless; it is just old Nestor rambling on in his customary way with no sense of times or seasons. But he is talking not only with a purpose but to the purpose. He is reminding Patroclus of the normal ways, the normal lives, the normal ideals of heroic young men. He tells him of the first raid he was engaged in, and how successful it was and how pleased his father was with him. He keeps the story going as long as he can, with details about the plunder and how it was divided, and when at last it seems to have reached its end, he drifts into another. Leaf says[1] that the whole passage from 666 to 762 is "one of the clearest cases of interpolation in the Iliad. It is altogether out of place at the moment when Patroclus has refused even to sit down, owing to the urgency of his mission." On which Andrew Lang remarks: "If Mr. Leaf has never met an intelligent old bore, whom no one could check by refusing to sit down, we envy his inexperience of misfortune." Homer has made us see the hurried manner of Patroclus, how anxious he is to get away, in order to give comic point to Nestor's procedure. In the light of that one can imagine him at this point when the story seems to be running out, taking another hopeful step doorwards and Nestor following him up with οἱ δὲ τρίτῳ ἤματι (707) ("Three days afterwards"); and so he goes on to describe the siege of Thryoessa and how his father tried to keep him out of the Pylian force that went to its relief, and hid his horses; but he was so keen that he went on foot; and how he, the mere youth, killed the great captain of the enemy, causing the flight of their army, and besides, incidentally, killed one hundred men with his own hand. And when they returned home with their booty "all gave praise, among the gods, to Zeus, and to Nestor among men. That is what I was like among warriors —but Achilles" (761-762). Nestor no doubt has been somewhat carried away by his glorified memories, but he has kept his main object in view. He has been surrounding Patroclus

---

[1] *Commentary*, Introduction to Book XI.

with a different atmosphere, reminding him of the world out-
side Achilles' tent, and the sort of things it deems glorious in
a young man's life, and then suddenly he flashes the conduct
of Achilles into the light of that world. He is making
Achilles' magnificent indignation, which he thinks so fine,
and Patroclus doubtless thinks so fine, appear a paltry thing.
He hints that Achilles will lose his reputation. All he
will get from his valour is what he thinks of it himself[1]—
οἷος τῆς ἀρετῆς ἀπονήσεται (763). And then comes the appeal,
beginning

> ὦ πέπον, ἦ μέν σοί γε Μενοίτιος ὧδ᾽ ἐπέτελλεν
> ἤματι τῷ ὅτε σ᾽ ἐκ Φθίης Ἀγαμέμνονι πέμπε.

(765-766)

("Dear friend, that day when your father sent you from
Phthia to Agamemnon, he urged you thus.")

"You have a responsibility in the matter." And he recalls to
his mind that farewell scene, painting it in detail so that
Patroclus will see it all in his mind's eye again exactly as it
occurred. Therefore he urges him to tell Achilles what he
(Nestor) has told him, and use his influence to persuade him.
Then with the little stinging suggestion as to Achilles' real
reason for staying out of the fight (794-795) he proposes as a
possible compromise the fatal plan:

[1]. cf. Arnold: *Sohrab and Rustum*
> Take heed lest men should say
> Like some old miser Rustum hoards his fame.

and *Troilus and Cressida* III. 3. 180-6:
> Then marvel not, thou great and complete man,
> That all the Greeks begin to worship Ajax;
> Since things in motion sooner catch the eye
> Than what not stirs. The cry went once on thee,
> And still it might; and yet it may again,
> If thou wouldst not entomb thyself alive
> And case thy reputation in thy tent.

ἀλλὰ σέ περ προέτω, ἅμα δ' ἅλλος λαὸς ἐπέσθω
Μυρμιδόνων, αἵ κέν τι φόως Δαναοῖσι γένηαι·
καί τοι τεύχεα καλὰ δότω πόλεμόνδε φέρεσθαι
αἵ κέ σε τῷ εἴσκοντες ἀπόσχωνται πολέμοιο
Τρῶες, ἀναπνεύσωσι δ' ἀρήϊοι υἷες Ἀχαιῶν.

(796-800)

("Let him send you forth, and let the rest of the Myrmidons
follow with you, in the hope that you may prove for the
Danaans a light in their darkness; and let him give you his
fair arms to carry into the field, on the chance that, taking
you for him, the Trojans may hold back from the battle, and
the sons of the Achaeans get their breath again.")

Patroclus, much troubled by the immediacy of the danger,
goes hurrying back to the ships of Achilles. But on the way
he meets Eurypylus wounded and limping back alone; and
he stops to ask him what he thinks of the fight. Eurypylus
fully confirms Nestor's account and takes the gloomiest view
of the situation—"the Achaean defence is over," he says
(823); but he begs Patroclus to help him with his wound as
there is no one to look after him. Patroclus is perplexed; he
is full now of the imperative necessity of conveying Nestor's
suggestion to Achilles.

ἀλλ' οὐδ' ὣς περ σεῖο μεθήσω τειρομένοιο.

(841)

("But not even so will I desert you in your distress.")

Why has Homer deliberately made Patroclus meet Eurypylus?
Simply, surely, because the situation is not yet ready for the
completion of Patroclus's message. It all makes for clearness.
As the poet is not yet ready to describe the appeal of Patroclus
to Achilles, he shows us that Patroclus has stopped on his way
back. The interruption in his narrative he dramatizes as an
interruption in the actual events.

BOOK XII

W ITH Bk. XII we return to the battlefield to watch the progress of the Achaean defeat. This being the main battle of the poem, the poet is making the most of each step; he invents devices to hold it and to draw it out. What happens in Bk. XII could be stated in one sentence—Hector crosses the wall; this book is Homer's way of making the statement. Unlike so many of the books into which the Iliad has been divided, it constitutes a distinct unit. Everything in it is pointing to the moment when Hector crosses the wall, and is designed to emphasize the significance of that event. We are warned at the beginning that it is going to happen (3-4), and our attention is fixed on the wall as the centre of interest by the account of its subsequent destruction at the hands of Poseidon and Apollo (10-33), in accordance with the promise given to Poseidon by Zeus at the time of its erection (VII, 459-463). Thus casually the poet wakens again the feeling that the earlier passage in its context aroused—the sense of the transitoriness of the interests for which men strive with such intensity—, and its presence gives an ironic colouring at the outset to the picture of Hector's triumph, which supports and enhances the note of menace running through the book.

Next, he focuses attention on the chief actor—Hector—by means of a simile:

ὡς δ' ὅτ' ἂν ἔν τε κύνεσσι καὶ ἀνδράσι θηρευτῇσι
κάπριος ἠὲ λέων στρέφεται σθένεϊ βλεμεαίνων·
οἱ δέ τε πυργηδὸν σφέας αὐτοὺς ἀρτύναντες
ἀντίον ἵστανται καὶ ἀκοντίζουσι θαμειὰς
αἰχμὰς ἐκ χειρῶν· τοῦ δ' οὔ ποτε κυδάλιμον κῆρ
ταρβεῖ οὐδὲ φοβεῖται, ἀγηνορίη δέ μιν ἔκτα.

(41-46)

("As when among dogs and hunters a boar or lion keeps
wheeling about, in the glory of his strength, and they, forming
themselves in a wall against him, pour javelins thick and fast
upon him; but his valiant heart quakes not nor quails, and his
courage slays him.")

This simile has been criticized by the literalists as unsuitable
because Hector is not at bay, but is attacking. Miss Stawell
well replies[1]: "The leading note is surely just the irresistible
daring of the boar, a daring that is to prove fatal to himself:
'Nothing can daunt him nor make his heart afraid, and his
courage slays him.' We are reminded, or reminded we ought to
be, of Andromache's words to her husband (VI, 407) 'Your
daring will be your ruin' (φθίσει σε τὸ σὸν μένος)." That is the
key-note of the book, and the simile is designed to strike it.
All through the poet makes us feel the shadow of impending
doom, so that we who know watch his triumph as Hector
shaping out of his own nature the decrees of destiny.

The Trojans advance to the edge of the trench, and
Polydamas advises that they should leave their chariots behind
and attack on foot. Hector approves the wisdom of the sug-
gestion, and descends from his chariot, and the others do
likewise (60-87). But one of the Trojan leaders, Asios, dis-
regards the advice of Polydamas and in consequence involves
himself and his followers in disaster. He drives for the open
gate through which the Achaean fugitives are pouring, but

[1] *Homer and the Iliad*, p. 54.

is held before it by the strong stand of two warriors, while
the defenders on the wall above rain down missiles upon the
baffled attackers.

$$νιφάδες δ' ὡς πῖπτον ἔραζε,$$
$$ἅς τ' ἄνεμος ζαής, νέφεα σκιόεντα δονήσας,$$
$$ταρφειὰς κατέχευεν ἐπὶ χθονὶ πουλυβοτείρῃ.$$

(156-158)

("The stones fell upon the ground like snowflakes that a
stormy wind, whirling the shadowing clouds, pours thick
upon the bounteous earth.")

Asios protests angrily to Zeus for deceiving them with false
promises.

With this immediate confirmation of the wisdom of Poly-
damas we are carried back to Hector, and hear him reject the
advice he gives as the result of the omen that appears to them
as they stand at the trench (195-250). This would lose much
of its significance if the incident of Asios were omitted, or
rather it would lose the immediate recognition of its signifi-
cance. Hector is heading for his doom. The shadow of the
coming tragedy is falling across the scene of his triumph,
and Homer makes us see the shadow. That is what the omen
is for, and that is what Polydamas's interpretation of it is for.
He sees that all this extraordinary fortune is a delusion, that
it does not mean what it seems to mean, and of course we
who have been behind the scenes are thereby reminded of
what we have heard. Coming events are casting their shadows
before. We feel here very distinctly the forward movement of
the poem.

Hector's reply of rejection (231-250) strikes emphatically
the other dominating note of the book, the note which was
struck in the simile of the boar. Polydamas is right, as we
know, but there are greater things than being right, as every

tragic hero has shown, and Hector here rises to that rank. There is a depth of tragic irony in his speech for us who know what is preparing. A few lines further back this was Homer's comment on Asios' refusal to listen to Polydamas:

νήπιος, οὐδ' ἄρ' ἔμελλε κακὰς ὑπὸ κῆρας ἀλύξας
ἵπποισιν καί ὄχεσφιν ἀγαλλόμενος παρὰ νηῶν
ἂψ ἀπονοστήσειν προτὶ Ἴλιον ἠνεμόεσσαν.

(113-115)

("—the fool, who was not to escape the evil fates and return home, glorying in his chariot and horses, back from the ships to windy Ilios.")

It would have jarred if Homer had written such a comment on Hector's noble speech. It applies none the less, and perhaps originally Homer wrote it, or something like it, here, and, feeling how it jarred, invented the Asios incident to make the comment. Anyway, that incident sets forth as in a parable the significance of this one; the truth about Asios is the truth about Hector. Hector is trusting to the promises of Zeus, and so he pays no heed to the birds whether they fly to the dawn and the sun, or the left and the darkening west. And yet the omen represents the facts as we know them. The bird of Zeus is bitten by a snake, which, though torn and bleeding, is yet alive—as Polydamas says, the interpretation is obvious to any-one who knows anything of portents. For what were the promises of Zeus in which Hector trusts?—"I will give him might to slay, until he reaches the ships, until the sun sets and the sacred darkness comes on" (XI, 207-209). We can say (and see that in a sense it is true) that Hector is infatuated, that this is where he in his turn makes his fatal choice, and thereby ensures his doom. But it has been said before, and said differently: δαιμόνιε, φθίσει σε τὸ σὸν μένος, said Andro-mache, and it is this aspect of his conduct that is stressed in

the rest of the book.   All the incidents that follow are the
comment on his speech.   The voice of prudence and foresight
says "Go back! That is the way of safety." μὴ ἴομεν, says Poly-
damas (216).   But Hector cries "Forward!", and that becomes
the key-word of the book, and the spirit of the heroic age
seems to blaze out all around him in response to his cry.   The
two Ajaxes take up the word as they exhort the Achaeans on
the wall:

μή τις ὀπίσσω
τετράφθω ποτὶ νῆας ὁμοκλητῆρος ἀκούσας.
ἀλλὰ πρόσω ἵεσθε καὶ ἀλλήλοισι κέλεσθε.

(272-274)

("Let no one turn back to the ships, when he hears the call of
the foeman, but forward press you all and urge one another.")

They are the two warriors that hold back Hector in his turn,
and the parallel with Asios is sustained as the music of the
snow-storm simile rises once more, but more elaborate, more
complete (278-286).

Then Sarpedon comes forward to make what is implicit
explicit.   "Hector has made his tragic, noble choice, and
is going forward.   That is the moment chosen by the poet
for Sarpedon's famous apologue to Glaucus, the perfect
exposition of the heroic view of tragic life."[1]

ὦ πέπον, εἰ μὲν γὰρ πόλεμον περὶ τόνδε φυγόντε
αἰεὶ δὴ μέλλοιμεν ἀγήρω τ' ἀθανάτω τε
ἔσσεσθ', οὔτε κεν αὐτὸς ἐνὶ πρώτοισι μαχοίμην
οὔτε κε σὲ στέλλοιμι μάχην ἐς κυδιάνειραν·
νῦν δ' ἔμπης γὰρ κῆρες ἐφεστᾶσιν θανάτοιο
μυρίαι, ἃς οὐκ ἔστι φυγεῖν βροτὸν οὐδ' ὑπαλύξαι,
ἴομεν, ἠέ τῳ εὖχος ὀρέξομεν, ἠέ τις ἡμῖν.

(322-328)

[1] Sheppard: Pattern, p. 119.

("Dear friend, if, by escaping alive from this battle, we were going to be ageless and deathless for ever, neither would I myself fight among the foremost nor would I send you to win glory in battle; but now—since in any case countless fates of death beset us, which no mortal can escape or avoid—let us forward, whether we shall give glory to another or another to us.")

This is the true commentary on Hector's speech. This is the spirit and outlook that actuates him. It is the same as he expressed in his answer to Andromache's appeal in Bk. VI— since Troy and all its people will perish, therefore he will fight. Out of hopelessness he will make not hope, but glory. The nobleness of life is to do thus. Since death in countless forms threatens us anyway, let us forward.

This book is, as I have said, markedly a unit, and if we read and reread it until we can hear it both as music and meaning, the music as the meaning, and the meaning as the music, we shall have a better appreciation of the artistry of the Iliad than any explanation can give. For it illustrates in small compass how the poet throws out his net to catch all sorts of disparate interests, how he flashes from one person to another, from one topic to another, and yet fuses them into one significance, crystallizes varieties of effects into a unity of effect.

Here he seems to be merely describing the battle first at one point, then at another; and it is a series of pictures designed to convey as clearly as narrative can something of the turmoil of events and feelings which must mark such a struggle. The real purpose of the book is just to describe how Hector crossed the wall, and the poet pads it out with what

others did or said, first on one side, then on the other, passing
rapidly from incident to incident, from person to person. So
we may say; and yet when Hector does burst through the
wall, he does so with the splendour of all these things around
him. It is his spirit that fills the battlefield; it shines all about
him and makes the fitting background for his triumph. He
moves as it were to great music that expresses, that interprets,
the spirit that inspires him. The poet comments on the signifi-
cance of his act, but comments by incidents which at the same
time spread the battle before us.

The folly of Hector—that is what is emphasized and what
we who know the end feel in the first half; the splendour of
that folly, worth all the wisdom in the world, is what the
manifold music of the second half proclaims. Homer is
calling the world to witness the triumph of Hector. He has
been careful to keep reminding us that he is choosing the way
of death; he presents the plain foolishness of the thing, con-
fronts it with prudent words, with the wisdom that looks
before and after, and then drowns out these voices in the
applause of Hector's world. It all climbs up to the thrilling
description of Hector's break through the wall, and when
that comes, it reveals and creates the unity of the whole
design. All the incidents fall into place, become part of the
glorification of his deed. It is as if, above the voice of prudence
and common sense, the trumpets of heroism sounding the
charge rang out triumphantly around Hector as he leapt
within the gates.

BOOK XIII

THE poet then coolly announces that Zeus chose this moment to let his eyes wander from the battlefield (1-9). No one can doubt the purpose of that announcement. It is a direct intimation to his audience to be prepared for a digression from the main story. He has brought us at the end of Bk. XII to a crisis in the action. Now he deliberately arrests its course, holds it back for two books and a half, and then has to reconstruct the situation he had already reached. We know what is to happen, the poet has told us: Patroclus is to be killed, and then Hector's brief day of glory is over. And now events are in train for this: Patroclus is on his way back to Achilles with Nestor's proposal, and Hector is across the wall. Then, instead of the immediate development we are expecting, comes the surprising reversal of the situation. Poseidon, seizing the opportunity of Zeus's inattention, inspires the resistance of the Achaeans, and they halt the Trojan advance (Bk. XIII). Hera backs up Poseidon's efforts by beguiling Zeus with her charms and luring him to sleep; while he is sleeping, the battle turns definitely against the Trojans; Hector is wounded and the Trojans driven back in confusion (Bk. XIV). In Bk. XV Zeus wakes, and the situation already reached at the end of Bk. XII is restored again.

It is obvious that this excursion contributes nothing to the advancement of the story; it merely prolongs the poem by

126

further incidents, and perhaps the poet's chief purpose was
to make room for the material he has used here. "Homer was
the creator of the spacious epic," says Bury,[1] "and his epic
conception, if the term may be used, was not that of a poem
in which the interest is concentrated, as the dramatist concen-
trates it, exclusively on the one motif which gives it its unity
and on a few central figures, and in which nothing is admitted
that does not bear more or less directly on the *dénouement.* . . .
The epic on the grand scale conceived by Homer was to be
a composition in which the interest is extended to the whole
background and environment. The means for combining this
design with a dramatic plot was *delayed action,* and one of
the principal functions of the gods who play such a large part
in the Iliad was to provide devices for delaying the movement
which conducts from Agamemnon's repulse of Chryses to
the deaths of Patroclus and Hector." Here is delayed action
plainly enough, and it is brought about through the action of
gods. In fact, the story of the quarrel on Olympus reaches its
culmination in this revolt. From the beginning the other
gods have been raising our expectations of some overt act by
threatening and making tentative efforts to thwart the will
of Zeus, *i.e.* to divert the course of the story. Here our hopes
are realized (for, in a story, what we have been led to expect,
we unconsciously hope for), and in a form that has been
specifically foreshadowed; it is Hera's wish in Book VIII
come true; Poseidon acts, as Hera there prayed he would.

Justification for this long interruption is not hard to find
from the point of view of the poem, although undoubtedly
modern readers grow tired of the multiplication of battle
incidents. We must here discount our own feelings. The type

[1] *Cambridge Ancient History,* Vol. II, p. 499.

of narrative poetry that developed into the Iliad probably consisted of just such accounts of single combats as we have in such abundance here, so that it would be a feature that the Homeric audience chiefly looked for and desired. Fights were the first essential, and the rest, in origin, a framework to hold them and increase their interest by relating them together. Thus it would be artistically right to make the most of the opportunity afforded by this central battle and insert enough of such combats to satisfy the taste of his audience. He has done the same thing in the first part of the poem, and the symmetry in the structure has been (inadvertently) noted by Leaf[1]: "There is indeed a plot," he says of the Iliad, "a most magnificent story underlying the whole; yet for large portions of the poem at a time this main plot seems to be entirely forgotten in the long series of brilliant episodes which form the beauty of the Iliad. From the second book to the seventh we hear nothing of the counsel of Zeus which is to avenge the wrong done to Achilles. . . . So also in the thirteenth and fourteenth and the first part of the fifteenth books no advance whatever towards the catastrophe is made; the battle surges forwards and backwards; whatever is gained by one party is exactly balanced by a success by the other; and at the end of this long section things are in precisely the same position as at the opening." Thus, after the opening act which sets the story moving, we have a long delay in which the poet puts before us "the sea of character and circumstance that surrounds the initial deed"; and after the second great act in that story there is spread before us at sufficient length to make it adequate to the occasion a picture of the calamitous results which followed Achilles' refusal to fight. The longer he can make the list of

[1] *Companion*, p. 22.

warriors slain in the struggle resulting from the wrath of Achilles, the greater is the impression of the terribleness of that wrath; the more valiant souls that he can send to Hades, the better for his purpose, so long as he can in the process maintain the interest of his hearers. To accomplish this, he has recourse to the same technique as he used in the earlier battles of Bks. V and VIII; there is an apparent turn in the tide of battle; the issue seems for a time doubtful. The holding incident is here developed on a much larger scale, to fit the dimensions of this all-important battle.

It should be noted too that it is necessary to keep some balance in the fighting; the Achaeans must not be represented continually in defeat, not for patriotic, but for artistic reasons. The plan of the poem as begun in Bk. I called for their defeat, and that is therefore what we are expecting; but the poet has so managed it that we feel that the Achaeans are, of right, the stronger side, notwithstanding their fairly continuous misfortunes. By their successes in these two digressions the poet gives us the right perspective for Hector's triumph, and allows of the exploits of his great figures, who are all Achaeans except for Hector. It is something of a triumph in construction that as a fact the Trojans are on the whole the winning side while Achilles is absent and yet we have no doubt that the Achaeans are the better men.

But in fulfilling these purposes the episode has a direct dramatic value coming at the very point that it does. The prolonging of the battle by the desperate resistance of the Achaeans gives us time to realize the seriousness of the situation when Hector crosses the wall. The poet makes his hearers pause to take it in by translating the excitement aroused by that happening into incidents that express its

seriousness. Hector is through the wall: how can the poet
better make us realize, or, rather, express our realization of,
what this means than by showing the Achaeans fighting back
with the courage of despair? What happens is indeed the
natural sequel of the event that closed Bk. XII; the breaking
through of the defences of the ships would naturally spur the
Achaeans to a more desperate resistance, and this it is which,
leaving the gods out of account, is being depicted here. What
Homer wanted to do, artistically, when he had brought Hector
and the Trojans within the wall, was to hold the situation.
It is too good and dramatic to be covered up by rushing to his
climax. And so the Achaeans are represented as making a last
stand before their ships—their only hope of safety. They
have turned at bay. Our realization of the crisis that has been
reached is expressed as their realization of it.

In this way too the poet achieves the difficult but desirable
feat of repeating his climax. He makes the crossing of the
wall and the reaching of the ships two separate crises instead
of running them together. Hector breaks through the wall
at the end of Bk. XII; he reaches the ships at l. 704 of
Bk. XV. Now if one had followed hard upon the other,
we should have felt them both as two stages of one crisis. It
would be just one excitement rising to a climax. But by this
means he gets the effect of the excitement twice over. When
Hector breaks through with such *éclat*, we feel that the great
moment has come, that the event for which we have been
prepared is almost upon us; Achilles must do something.
Owing to the delay, we have the feeling all over again when
Hector lays his hand on the ship, and calls for fire. We get,
then, out of one event the effect of two climaxes, and that is
sheer gain.

But to prolong the battle for the ships by this unexpected change of fortune it was necessary to remove the guiding hand of Zeus, and so there was suggested the insertion and elaboration of an incident which would adequately account for his continued negligence and at the same time relieve the long narrative of battles with a scene having an entirely different kind of interest and with a complete change of tone. Indeed it may be that the nucleus and occasion of the whole digression is the episode of the beguiling of Zeus; that Homer deliberately diverted the course of the story to make a place for it, and built up this elaborate framework to hold it.

Poseidon, noting the wandering attention of Zeus, comes driving over the sea to help the Achaeans (10-31). In the likeness of Calchas, he urges the two Ajaxes to concentrate on resisting Hector, and the shame and indignation of the Achaean warriors generally at what has happened are dramatically expressed as his admonition to them (95-124). They accordingly rally round the two Ajaxes, and the oncoming phalanxes of Trojans are halted. Various details of the fight are given to get the situation established in our minds (155-205). Then, as his manner is, the poet turns to an individual and we follow for some time the fortunes of Idomeneus.

Poseidon, now in the likeness of one Thoas, passing to the tents of the Achaeans, meets Idomeneus coming from attendance on a wounded comrade. There is a brief conversation, in which we get something of the feeling which Achilles' indifference at their peril is rousing in the army (232-238). Idomeneus, having donned his armour and hurrying out to the battle, meets Meriones coming from the fight against Hector's division, for a new spear. Idomeneus offers to lend him one of the many spears he has captured from the enemy, and Meriones, while accepting the offer to save time, is careful to point out that he has likewise plenty of his own, also taken from the enemy. The conversation is no doubt pure elaboration of a detail, but delightfully spirited and human.

They go out together deciding not to rejoin the Ajaxes in their fight against Hector but to add their weight to the defence on the left. This was the point where Asios had attempted to drive in with his chariot, when we were told that he was to fall by the spear of Idomeneus (XII, 117). It is, then, the fight the description of which was broken off at l. 194 of Bk. XII that is picked up again at 361 of this book; and with what would seem quite unnecessary care Homer disposes of all that are left of the persons mentioned as belonging to the company of Asios.[1]

Thus the so-called *aristeia* of Idomeneus is the poet's way of completing the account of Asios' ill-advised attempt, and by including it here in connection with the fierce rally of the Achaeans he brings back sharply the thought of Polydamas; and when we turn from the fighting on the left where the Trojans are thus having the worst of it, to Hector's division in the centre, the same point is emphasized. This passage (from 673) resumes the fight which we left at l. 205, and we are shown the Trojans there also losing heart at the determined stand of the Achaeans (721). Then come Polydamas's words

---

[1] Ἄσιον ἀμφὶ ἄνακτα καὶ Ἰαμενὸν καὶ Ὀρέστην
  Ἀσιάδην τ' Ἀδάμαντα Θόωνά τε Οἰνόμαόν τε. (XII, 139-140)
Iamenos and Orestes fell in the first attack along with many others not otherwise mentioned (XII, 182-194). Here in Bk. XIII there are Asios himself (384-401), Oenomaus (506-511), Thoon (545-550), Adamas (560-575).

to Hector (726-747), which, for us, point the moral of what is happening here. It is to this state of things that Hector's refusal in Bk. XII to listen to Polydamas's advice has brought them. The omen had shown him before the attack began that their apparent opportunity was their deadliest peril; the events that are now occurring seem to him the fulfilment of the omen; the snake is striking back. He obviously wishes to propose withdrawal, for he realizes, not as an augur, but as a soldier, that Achilles and the Myrmidons are in effect troops in reserve which can be let loose on the confused ranks of the Trojans whenever their leader chooses (740-747). But what his speech shows the audience is that the present check is itself an omen, a warning of what is to happen. They know that the end is not yet, for Zeus's purpose is not yet fulfilled, so that this is for them a repetition of the omen, reminding them, as it did, of the real nature of Zeus's plans.

All that Polydamas ventures to suggest is that Hector should consult with the other Trojan leaders whether they should press on or withdraw now. Hector approves, but when such of the leaders as are still unwounded have gathered he instantly leads another attack on the centre where Ajax is still heading the Achaean defence. Thus the action comprised in Bk. XIII is limited to the check of the Trojan attack.

BOOK XIV

NESTOR is the first of the absentee Achaeans to begin to move. He is stirred by the realization that the noise of the fighting is coming nearer to the ships to leave the wounded Machaon (1-8).

Critics have pressed too heavily on the inconsistency between the situation at the end of Bk. XIII and that which Nestor finds when he views the battlefield at the beginning of Bk. XIV. We read at l. 835 of Bk. XIII:

'Αργεῖοι δ' ἑτέρωθεν ἐπίαχον, οὐδ' ἐλάθοντο
ἀλκῆς, ἀλλ' ἔμενον Τρώων ἐπιόντας ἀρίστους.

("The Argives shouted on their side, and forgot not their valour, but abode the oncoming of the best of the Trojans.")

But when Nestor looks out (XIV, 13),

εἴσιδεν ἔργον ἀεικές,
τοὺς μὲν ὀρινομένους, τοὺς δὲ κλονέοντας ὄπισθε,
Τρῶας ὑπερθύμους· ἐρέριπτο δὲ τεῖχος 'Αχαιῶν.

("He saw a shameful thing, the Achaeans in rout and the high-hearted Trojans pressing upon them; and the wall of the Achaeans was down.")

Now the natural conclusion anyone would draw is that the poet has gone back in time and that he is of necessity giving consecutively events which are really concurrent. That is obvious on the face of it. And yet, the critics point out, this explanation is spoilt by the way the two incidents are linked together. Bk. XIII ends with the line (which follows immediately on the two quoted above)

ἠχὴ δ' ἀμφοτέρων ἵκετ' αἰθέρα καὶ Διὸς αὐγάς

("The cry of both hosts arose to the height of heaven")

and Book XIV begins

Νέστορα δ' οὐκ ἔλαθεν ἰαχὴ πίνοντά περ ἔμπης

("Nestor failed not to hear the cry though at his wine.")

No one, it is said, could help taking the ἰαχή of the one line as the same as the ἠχή of the other. That is clearly right, too. But I find no difficulty in accepting both propositions—that the cry that roused Nestor was the cry uttered by the Trojans and Achaeans as described in the preceding line, and that what Nestor saw was the battlefield as it was before that cry was uttered. That is, this is an example of Homer's inability to handle artistic perspective, or rather his primitive way of handling it. He is giving a series of simultaneous scenes, but the exigencies of narrative compel him to give them one after the other; and as this incident is the next thing to be narrated, he finds it simpler to describe it as if it happened next. He simply goes on even when he goes back.

The same thing applies to the episode of the beguiling of Zeus. All these incidents are overlapping in time, but the poet cannot narrate them all at the same time. The events that occur on the battlefield are plainly these, and in this order: the Trojans, led by Hector, are attacking again, and the Achaeans are standing firm, as related in the closing lines of Bk. XIII; at this juncture they are joined by Nestor, Agamemnon, and Diomedes, as related in Bk. XIV, 379-387. It is at the moment, or shortly after the moment, described in

147-152 that the god Hypnos (Sleep) comes to Poseidon with the message from Hera. The three incidents then—the impending fight at the end of Bk. XIII, the return of the wounded warriors, and the beguiling of Zeus—all converge on the one point, that described in 379-390, and that point is, in time, immediately consecutive to the end of Bk. XIII.

Objection has been taken to the place of the Hera episode in relation to Poseidon's activities. Leaf asks[1]: "Why, when Poseidon has been successfully helping the Greeks for a long space of time, should it only now occur to Hera to come to his aid, and distract the attention of Zeus? Her intervention should evidently have come at the beginning of Book XIII." And so it has been suggested that XIII 39 to XIV 152 is an interpolation. But, it must be remembered, such objections are being looked for; these critics are trying to find passages to leave out; their ingenuity therefore is directed towards detecting any flaw in the strict logic of events which may serve as an excuse for a cut. Here the poet arranges his incidents with a view to dramatic effect; he is leading up to the complete disruption of Zeus's plan in the wounding of Hector and the flight of the Trojans, and therefore makes his motivation of it a progress of emotional interest, grading it up to the crisis by two steps.

Zeus has let his eyes wander from the battlefield. That is the first step. (Monro says "The sudden indifference of Zeus comes as a surprise: there is nothing to make it natural for him to turn his eyes away." Certainly it is a surprise, and therefore dramatically good; it may even be exasperating to hear at such a point—as it is exasperating when an instalment of a serial story stops on the edge of an apparent catastrophe.

[1] *Companion*, p. 242.

But it is not true that there is nothing that makes it natural; there is the character of Zeus himself as he has already been set before us in the poem. He is, from the point of view of those who would have the business of the poem carried through as expeditiously as possible, a maddening person. He has never shown the interest in the Trojan affair felt so intensely by the other gods. He was forced by Thetis's importunity to adopt a definite policy towards it, but his heart is not wholly in the fulfilment of his promise, and he has been distinctly casual and dilatory about it, as the critics have complained, giving the poet, incidentally, plenty of time to spread his scene before us. So now, satisfied that events are progressing in the promised direction, he—quite naturally for him—lets his eyes and thoughts wander elsewhere in search of variety.) The fact of his wandering attention provokes of itself an expectation of some immediate effect on the battlefield. This is supplied just sufficiently to the extent of his lapse by seeing the Trojans cease to make headway. In this first stage the Achaeans merely check their advance and Poseidon sneaks about cautiously in disguise. But something more than an averted glance is needed to key us to hear and acquiesce in a complete Trojan reverse. Some new incident is not only logically necessary, but, more important, imaginatively necessary. An intensification of Zeus's inattention is needed to make their defeat credible, and to build up an effect of climax in the approach to it. So to him in his idle, easy mood, comes Hera with her allurements; at what exact point chronologically during the previously related incidents does not matter; Hera has chosen her moment with the skill of a woman, and the poet his with the skill of an experienced narrator. Zeus is obviously off his guard and in the mood for dalliance. (The deliciously humorous reminiscence by Zeus of his own infidelities helps to motivate the event; he is very susceptible to feminine beauty.) The episode is excellently well placed to break the account of the long day's battle. Set in the midst of the endless fighting, there is in it the relief of beauty, of humour, a complete change of scene, character, tone. We are back in the light frivolous atmosphere of Olympus. There seems also, in its sharp contrast with the bitter scenes of human suffering, something of irony. This is the heavenly aspect of that desperate struggle on the plain below. Perhaps the poet did not intend this effect; and yet the words he gives to Achilles later on seem to show him aware of the contrast:

$$\text{ὡς γὰρ ἐπεκλώσαντο θεοὶ δειλοῖσι βροτοῖσι,}$$
$$\text{ζώειν ἀχνυμένοις· αὐτοὶ δέ τ' ἀκηδέες εἰσί.}$$

(XXIV, 525-526)

("For this is the lot the gods have spun for miserable mortals, that they should live in pain, while they themselves are without sorrow.")

The catastrophe, thus elaborately prepared, is formally introduced by the great three-ply simile (394-399), and its startling effect is reproduced by the rapidity with which it is told. It all happens in a moment: Hector is wounded by Ajax and carried unconscious off the field to his chariot; after a brief stand the Trojans break and flee. The whole carefully built plan, the situation so long and laboriously arrived at through Bks. XI and XII—the carrying of the Achaean defences—a situation essential to the projected continuance of the story, has been deliberately jettisoned, and if the story is to proceed, everything will have to be done all over again.

BOOK XV

THE poet's method of meeting the difficulty he has
created is very simple. He is telling a story, and his business
is to interest and delight, and he is not bound by the necessities
of real life. Having, for the further delectation of his audience,
broken off the development of his plot when it was just on its
way to fulfilment, he now aims to continue from the point
where he left it off without the tedious repetition which strict
verisimilitude would require. He avails himself, accordingly,
of the convenient resource afforded him by his divine
machinery.

Zeus wakes in the nick of time, and sees what has
happened. But the poet does not hasten at once to his
restoration of the battle; being a good story-teller he knows
that a minor curiosity has been raised and should be satisfied.
For Hera's trick provokes more than the question: What will
Zeus say and do when he finds what has happened while he
slept? It raises also the subordinate question: What will he say
and do to *Hera* when he discovers that she has purposely
tricked him? Accordingly, we see him turning in fury upon
Hera. But the resolution of the scene of the beguiling main-
tains its note of levity. Though Zeus hints at a terrible retri-
bution, he dismisses her unpunished to Olympus, obviously
amused at the outrageous prevarication of her oath of denial
and choosing to be convinced. It is further rounded off by the
scene on Olympus. Hera has been ordered to send Iris and

Apollo to Zeus, but the poet apparently cannot resist developing the scene beyond the absolute requirements of the plot. Hera's struggle between her rage at her failure and her efforts to preserve her dignity is beautifully drawn, and her malicious attempt to get Ares into trouble, though it leads to nothing, was well worth putting in for its own sake. It is just this "finish" of imagination that makes us accept these events for the time being as actualities; we see them, as it were, in the round.

But before Hera departs, Zeus takes occasion to give her a further glimpse of what he is preparing, and so the goal of the hearers' interests is set forward again. Homer has followed this practice throughout, and, as I have noted, the artistic advantage is plain: one can see the significance of an event in a series much more clearly when one knows to what they are tending; one's interest is oriented. In Bk. VIII (to go no further back) we had:

οὐ γὰρ πρὶν πολέμου ἀποπαύσεται ὄβριμος Ἕκτωρ,
πρὶν ὄρθαι παρὰ ναῦφι ποδώκεα Πηλεΐωνα,
ἤματι τῷ ὅτ᾽ ἂν οἱ μὲν ἐπὶ πρύμνῃσι μάχωνται
στείνει ἐν αἰνοτάτῳ περὶ Πατρόκλοιο θανόντος.

(473-476)

("For Hector will not cease from battle before the swift-footed son of Peleus rises up beside the ships on that day when they are fighting at the sterns in direst straits around the dead Patroclus.")

This prophecy has coloured and pointed our reading of the Embassy and of Patroclus's activity in Bk. XI.

In Bk. XI came Zeus's promise to Hector:

οἱ κράτος ἐγγυαλίξω
κτείνειν, εἰς ὅ κε νῆας ἐϋσσέλμους ἀφίκηται
δύῃ τ᾽ ἠέλιος καὶ ἐπὶ κνέφας ἱερὸν ἔλθῃ.

(192-194)

("I will give him might to slay until he reaches the ships, until the sun sets and the sacred darkness comes on."

It is within that frame that Hector's triumph is set; it conditions for us every move he makes.

And now we hear:

ὁ δ' ἀνστήσει ὃν ἑταῖρον
Πάτροκλον· τὸν δὲ κτενεῖ ἔγχεϊ φαίδιμος Ἕκτωρ. . .
τοῦ δὲ χολωσάμενος κτενεῖ Ἕκτορα δῖος Ἀχιλλεύς.

(64-68)

("He will raise up his comrade, Patroclus; him will Hector kill; in rage for him Achilles will kill Hector.")

When Iris and Apollo descend, Zeus sets himself to restore the battle. Iris is despatched to dismiss Poseidon, who sullenly retires, and Apollo to revive Hector. And Homer dismisses the interruption to his plot as brusquely and as easily. Just as in Bk. VIII, he uses a god to bring the situation rapidly to the point he wishes. Apollo puts a panic into the hearts of the Achaeans. We are not to have the struggle for the wall all over again, so Apollo simply knocks it down and makes a way for the Trojan chariots across the trench (360-366). This is to be a struggle for the ships.

But another loose thread has to be now picked up. We read (381 ff.): "As a great wave in the broad paths of the sea breaks over the bulwarks of a ship . . . so the Trojans with a great cry came down over the wall, and driving in their chariots fought at the sterns with double-pointed spears hand to hand—they in their chariots, and the Achaeans mounting their black ships fought from them with the long pikes that were lying on the decks ready for use in a sea-fight, jointed and shod with bronze. And Patroclus. . . ." At last! This is what we have been waiting for ever since the beginning of

Bk. XIV at least, when Nestor set the example by leaving
Machaon. What is Patroclus doing? Of course Homer has
been keeping Patroclus back for an artistic reason. He wants
to delay his appeal to Achilles till the firing of the Achaean
ship. It would doubtless be more natural if Patroclus had
noticed the seriousness of the situation earlier, but then that
would have dislocated the poet's plan of synchronizing the
appeal to Achilles with the firing of the ship. Besides, it is
clear that these events, though they have taken long to tell,
have happened rapidly: Hector and the Trojans broke through
the wall; the Achaeans, desperate, rallied and held back the
Trojan advance; Nestor and the wounded chieftains rushed
out to aid in the battle; Hector fell wounded and the Trojans
were beaten back; Hector revived and led another attack, re-
taking the wall and hurling the Achaeans back to the ships.
That is, as we may say, what actually happened.

But Homer has made a bold attempt to obscure any un-
naturalness in Patroclus's delay by speaking of two moments
as if they were one (390-398): "And Patroclus, so long as the
Achaeans and Trojans were fighting about the wall outside
the ships, sat in the tent of Eurypylus, cheering him with talk,
and upon his wound spread remedies to soothe the dark
pains. But when he saw the Trojans rushing over the wall,
and the shouting and flight of the Danaans began, he groaned
and smote his thighs with the flat of his hands."

The poet may have "got by" with this in the case of his
unsuspecting audience, but it has not escaped the close scrutiny
of his later critics. "Are we to suppose then," Leaf asks
sternly,[1] "that Patroclus never noticed all the disasters of
XIII and XIV, and only remarks when the wall is carried a

[1] *Commentary, ad. loc.*

second time?" It seems to me that Homer may indeed have
been aware of the difficulty, and has tried to cover it up by
assuming an air of complete naturalness as he telescopes the
two events together.

At any rate, this is just the right time to set Patroclus
moving. The fight for the ships has begun, and that is to
culminate in the firing of the ship by Hector, which happen-
ing is to cap and clinch Patroclus's appeal. So Homer flashes
this scene upon us and then returns to the battle, so that we
may feel that it is a race between Patroclus and the advancing
lines of the Trojans. Will he be in time?

From this point (405) the poet sets the scene for Patroclus's
appeal, in the desperate struggle of the Achaeans to hold back
the Trojans from their ships. In the description he alternates
from one side to another, thus through the feelings of those
engaged making us realize the sense of crisis. At first the
battle line holds firm (405-414). Ajax and Hector are the
central figures. Ajax kills a Trojan who was rushing upon
the ship with a burning brand, and Hector calls upon his
comrades to rescue the body (419-428). Then an Achaean is
killed by Hector, and Ajax shouts to Teucer to shoot at Hector,
and for a time we watch the battle from their side. At l. 463
Teucer's bowstring breaks, and, as it was new, he cries out in
despair that the gods are fighting against them. Ajax replies
"Never mind, get a spear and shield. The thing to do is to
fight, whoever is against us." Hector, seeing what has
happened, draws the same conclusion as Teucer, and cheers on
his men: "Zeus is on our side, their strength is diminishing.
Fight on! Who dies, let him die. It is not unseemly for him
to die in defence of fatherland; his wife is safe and his children
if only the Achaeans sail away to their own country."

Then back to Ajax again, with his exhortation that the final decision is at hand (502-513)—a splendid and stirring speech as all Ajax's are. This is followed by a general description of the battle (515-545), and out of it comes the voice of Hector urging on one Melanippus. Why should an unknown person like Melanippus, invented for the occasion, be chosen for this purpose? Perhaps again because it increases the impression of actuality—gives one the feeling that the only possible reason Homer says it was Melanippus that Hector called upon must be because it really was. But also he is to be the immediate victim of Antilochus. That is all he is for. Antilochus is to play an important part presently, and the poet begins to fix our attention upon him. So Menelaus's exhortation to Antilochus answers Hector's exhortation (569-571).

At l. 592 the poet sums up again the significance of these events, pointing to the goal, and showing us how near it is: "For this was what Zeus was waiting for, to see the flash of the burning ship. From that moment he was going to ordain the flight of the Trojans back from the ships" (599-602). This may not be literally true, but it is substantially: the firing of the ship is the signal of the beginning of the end.

Hector is fighting like a madman, inspired by the strength and help of Zeus, "for his time was short; already Pallas Athena was hurrying on his day of destiny at the hands of the son of Peleus" (612-614). The Argive line however still holds (617-622). Then with a rush Hector leads another attack, and the line begins to break (623-652). And now the Trojans are among the ships (653 ff.). Homer is holding his crisis. Nestor implores the Argives to stand firm. Ajax is still fighting desperately from the ships. "He went up and down the decks of the ships with long strides, wielding a long pike in his hands . . . like a man skilled in riding who harnesses four horses together, and drives them from the plain towards a great city, and many men and women marvel at him as he leaps from one to another, while they fly along, so Ajax went from deck to deck of the swift ships." Is not that the Ajax we have come to know? As brave as a lion, and as stubborn as a donkey.

At last Hector lays his hand on the stern of a ship (704) and again the poet holds the moment (705-715). And Hector, clinging to the ship, calls for fire: "Bring fire, and all with one voice raise the war-cry. Now has Zeus given us the day that compensates for all."

BOOK XVI

AT the exciting moment when Hector is calling for fire and Ajax is still chivying Trojans from the threatened ship, the picture of the fight fades out, and we see Patroclus with Achilles. Achilles greets him and his woe-begone face with affectionate mockery: "Why are you in tears, Patroclus? You remind me of a little girl that runs beside her mother and begs to be picked up, clinging to her dress and delaying her though she is in a hurry; and in tears she looks up at her, to make her pick her up" (7-10). The implied comparison of himself to a mother is not without a certain grim humour, but, aside from that, there is something extraordinarily effective in the tone of the speech. It is the tone of familiar friendship, and thus by this passing touch the poet evokes the emotional background that dramatizes the moment. Nothing has been made so far of Achilles' affection for Patroclus; at the most it has been only implied. This is the first time we have heard them talking together, and it is the first time we hear Achilles talking friendlily, not at a tension. And so when Patroclus outspokenly condemns his conduct, he shows no resentment, but tries to explain his feelings, not defiantly, but as to himself.

It is the most telling place for making us think of their close friendship, because, in the first place, it now becomes the vital factor in the story, and also because we know that it is the last time they ever talk together. That knowledge gives poignancy to the light mockery of Achilles' first words. He

146

has no notion that there is but one step between him and his great sorrow; but we know—or, if we don't, the poet tells us so (46-47)—and we see that his very affection for his friend is to play its part in inducing him to take that step. As soon as Homer says τὸν δὲ ἰδὼν ᾤκτιρε (5),—"seeing his tears, he pitied him"—it becomes plain that conditions are favourable for the success of Patroclus's appeal. The plan of Zeus is working out through the characters of the human agents. Zeus, we might say, did not *will* the death of Patroclus but, knowing the men he was dealing with, saw what was involved in the fulfilment of Achilles' prayer. In his own way he recognized that character is destiny.

This is the beginning of the repentance of Achilles. For by consenting to the suggestion Patroclus brings he is really giving up the full satisfaction of his revenge. It is just the letter of his resolve he sticks to, the spirit of it is broken. The effort to disguise this fact and to justify it at the same time is what causes the difficulties in his reply to Patroclus's appeal. The struggle in his own heart makes his speech illogical and inconsistent; that is, the speech is deliberately made illogical and inconsistent to represent dramatically and externally the internal struggle.

Achilles is obstinately clinging to his wrongs, just because he is tempted to forget about them and go into the fight himself. Homer has already given us an inkling of this change of mood. On the day after his passionate rejection of Agamemnon's offer had come the turn in the battle for which he had prayed, and we saw Achilles no longer sitting in his tent proudly aloof, but standing on his ship, eagerly watching the battle. He was evidently even then finding his resolution hard to retain in its rigidity. And now Patroclus has come with a compromise suggestion, and he sees in it a way out of his difficulty, and at the same time objects to it for two opposite reasons—because he longs to go out himself and because it is a virtual surrender of his position. These are the three thoughts that are contending within him and confusing his words, as his mind jumps from one to another.

He sees the insinuation in Nestor's suggestion (quoted by Patroclus) that his motive in staying out of the fight may be really to avoid the death prophesied by his mother (a malicious interpretation of Achilles' words in Bk. IX), and is quick to resent and deny it (48-51), and he tries to explain quite honestly what his feeling is. He cannot stand the insolence of office; it fills him with an agony of rage,

> ὁππότε δὴ τὸν ὁμοῖον ἀνὴρ ἐθέλῃσιν ἀμέρσαι
> καὶ γέρας ἂψ ἀφελέσθαι, ὅ τε κράτεϊ προβεβήκῃ.
>
> (52-54)

("when a man wishes to humiliate his equal and take back the prize he had won, because his position gives him the power.")

And as he recalls the wrong done him, the bitterness of his former mood echoes through his words:

> κούρην ἣν ἄρα μοι γέρας ἔξελον υἷες Ἀχαιῶν, . . .
> τὴν ἂψ ἐκ χειρῶν ἕλετο κρείων Ἀγαμέμνων
> Ἀτρεΐδης ὡς εἴ τιν' ἀτίμητον μετανάστην.
>
> (56-59)

("The girl whom the sons of the Achaeans chose out as my *geras*, royal Agamemnon the son of Atreus has taken back from my hands as if I were an outlander without rights.")

This has been his point all along; the offence is done, atonement or no atonement. All the compensation in the world would not remove it; what he wants is revenge.

I get the impression, however, that he is really trying to lash himself back into rage, as he realizes the presence of warring feelings in his mind. For his next words are:

ἀλλὰ τὰ μὲν προτετύχθαι ἐάσομεν· οὐδ' ἄρα πως ἦν
ἀσπερχὲς κεχολῶσθαι ἐνὶ φρεσίν·

(60-61)

("But we will let bygones be bygones; it was not after all
possible to keep anger for ever in my heart.")

Is he renouncing his wrath? Almost; he is on the verge of it.
But ἤτοι ἔφην γε—"verily I *did* say . . ." He cannot do it; he
has committed himself. His pride conquers his desire. And
then he hurriedly seizes on the suggested compromise,
illogical as it is (64-69). As he describes the necessity which
forces his hand, one can feel in his words the satisfaction at
the proof it affords of his vital importance to the Achaeans
clashing with his irrepressible desire to see the Trojans once
more flying before him; he cannot really bear to see them
triumphant. And as that feeling, that strong desire, rises in his
heart, with a childish but natural petulance he turns his resent-
ment at his enforced inactivity against the ultimate cause of it,
Agamemnon. "It's all Agamemnon's fault." It has been
absurdly objected to the clause εἴ μοι κρείων Ἀγαμέμνων ἤπια εἰδείη
("if Agamemnon dealt fairly with me") that it is hopelessly
inconsistent with the facts of the case, considering the
sending of the Embassy.[1] Of course it is. Homer no doubt
assumed that his audience would remember the Embassy,
would interpret Achilles' words on the understanding that

[1] "The words of Achilles are entirely inconsistent with the ample
and indeed abject humiliation of Agamemnon in IX. This is not a mere
superficial inconsistency such as may be due to a temporary forgetfulness;
it is a contradiction at the very root of the story. To suppose that the
same intellect which prepared the embassy to Achilles in the eighth book
and wrought it out in such magnificence and wealth of detail in the
ninth, could afterwards compose a speech, so different and yet so grand,
in entire oblivion of what had gone before, is to demand a credulity
rendering any rational criticism impossible." Leaf: *Commentary*.

it had taken place, and therefore take them as revelatory of his mood at this juncture, that is, would see that he is still being perverse and foolish. The contradiction is not "at the root of the story"; it is in Achilles' mind. It is, ultimately, Agamemnon's fault that Achilles finds himself involved in his present difficulty, and the realization that he has been a fool not to accept Agamemnon's offer of reconciliation would make him not less angry, but more, with the man whose injustice has put him into this quandary. These words are his explanation or justification to himself of why he is not doing what he plainly longs to do. As the glorious picture of the Trojans flying before him crosses his mind, he asks himself, as it were, why he does not do it; and, in exasperation at feeling how he has tied his own hands, makes out, in defiance of the facts, as men have a habit of doing on such occasions, that he is still acting on principle, he is still protesting against rank injustice.   '

Then, as he contemplates the facts of the situation as it now is, another realization arises in his mind:

οὐ γὰρ Τυδείδεω Διομήδεος ἐν παλάμῃσι
μαίνεται ἐγχείη Δαναῶν ἀπὸ λοιγὸν ἀμῦναι·
οὐδέ πω Ἀτρείδεω ὀπὸς ἔκλυον αὐδήσαντος
ἐχθρῆς ἐκ κεφαλῆς· ἀλλ᾽ Ἕκτορος ἀνδροφόνοιο
Τρωσὶ κελεύοντος περιάγνυται, οἱ δ᾽ ἀλαλητῷ
πᾶν πεδίον κατέχουσι, μάχῃ νικῶντες Ἀχαιούς·
ἀλλὰ καὶ ὣς, Πάτροκλε, νεῶν ἀπὸ λοιγὸν ἀμύνων
ἔμπεσ᾽ ἐπικρατέως.

(74-81)

("For not in the hands of Diomedes, son of Tydeus, rages the spear to ward off destruction from the Danaans; nor have I yet heard the voice of the son of Atreus shouting from his hated head; but all round rings the voice of man-slaying Hector urging on the Trojans, and they with their yelling fill all the plain, as they vanquish the Achaeans in battle. But even so, Patroclus, fall mightily upon them and ward off destruction from the ships.")

That ἀλλὰ καὶ ὣς ("but even so") shows the direction in which his thoughts are running. He sees that if he consents to the intervention of the Myrmidons under Patroclus he is giving up his contemplated revenge when the goal is actually in sight. His plan, we can conjecture, had been something like this: to take no part whatever with the Achaeans as such; that is Agamemnon's concern; let them see to what he leads them, what he is worth. He himself, as a free and independent prince, will not interfere with the Trojans until they attack his own separate, independent camp. This is to be his triumph; when he, acting simply for himself and his army, has defeated the Trojans (and we must believe that he has no doubts about his success), he will be in a position to dictate his own terms to the defeated Agamemnon. To intervene now means that it will still be Agamemnon's army that is victorious, whereas what he wants is that Agamemnon should be unequivocally defeated and therefore completely discredited, and that he himself, acting separately and on his own initiative, should be contrastingly victorious. By that, and that alone, he feels his honour can be vindicated, his shame wiped out, and his revenge completed. Everything is now in train for just that result. The Achaeans, without him, are on the verge of complete disaster. What he longed for, or thought he longed for, is just going to happen. . . . "But even so, Patroclus, fall mightily upon them and ward off destruction from the ships."

But there is another thought disturbing him. He is not only throwing away his chance of the full revenge he contemplated when it is actually within his grasp, he is risking his whole position; if Patroclus is too successful, Agamemnon may not renew his offer of gifts, and Achilles will be simply left in the lurch, like Meleager in Phoenix's story. That is part of his thought, but there is something more—a sudden fear or foreboding for Patroclus, which he hesitates to acknowledge. Three times he urges him to confine himself to driving the Trojans from the ships. First he solemnly impresses upon his friend the importance of restraint on his part for his leader's sake (83-87); and, not satisfied, puts it in another form as if he hoped the repetition would ensure his obedience. Again he repeats his order, and this time gets nearer to his real anxiety, but still keeping it vague and general: "Do not in the excitement of the fighting lead on to Ilios, lest some god step in; Apollo loves them very much; but turn back when you have brought salvation to the ships, and leave the fighting in the plain to others" (91-96). Then the thought he has been repressing breaks out incontinently: "Oh, Father Zeus and Athena and Apollo, would that neither a single Trojan might escape death nor any Argive, but that you and I might come out alive, and all by ourselves destroy the towers that veil the head of Troy!" A sudden passionate outburst against the net of circumstances in which he feels himself entangled—hatred for the Trojans because of the danger to his friend, hatred for the Achaeans because by reason of his quarrel he cannot go in Patroclus's place. "I wish we were rid of the whole lot of them, and there were just you and I and glory.—'A plague on both their houses!' " Illogical, wrongheaded, even absurd, the whole speech is, no doubt, but all the same magnificently dramatic as the intensely imagined depiction of a complexity of feelings.

"Why is it," asks Monro,[1] "that Achilles allows Patroclus to come to the aid of the Greeks but will not aid them himself? . . . It must be admitted that it is difficult to account for the action of Achilles on an intelligible principle, and still more difficult to trace any such principle in the text of Homer. What we do find in Homer is the art by which this want of motive is disguised. The sending of Patroclus in place of Achilles is first heard of in the eleventh book, where Nestor suggests a reason for it. 'If,' he says, 'Achilles is held back by fear of some warning given from Zeus, let him send thee forth.' This is duly repeated by Patroclus, and Achilles at once answers that that is not the reason of his holding aloof from the war. But he gives no reason which does not equally tell against sending Patroclus. His answer is virtually the confession of the poet that there is no reason. Yet the two speeches (20-100), though they do not logically account for the action of Achilles, nevertheless furnish it with a tolerable poetic motive. That is to say, the entreaty of Patroclus, and the reason that he gives are sufficient to prepare us for what follows and to remove the sense of harshness which entire absence of motive would involve."

Is this a complete account of the matter? "A tolerable poetic motive"—is that all the poet gives? While it is true that according to strict logic there is no reason and that in that sense Achilles' speech "is virtually the confession of the

[1] Vol. II, pp. 307-8.

poet that there is no reason", yet what the poet has made it show is that Achilles himself is the reason.

A character is ultimately made out of the requisite incidents of a plot or story, and Achilles is, in part, what he is to meet just such difficulties in the motivation of what is required by the given plot. Thus a story may gain depth and emotional perspective and power through its difficulties and illogicalities, and perhaps this sort of problem first forced upon a story-teller attention to character-study. When a man's required actions carry their motives on their face, one need not go beneath the surface; but when for the purpose of the plot he must act surprisingly, when the story calls upon him to act in one way at one moment, in a totally different way at another, and in a different way again at a third, the story-teller may either let it go at that, trusting to the excitement of the events to carry him through, or he may be led to seek in a diversity of incidents a diversity of motives and so develop a complex personality. He integrates the various and perhaps conflicting turns of the story in the mind of the actor as manifestations of a complex personality, which, therefore, if compellingly projected, seems to have a life independent of the story and to cause by its own conflicting motives the diverse turns of incident required.

However that may be, this is what Homer has done here. He has transferred this irrationality in the story to the mind of Achilles with immense gain to the tragic significance of the story. Supposing he had dodged this difficulty—let us say, by representing Patroclus as acting on his own initiative, borrowing Achilles' arms unasked and leading out the impatient Myrmidons—; would not the significance and impressiveness of the sequel dwindle at once? Gone would be

Achilles' realization that he had sent Patroclus to his death, gone therefore almost all the agony of mind which displays itself in the ruthless brutality of his revenge. It is essential to the effect (and effect is paramount, logic is subordinate to it) that Achilles should be tortured with the thought that he was responsible for Patroclus's death; and so the absence of a logical reason appears as the positive presence of conflicting and illogical passions in a complicated, many-sided personality, out of which comes with complete convincingness the Achilles of Bk. XXII and the Achilles of Bk. XXIV.

Their conversation is interrupted at this point to show what is going on at the ship meanwhile (101). It is remarkable that the scene in which Achilles is shown still holding back from his comrades' desperate battle for life is placed between the two pictures of Ajax's magnificent stand in defence of the ship the Trojans are attacking. It seems as if the poet were determined to thrust Achilles' conduct into the worst light possible.

Then comes Hector's great moment, solemnly marked by an appeal to the Muses. Ajax's spear is shorn in two, and the fire runs along the ship. The picture flashes out, and we see Achilles seeing it:

$$\text{αὐτὰρ 'Αχιλλεὺς}$$
μηρὼ πληξάμενος Πατροκλῆα προσέειπεν·
"ὄρσεο, διογενὲς Πατρόκλεες, . . .
λεύσσω δὴ παρὰ νηυσι πυρὸς δηΐοιο ἰωήν·
μὴ δὴ νῆας ἕλωσι καὶ οὐκέτι φυκτὰ πέλωνται·
δύσεο τεύχεα θᾶσσον, ἐγὼ δέ κε λαὸν ἀγείρω.

(124-129)

("And Achilles smote his thighs and spoke to Patroclus: 'Up, Zeus-born Patroclus, . . . I see the rush of deadly fire by the ships. Up! lest they take the ships and there be no more hope of escape! Get on your armour quickly, and I will gather the host.' ")

At this exciting point the poet holds up the action, not by an interruption this time, but by making us stop to witness all the details of the preparation. We see Patroclus putting on his armour piece by piece; since he is arming, as we know, for his death, this is a solemn moment, and rightly dwelt upon. And it is Achilles' armour he is putting on. "Only Achilles' spear he did not take" (140); our attention is drawn to this because there will come a time when Achilles is arming and the great spear is all that is left of his old equipment. We watch the horses being harnessed; Achilles' immortal horses, Xanthus and Balios, are pointed out to us, for they have a part to play in the sequel; and Pedasus, the trace-horse, we are told, was among the spoils taken in the capture of Eetion's city. Then we turn to the Myrmidons who under the direction of Achilles are mustering, fierce and hungry for battle. All these things, we can see, would in fact have to be done, and would take time, and the maddening slowness of it may perhaps be said to reproduce the feeling of the impatient actors themselves. Certainly the delay prolongs and sharpens the suspense, and gives us time to realize the great significance of the occasion; but one can hardly resist the suspicion that in much of what follows (168-256) the poet is deliberately teasing us—especially 173-197, where he lists the chief officers of the Myrmidons, and actually sketches the pedigree of two of them; and the sudden halt, when the force is apparently going forward (210-220), to watch every movement of Achilles as he goes to get the precious cup from his tent and ceremoniously cleanses it and himself before pouring a libation to Zeus (220-232). However that may be, Achilles' prayer and the poet's comment thereon (233-252) sharply rivet our attention again on the thought of the critical point we have reached in the story.

Then at last (though not till we have seen the cup restored to the chest) comes the charge of the Myrmidons. Their sudden onset and the appearance of Patroclus dismay the Trojans; they give back from the burning ship, and the fire is put out. The other Achaeans come pouring out from among the ships;

> ὡς δ' ὅτ' ἀφ' ὑψηλῆς κορυφῆς ὄρεος μεγάλοιο
> κινήσῃ πυκινὴν νεφέλην στεροπηγερέτα Ζεύς,
> ἔκ τ' ἔφανεν πᾶσαι σκοπιαὶ καὶ πρώονες ἄκροι
> καὶ νάπαι, οὐρανόθεν δ' ἄρ' ὑπερράγη ἄσπετος αἰθήρ,
> ὣς Δαναοὶ νηῶν μὲν ἀπωσάμενοι δήϊον πῦρ
> τυτθὸν ἀνέπνευσαν.

(297-302)

("As when from the lofty summit of a great mountain Zeus, the lord of lightning, moves a thick cloud, and there shine out all the peaks and sharp headlands and valleys, and to heaven opens the infinite sky; so the Danaans, having thrust back the deadly fire from the ships, for a little breathed again.")

The battle is handled in the usual manner. The first struggle, while the Trojans are making a stand, is described comprehensively with various victors and vanquished listed (303-363). A storm-simile heralds the flight of the Trojans, and this is supported by another and more extended one that pictures the wild confusion (364-393). The narrative then begins to narrow down to the exploits of Patroclus as he sought to cut off the retreat of the Trojans, and at l. 419 one of these spreads into an episode—the slaying of Sarpedon.

As was noted earlier, one of the difficulties that faced the poet was to supply his heroes with victims worthy of their prowess without killing off prominent persons in the story; his subterfuges in this regard have been very successful, for no one has ever felt that the poet has been restraining himself in the matter of bloodshed, and yet when one comes to count them up, one finds that he emerges at the end with only two casualties among his major characters, *viz.,* Patroclus and Hector. His handling of Sarpedon is perhaps the most notable example of his subterfuges. He has built him up for this one purpose, and has established him in our minds as a remarkable and attractive figure. The disadvantage of so doing, namely that the audience may resent the sacrifice of a person they have come to know and like to what is after all an incidental requirement of the story, he turns to enormous advantage. As Sarpedon comes to the fore now and we suspect that his role here is what it is—to give glory to Patroclus—, the poet, sensing our feelings (perhaps through his own), gives them expression in the words of Zeus, to soften the shock, to mitigate our resentment (433-438): "Ah, woe is me, that it is the loved Sarpedon's lot to fall beneath the hand of Patroclus! My heart is divided, and I am considering whether I shall catch him up out of the fight and set him down safe and sound in Lycia, or let him fall now beneath the hands of Patroclus."

We all applaud Zeus's reluctance, and if such had been the poet's plan when he gave Sarpedon so notable a personality, we hope that he is thinking better of it and will find another way. In Hera's reply comes the rebuke of the ruthless artist in Homer to his own apparent hesitation,[1]

---

[1] Poets are not always so conscientious. See Raleigh's *Shakespeare,* p. 148, on Barnadine in *Measure for Measure.*

or, we might say, the poet seeks to transfer the resentment from himself to Hera:

αἰνότατε Κρονίδη, ποῖον τὸν μῦθον ἔειπες.
ἄνδρα θνητὸν ἐόντα, πάλαι πεπρωμένον αἴσῃ,
ἂψ ἐθέλεις θανάτοιο δυσηχέος ἐξαναλῦσαι;

(440-443)

("Most dread son of Kronos, what is this you have said? A man who is a mortal long predestined to his lot, do you wish to snatch back from mournful death?")

"A man long predestined to his lot"; let us not obscure the point by speculations on the relation between Zeus and fate. This is not metaphysics but art, and the necessity is an artistic, not a theological one. It was by the poet that the man was long predestined to his lot; fate is here what the poem demands.[1]

Sarpedon, accordingly, fulfils his destiny and is slain by Patroclus. Then follows a long and desperate fight for possession of the body (508-665). It is this fight which accomplishes the purpose of Patroclus and of Zeus, causing the flight of the Trojans back from the camp towards the city (644-62). The Achaeans strip Sarpedon's body of its armour. But the poet here pauses again, and makes the regret he has aroused serve as an excuse for a very welcome breathing-space of beauty and compassion in the midst of the savage slaughter: "Go now, dear Phoebus," says Zeus, "and beyond the range of the spears cleanse the black blood from Sarpedon, and then far away bear him and wash him in the streaming waters of the river; anoint him with ambrosia, and put immortal robes upon him, and send him to be borne under swift escort, that Sleep and his brother, Death, may quickly set him down

[1] See Leaf: *Homer and History*, pp. 17-18.

in the broad rich land of Lycia. There will his kinsmen and
clansmen bury him with mound and column, which is the
due and glory of the dead." It has the soothing quality, it
is the Homeric version of "Good night, sweet prince, and
flights of angels sing thee to thy rest." And just as perhaps
Shakespeare put these words in chiefly for the emotional
satisfaction of the audience (for the tone does not seem par-
ticularly appropriate either to the speaker or to the dead
Hamlet), so this passage is inserted with a view to the feelings
of the audience, even if it has also a practical use in getting
rid of the dead body, as Leaf suggests.[1] But is it not out of
proportion to the need? Does the death of Sarpedon matter
to us enough to deserve so much attention? We could have
dried our tears for him on less than this. I venture to suggest
that the reason why Sarpedon, the son of Zeus, was chosen
to be the prominent victim of Patroclus was because the poet
wished to insert this passage just here. His fall naturally calls
forth an expression of sorrow from his father and his inter-
vention on behalf of the body. The incident may be a digres-
sion within the episode, but it is structural in the poem. It
gives us the emotional clew that serves to guide our feelings
in what is to come. We are soon going to enter upon the
cruellest, the most terrible part of the story, the slaying of
Hector, and Homer has built up the incident of Sarpedon's
death into a preparatory statement of the theme to be devel-
oped. We go through by anticipation, in miniature as it were,
the range of emotions we are to experience on a greater scale
through the conclusion of the poem. Here we have a death

[1] *Commentary, ad loc.*: "The intervention of Zeus on behalf of
Sarpedon's body was rejected by Zenodotus, and the only reason for
doubting the *athetesis* is that we should then hear nothing of the fate of
the body."

which we resent followed by a merciful picture of the broken
body laid reverently in its native earth. There, in the closing
books, a death which we much more bitterly resent, and,
worked up to with immense elaboration and power, the final
scene in which the poor abused body of Hector is at last borne
home. The poet is beginning to attune the ear to the *dénoue-
ment*. The completed theme is given out compactly in simple
outline, to focus and control our response to the major move-
ment that is about to begin.

After this breath of healing pity we return at once to the
mercilessness of the battlefield. Apollo comes from his
mission of mercy to superintend the slaying of Patroclus.

Patroclus has forgotten the injunction of Achilles. He in
his turn is in the power of Ate and is rushing blindly to his
death (684-691). Homer now rapidly sets the stage for his
death. Patroclus is fighting beneath the walls of Troy, with
proud thoughts of himself leading the final victorious attack
upon the city. But Apollo stands before it (as Achilles warned
"Apollo loves them very much"). At his rebuke (707-709),
Patroclus, like Diomedes before him, draws back, and Apollo
gives the signal to Hector. It is of course essential to the story
that Hector should be responsible for Patroclus's death.
Summoning his half-brother, Kebriones, to act as his driver,
he advances to the attack. Patroclus, hurling a stone at the
oncoming chariot, kills Kebriones and lightheartedly scoffs
at the fallen man. As he springs forward to strip his victim,
his fate is foreshadowed in the simile that describes the act:

οἶμα λέοντος ἔχων, ὅς τε σταθμοὺς κεραΐζων
ἔβλητο πρὸς στῆθος, ἑή τέ μιν ὤλεσεν ἀλκή.

(752-753)

("He sprang like a lion that, while ravaging the sheepfolds,
is struck in the breast, and his valour destroys him.")

—an echo of that which was applied to Hector in Bk. XII, 41-46.[1] And so the two lions grapple:

τὼ περὶ Κεβριόναο λέονθ' ὣς δηρινθήτην,
ὥ τ' ὄρεος κορυφῇσι περὶ κταμένης ἐλάφοιο,
ἄμφω πεινάοντε, μέγα φρονέοντε μάχεσθον.

(756-758)

("They strove round Kebriones like two lions that on the peaks of a mountain fight fiercely in their hunger for a slain deer.")

And above this final battle, as Trojans and Achaeans join, sounds the thunder of another storm simile (765-769).

It is now late afternoon—without turning aside, the poet with a word calls up a picture of the peaceful summer evening (779)—and the time has come for Patroclus to die. Phoebus was moving towards him through the throng of fighters but Patroclus did not see him, for he was hidden in thick darkness. "And the god stood behind him, and struck him on his back and shoulders with the flat of his hand, and his eyes turned dizzy. And from his head Phoebus Apollo struck the helmet, and it rolled rattling under the horses' feet, and its plumes were begrimed with blood and dust. . . . His spear was broken . . . his shield slipped from his shoulders, Apollo loosed his breastplate, his mind became clouded, his limbs failed him, and he stood dazed. Then there came behind him, and struck him in the back with his sharp spear a Dardanian, Euphorbus . . . but he did not bring him down, and he ran back and mingled with the throng . . . and Patroclus, unnerved by the blow of the god and the spear, drew back under cover of his men. But Hector seeing it forced his way through the ranks,

[1] See above, p. 120.

and stabbed him in the belly, and drove the bronze point home; and he fell with a crash, and a shudder ran through the Achaean host" (788-822). Hector exults over him and jeers at him for his failure.

The poet has piled up point after point in his description of the circumstances of Patroclus's death, so that even the least imaginative reader must burn with indignation at the way it is accomplished. That is what Homer wants, for he is motivating the terrific fury and grief of Achilles. We can sympathize much better with the extravagance of his feelings because we too have resented the manner of his slaying.

The final scene (843-857) explicitly foreshadows the similar scene in Bk. XXII, in the dying man's prophecy of Hector's death. The repetition of the same effects well shows Homer's confidence in his ability to control and direct the sympathies of his listeners to suit his immediate purpose. Here he deliberately takes away from Hector the glory that would naturally redound to him as the conqueror of Patroclus; Apollo and Euphorbus are given a hand in his death—Apollo, to allow of Euphorbus taking a part without diminishing the honour of Patroclus. The glory is all his, in that it takes two men and a god to overcome him. Thus Patroclus has all our sympathy here, and it is not qualified by any sense of the glory of his vanquisher. Everyone must feel at this point only a fierce desire to see him avenged.

BOOK XVII

THE next step in the story is delayed for 761 lines
by an account of the fight for the body of Patroclus. "No-
where else," says Leaf,[1] "do we feel the fighting so unduly
drawn out. The scene is often confused and the individual
incidents are, with hardly an exception, not such as to reward
us for the delay in returning to the main story, to Achilles
and the camp, whither we feel we should be taken imme-
diately after the fall of Patroclus." Precisely; that is what we
are impatiently waiting for—to see Achilles receiving the
news of Patroclus's death. And again it is just when we are
on the verge of a crisis, when we are all agog to get on, that
the poem lingers to add detail after detail. Like so many
story-tellers after him, Homer thinks the great moment comes
more tellingly from being delayed. And this time we cannot
say it is done in order to find room for additional material; the
events are clearly created just to protract the action, and not
the action protracted to supply the occasion for the events.
They are all small incidents and have no standing-ground
apart from the action to which they are related. That is what
Leaf means by saying "they are not such as to reward us for
the delay". But all the same there is a basis of necessity in
what he has done here; the fight for the body, in some form
or other, is essential to the economy of the poem. Critics have
quite rightly seen that what the constructor of the Iliad has

[1] *Companion,* p. 286.

for some time been preparing a place for is the making of
the new armour for Achilles—"the source of the great disturb-
ing element" running through Bks. XVI and XVII. That
is the real reason why Patroclus was sent out in Achilles'
armour—to lose it and so necessitate the preparation of new
armour. Therefore it is essential for the poet to describe the
taking of the armour from Patroclus's body; that must be
made an event.[1] And also his body must be rescued; for if
the Trojans possessed it, Achilles would not afterwards be
able to hold back Hector's body. The poet then has to
describe how the body of Patroclus was rescued and yet the
armour taken by the Trojans. Out of these two necessities
(chiefly) he has built up the fabric of the part we call Bk.
XVII. Instead of relating them as briefly as possible, he makes
as much of them as he can on his usual principle of ampli-
fying whenever he can find or make artistic justification for it.

That he has here justified it is amply proved if we read
straight on and do not regard these books as separate units.
The poet is preparing for one of the great moments in the
poem—the return of Achilles. The final salvaging of the
body of Patroclus is to be due to Achilles himself. Therefore,
to lead up to that, to make it necessary and fully effective, he
must give the impression that the struggle for the body was

[1] It is perfectly clear that the armour is not taken from him until
l. 125 of this book, and there is no discrepancy with Bk. XVI. What
happens in Bk. XVI is described in ll. 793-804; his helmet is knocked
off, his spear broken, his shield slips from his shoulders, and the fasten-
ings of his breastplate break; and it is to that Patroclus refers in l. 846.
It is the most crudely literal interpretation to say that this means Apollo
has actually removed his armour as a triumphant enemy would do.
Patroclus means that he was practically unarmed when Hector stabbed
him because all these mischances had happened to him.

very desperate, very difficult, and hence very prolonged. As we study his plan, we can see the thing growing in his hands. It is never his way, as we have seen over and over again, merely to state that a battle was very desperate or prolonged, nor to describe it in a massive, comprehensive way. He makes us feel it as such. He builds it up by a number of vivid incidents centred round the exploits of definite persons, so that our eyes follow the battle by following this or that individual figure, and thus each moment supplies a little plot of its own to engage our attention while the general impression is being created. That is, a battle is shown to be desperate by making us watch a number of desperate little struggles, and is shown to be prolonged by prolonging it through a multiplication of such personal incidents. That is his method throughout the poem, and one of the secrets of his power. We are always feeling the story for ourselves, never just listening to it being told.

This battle also undoes what Patroclus had accomplished, bringing the Trojans back across the plain to the ships, and thus the stage is cleared for Achilles' entrance.[1] Also it should be observed, we are beginning to move through the same

[1] See Monro, vol. II, p. 323: "Patroclus having led the Greeks far across the plain of Troy, it becomes necessary to bring them back, on the one hand to show the immediate effect of his fall, and on the other hand because the fullest room has to be left for the impending victories of Achilles. Again, the book serves to prepare us for the scene in which Achilles hears of the death of his friend. This, the critical moment in the history of the wrath, is intentionally delayed, obviously with the view of raising expectations to the highest pitch. The poet even stops in the middle of the desperate battle over Patroclus to tell us that Achilles had not yet heard the tidings. The successive steps taken by Ajax and Menelaus, and the shock which the message gives to Antilochus, have the same poetical purpose."

sequence of events as we had in the case of Sarpedon. The theme is being reinforced. As Sarpedon's fall was followed by the long struggle for his body and the taking of his armour, so the fall of the much more important Patroclus is succeeded by the longer struggle for his body.

Thus, though these incidents are not individually necessary, cumulatively they are; and since therefore he has to concoct incidents, we must admit that he shows remarkable resource in inventing variations on the same general theme. The poem is not only longer but richer for this multiplicity of little incidents. It is interesting to observe out of what he contrives them. To begin with, he is restricted in the matter of his personnel; Agamemnon, Odysseus, Diomedes are wounded; though they returned to the field at the beginning of Bk. XIV, it was only to encourage the others. It is true that the poet has no scruple about healing wounded men as he needs them, but here he has his reasons for keeping them *hors de combat*.[1] Therefore the most prominent that he has left are Menelaus and, of course, the incomparable Ajax. These with such minor figures as Idomeneus and Ajax, son of Oileus, must bear the brunt of this struggle, must form the centres of interest.

At the end of Bk. XVI Hector has been lured away from the dead body by the hope of capturing the famous horses of Achilles. Menelaus rushes to its defence. He is attacked by Euphorbus, and kills him. As Euphorbus had a hand in the slaying of Patroclus, his fate is an appropriate theme to make an incident of here. In fact it may be said with confidence that Homer chose him instead of a more prominent Trojan as the co-slayer of Patroclus, because he was intending to have him

[1] See below, p. 194, on XIX, 47 *ff.*

killed here and now. He has been characterized with this in view. He is very young, is having his first taste of real fighting (XVI, 811), and having enjoyed astonishing success quite genuinely feels that the taking of the arms of Achilles is not an honour in excess of his merits. Thus does Homer work up this little incident and give it an interest of its own. The youth of Euphorbus makes it what it is, as explaining his extraordinary cheek in claiming the spoils as his right, Menelaus's bantering tone—"Good God! a man oughtn't to boast like this. Why, a panther, a lion, a boar, is not so fierce as these sons of Pantheus . . . now, you had better run back or you'll get hurt"—, the boy's fury at hearing that the man before him is the slayer of his brother, which spurs him to strike and so forces Menelaus to kill him, the suggestion, so pathetic now, of his youthful vanity, as you picture him before the battle laboriously dressing his hair; and then the poet very pleasingly pats him on the back, does honour to the passing of the gallant young spirit by a simile which sounds more emphatically the recurrent note of regret at the destruction of youth and beauty:

> οἷον δὲ τρέφει ἔρνος ἀνὴρ ἐριθηλὲς ἐλαίης
> χώρῳ ἐν οἰοπόλῳ, ὅθ' ἅλις ἀναβέβροχεν ὕδωρ,
> καλὸν τηλεθάον· τὸ δέ τε πνοιαὶ δονέουσι
> παντοίων ἀνέμων, καί τε βρύει ἄνθεϊ λευκῷ·
> ἐλθὼν δ' ἐξαπίνης ἄνεμος σὺν λαίλαπι πολλῇ
> βόθρου τ' ἐξέστρεψε καὶ ἐξετάνυσσ' ἐπὶ γαίῃ.

(53-58)

("As a man grows a healthy young olive tree in a special place, where there is plenty of water—a fair thing, full of life, tossed by the breath of every wind, and covered with white blossom; suddenly a wind comes with a mighty blast and wrenches it from its place and stretches it upon the earth.")

While Menelaus is stripping off Euphorbus's armour, and the other Trojans round are hesitating to attack him, Apollo recalls Hector, and Menelaus, seeing him approaching and knowing that the others will no longer hang back if Hector attacks, sees no recourse but to withdraw and get help, that is, to get Ajax; only he can be equal to the task they have before them. It is during this absence that Hector takes Patroclus's armour, and as Ajax and Menelaus return he is in the act of dragging away the body. On seeing Ajax he drops the body but withdraws with the armour to his chariot, and orders it to be taken to the city, while Ajax bestrides the body with Menelaus by his side. Glaucus, thinking that Hector intends to drive away, turns furiously upon him; he is of course certain that Sarpedon's body has been taken to the Achaean camp, and is anxious that the Trojans should have that of Patroclus to exchange against it (160-163). Thus does the poet get matter for this enlargement from the events of Bk. XVI. Hector now astonishes the critics by doffing his own armour and putting on that of Achilles. But his intention in so doing is made perfectly plain. Glaucus has taunted him with being afraid. "Afraid, am I?" says Hector in effect. "You watch" (179), and he goes and puts on Achilles' armour. He is not only going to attack Ajax, but he is going to flaunt his triumph in the face of the defenders of the body. Zeus's comment on the ominous significance of the act keeps before us the thought of Hector's approaching fate.

Ajax, seeing the Trojans approaching, bids Menelaus call for help, remarking simply that it is not now a question of the body of Patroclus, but of their own lives; it does not occur to him to withdraw. Ajax, the son of Oileus, Idomeneus, Meriones, and many others hasten to their assistance,

and the real battle for the body begins, announced by the
great simile:

ὡς δ' ὅτ' ἐπὶ προχοῇσι διιπετέος ποταμοῖο
βέβρυχεν μέγα κῦμα ποτὶ ῥόον, ἀμφὶ δέ τ' ἄκραι
ἠϊόνες βοόωσιν ἐρευγομένης ἁλὸς ἔξω.

(263-265)

("as when at the outpourings of a rain-fed river the great
waves come roaring against its stream, and the high shores
round boom to the bellowing of the sea outside.")

A darkness falls round the group, intended by Zeus to help
the defenders or at least to shelter the body. So he did also in
the fight for Sarpedon's body (XVI, 567-568); the parallel is
maintained. The struggle is described at length from l. 274 to
l. 425. The fortune varies from side to side. First the Trojans
press back the Achaeans and get hold of the body. But Ajax
rallies them and scatters the Trojans. This is followed by the
description of the death of an individual Trojan, balanced by
the death of an Achaean. Then it is the turn of the Trojans
to give back; they are rallied by Aeneas, who reminds them,
at Apollo's instigation, that Zeus is on their side. Again some
individuals are noted, Achaeans and Trojans as before being
exactly balanced. At l. 370 we are given a glimpse of the rest
of the field in the clear sunlight, and see for a moment the two
sons of Nestor, Thrasymedes and Antilochus, fighting in
ignorance of the fall of Patroclus; then we return to the
equal struggle for the body. The poet is thus making us feel
the length of the struggle, varying it from side to side, going
away from it and coming back to it. At l. 401 we are reminded
of Achilles and of the great moment that is being postponed.

Then the horses of Achilles are used to supply another
incident. They are refusing to move either back to the ships

or forward to the battle, because they miss their usual driver Patroclus. The picture of the mourning horses is no doubt intended to show the general sorrow at Patroclus's death. Their grief rouses the compassion of Zeus, that they, immortal creatures, have been doomed to share the sorrows of miserable men (443-447). But, he announces, they are not to be captured by Hector, and once more we are reminded of the purpose of Zeus in regard to him and the Trojan success:

ἔτι γάρ σφισι κῦδος ὀρέξω,
κτείνειν, εἰς ὅ κε νῆας ἐϋσσέλμους ἀφίκωνται
δύῃ τ' ἠέλιος καὶ ἐπὶ κνέφας ἱερὸν ἔλθῃ.

(453-455)

("For still I will grant glory to the Trojans, to go on slaying, until they reach the ships, until the sun sets and the sacred darkness comes on.")

This is Hector's day of glory, and the sun has not yet set. The poet is going to show that only Achilles can save the Achaeans.

The horses, inspirited by Zeus, suddenly begin of their own accord to play their usual part in battle, and we have an amusing picture of Automedon borne helplessly hither and thither, now charging into the thickest of the throng, now fleeing before the press of foemen, until, near the place where the conflict for the body is taking place, Alcimedon hails him and asks what on earth he is doing. Automedon explains his difficulty and apparently manages to stop the horses. Alcimedon mounts the chariot, and Automedon descends to take part in the fight. Hector and Aeneas turn aside from the body to attempt the capture of the horses. Automedon calls upon the Ajaxes and Menelaus, and a variation is made by describing their staving the Trojans off from the horses.

They return to the defence of the body. Athena, through the mouth of Phoenix, strengthens the determination of Menelaus. Apollo does the same with Hector, and Zeus gives the signal for the advance of the Trojans back to the ships (593-596). The Achaeans begin to break. Idomeneus flees from the field.

Ajax now sees that their one hope of saving the body is to get tidings to Achilles (640), and looks round despairingly for some one to send. He can see nothing beyond the immediate struggle because of the darkness, and angrily calls upon Zeus to let them at least die in the light. The poet characteristically, finding his picturesque device now in the way, invents this magnificent method of removing the obstacle. He knows how to load his rifts with ore.

> Ζεῦ πάτερ, ἀλλὰ σὺ ῥῦσαι ὑπ᾽ ἠέρος υἷας Ἀχαιῶν,
> ποίησον δ᾽ αἴθρην, δὸς δ᾽ ὀφθαλμοῖσιν ἰδέσθαι·
> ἐν δὲ φάει καὶ ὄλεσσον, ἐπεί νύ τοι εὔαδεν οὕτως.

(645-647)

("Father Zeus, deliver the sons of the Achaeans from the darkness; make it clear, and grant us to see with our eyes. Slay us if you want to, but at least let it be in the light.")

At this sublime rebuke, Zeus, who apparently finds it difficult to remember which side he is on, or, at least, to keep the balance between his promise and his ultimate intention, hastily removes the darkness, and Menelaus at the bidding of Ajax goes to look for Antilochus. Now we see why Homer has kept reminding us of Antilochus. Our attention has been called to him at intervals from the beginning of the fight around the ships in Bk. XIII, and in Bk. XV, 570, his speed of foot was especially remarked on by Menelaus, which is of course why Ajax has thought of him as the fitting messenger.

Menelaus is most reluctant to weaken the defence of the body, and before he goes urges the chief men left to remember it is Patroclus they are defending.

> νῦν τις ἐνηείης Πατροκλῆος δειλοῖο
> μνησάσθω· πᾶσιν γὰρ ἐπίστατο μείλιχος εἶναι
> ζωὸς ἐών· νῦν αὖ θάνατος καὶ μοῖρα κιχάνει.

(670-672)

("Now let everyone remember the kindliness of poor Patroclus; for he was gentle to all in his life, and now has death found him.")

It is very noticeable that Homer here and hereafter keeps stressing the attractiveness of Patroclus's character. For now is the time when it is effective for us to realize it.

Menelaus, having seen Antilochus start for the camp, returns to Ajax, and they make a desperate attempt to carry the body from the field. Menelaus and Meriones lift it upon their shoulders while the two Ajaxes strive to hold back the Trojans, and the poet drops the curtain on the scene in a series of similes, in which each group of participants is described in turn.

BOOK XVIII

To Achilles, watching the Achaeans pouring back in flight across the plain, with dread growing in his heart, comes Antilochus, and in three sentences tells him all:

κεῖται Πάτροκλος, νέκυος δὲ δὴ ἀμφιμάχονται
γυμνοῦ· ἀτὰρ τά γε τεύχε' ἔχει κορυθαίολος Ἕκτωρ.

(20-21)

("Low lies Patroclus; he is dead, and they are fighting about his naked body; Hector has his arms.")

The leisureliness and fullness of Homer's style are so marked that his terseness, when it comes, has a quite extraordinary force. Every one can see how dramatically right it is here. No doubt if we had had a long speech with a full recapitulation of the events of Patroclus's death and the struggle to save his armour and the body, we should have been ready to overlook, on the grounds of convention, the absurdity of Achilles waiting till it was over to drop to the ground in his grief. But Homer is surely seeking and certainly achieving something finer than the mere avoidance of unnaturalness. These brief, sharp sentences reproduce for *us* the effect of the news on Achilles. Put thus, we, though we already know the facts, get the effect of a sudden, stunning blow.

The difficulty that confronts every story-teller who works up to such a moment as this is not to let the audience down when the moment comes, to achieve the height of his climax. It is comparatively easy to build up to these intensely dramatic moments; the problem is to make the effect ade-

174

quate to the expectation. This is one of the supreme crises of the poem and must be felt as such. We are expecting Achilles to be as extreme in his grief as he is in his wrath, and, besides, the scene prepares us for the dreadful sequel; it is in the strength of this wild grief that Achilles goes forth to battle; it makes the fitting prelude for the slaughter he is to inflict upon the Trojans.

Homer does not fail us; he follows the artistic crescendo of feeling unfalteringly to its climax; unlike many poets in similar situations he takes his top note at full voice and does not drop to a different key and express the extreme of grief by not expressing it, trusting to the effect of surprise to compensate the hearer for the artistic disappointment.[1] Homer has not shrunk from the endeavour to express the extreme of grief, and the passage stands out as one of the poetical highlights of the poem. The poet elicits by his words the full quality of Achilles' emotion, the whole significance of the scene.

[1] The sort of thing I mean may be illustrated (unfairly) from Shakespeare: Romeo receiving the news of Juliet's (supposed) death (Act V, Sc. 1), or Antony the news of Cleopatra's (Act IV, Sc. 14). Of course the conditions are entirely different. Shakespeare has to put suitable words into the mouths of Romeo and Antony. He must express the emotion through the words of his actors. It is great and right that Homer makes Achilles say nothing, for utter speechlessness is in fact the extreme manifestation of overwhelming feelings. But it would never do for the dramatist to take refuge in a stage direction "Antony falls to the ground." The difference is that the narrative poet can describe Achilles falling to the ground. That is the point, we must have the emotion expressed in words; otherwise the poet is deserting us at our utmost need, asking us to imagine the feeling for ourselves. The dramatist is at a disadvantage because, precluded from intervening himself, he has to express the emotion without going beyond the bounds of reasonably convincing human speech; he has to show by the actor's words that words fail him.

Real grief is sheer pain, and in its manifestation an ugly, disfiguring thing. This fact Homer has conveyed in his description of the action of Achilles, but he has made his expression of it supremely beautiful. While Achilles falls, the poetry lifts; the magic of perfect diction is invoked to create the impression of beauty in something that is in itself painful and even repellent. It is the triumph of Homer that one reads this without thinking of the art of it; it is hidden by the apparently effortless simplicity of his expression; one feels that the reason it is expressed thus is because it happened thus, that he has just used the simplest and most natural words to describe what happened, and therefore that the effect of beauty produced is not something added by art, but inherent in the thing described. It *is* added by art, and yet the impression created does represent a reality too—the essential beauty of the feeling that lies behind the distorted face of grief. This effect is achieved by the sheer surface beauty of the words. Without disguising or palliating the unloveliness of its external manifestations, nor turning aside to comment, the poet, by surface means, pierces beneath the surface, and not by intellectual means to the intellect, but by the simpler, surer ways of direct emotional suggestion creates within the imagination a sense of the presence of that inner, essential beauty. By what magic it is achieved it is impossible to say. There are devices we can point to, such as the interweaving of contrasting words that suggests the beauty and power now fallen and marred:

χαρίεν δ' ᾔσχυνε πρόσωπον·
νεκταρέῳ δὲ χιτῶνι μέλαιν' ἀμφίζανε τέφρη.

(24-25[1])

[1] It is naturally impossible to reproduce the effect in English as it depends largely on the order of the words. The general sense is "He befouled his fair face; upon his fragrant tunic the black ashes settled."

It is a dreadful and awe-inspiring sight, awe-inspiring because of the contrast, because the beauty is marred, the power fallen —Achilles, the unbending, mighty hero, so strong and beautiful and proud, humbled in the dust. And perhaps the most magic line of all is

αὐτὸς δ' ἐν κονίῃσι μέγας μεγαλωστὶ τανυσθεὶς κεῖτο.

(26-27)

("Low too he lay, the mighty, stretched full length in the dust.")

In the echo here of the κεῖται Πάτροκλος of line 20 the intensity of his unutterable, bitter remorse seems comprehended and conveyed as the most explicit statement of it could not have expressed it.

There is no doubt that the strong impression of beauty made by this passage is due largely to the fact that this note is sustained and reinforced in the immediately succeeding lines. The grief of Achilles having risen to its culmination in his exceeding bitter cry (35), the poet suddenly follows it up by a passage which is almost nothing but beauty of sound. His cry has its echo in the depths of the sea, and in a moment we are far away from the bloody field of Troy. There are those who choose to reject the catalogue of Nereids because "it is rather in the manner of Hesiod than Homer." (These interpolators certainly had a great sense of style.) It is, to my mind, a stroke of perfect poetic judgment; a list of lovely names that by almost nothing but lovely sounds conjure up a lovely scene, comes to heal the pain. It is just the relief and release of feeling that was needed; the strain of thought is for the moment completely lifted, and the mind finds rest and refreshment in sheer beauty that requires not the slightest effort to apprehend it.

The effect is still further enhanced, I venture to say, by the fact that this scene in the lovely world of goddesses and sea-nymphs reflects the scene by the ship of Achilles. When Achilles falls to the ground before the shock of grief, the handmaids that he and Patroclus had captured flock about him with cries of sorrow,

$$\chi\epsilon\rho\sigma\grave{\iota} \; \delta\grave{\epsilon} \; \pi\hat{a}\sigma\alpha\iota$$
$$\sigma\tau\acute{\eta}\theta\epsilon\alpha \; \pi\epsilon\pi\lambda\acute{\eta}\gamma o\nu\tau o.$$

(30)

("They all beat upon their breasts.")

At the sound of Thetis' cry the sea-nymphs flock about her:

$$\tau\hat{\omega}\nu \; \delta\grave{\epsilon} \; \kappa\alpha\grave{\iota} \; \dot{\alpha}\rho\gamma\acute{\nu}\phi\epsilon o\nu \; \pi\lambda\hat{\eta}\tau o \; \text{'}\sigma\pi\acute{\epsilon}o\varsigma \cdot \quad a\grave{\iota} \; \delta\text{'} \; \ddot{a}\mu\alpha \; \pi\hat{a}\sigma\alpha\iota$$
$$\sigma\tau\acute{\eta}\theta\epsilon\alpha \; \pi\epsilon\pi\lambda\acute{\eta}\gamma o\nu\tau o.$$

(50)

("The silvery cave was filled with them; and they all beat upon their breasts.")

The pictorial and verbal echo seems to strengthen and yet soften the mournfulness of the former scene.

As Thetis rises from the sea in response to her son's cry, there rises with her the memory of her former coming when she promised to convey his prayer for vengeance to the throne of Zeus. As that scene necessarily comes back to the mind, the poem responds to the recollection; it comes back in the words. The verbal repetitions do not wake the recollection; they are the memory recording itself. What Homer wants to ensure our realizing is the full tragic irony of this grief-stricken figure grovelling in the dust. This is Achilles' prayer translated into reality. The events so far recorded have been the slow working out of the promise Zeus made in answer to his prayer, the immense complication of circumstances and characters through which his promise has had to find its tortuous way.

And now it is fulfilled; gods and men have put forth all their strength to thwart it, but the will of Zeus has prevailed. There is nothing now between the Achaeans and destruction but the arm of Achilles; everything else has been tried and has failed. Achilles' highest hopes have been fulfilled, and there he lies in bitterest agony of soul. The events which the prayer to his mother long ago set going have run their course. The wheel has come full circle, and, to mark its revolution, there rolls back with it a repetition of that fateful scene. The initial act rises before us visibly in its consequences.

So this was how the wrath of Achilles was to be allayed—not by gifts, as Agamemnon and the army thought, not by the humiliation of Agamemnon, as Achilles thought. The thing that stops it is the wrath of Achilles. By the simple device of the repeated motif we are made to look back through the long vista of events and see that we have reached a terminus, and yet that it is not a terminus, but a fresh beginning. The wrath of Achilles has taken a new direction. Achilles himself now takes the situation in hand; he seeks no promise and asks no help. It is Thetis who insists on the necessity of new armour.

Thetis's coming also reminds us of Achilles' approaching death. As always, she brings the thought with her. This association the poet stresses here in Thetis's words before she comes to Achilles (52 ff.), and the reason for underlining the point appears in her reply to his vow of vengeance:

ὠκύμορος δή μοι, τέκος, ἔσσεαι, οἷ' ἀγορεύεις·
αὐτίκα γάρ τοι ἔπειτα μεθ' Ἕκτορα πότμος ἑτοῖμος.

(95-96)

("Swift-doomed indeed you will be, my child, the way you talk; for straightway after Hector fate is waiting for you.")

That is, the fact is impressed upon us that Achilles is here deliberately condemning himself to death, so that, when later we watch him riding out to the battle, we know that in that act he is paying "the last full measure of devotion" to the memory of Patroclus; he is laying down his life for his friend.

The announcement to Achilles of the death of Patroclus and the effect of the announcement upon him have been naturally succeeded by the coming of Thetis, and it is not till she has departed on her errand to procure new armour for him that we have time to remember that the body of Patroclus is still in danger. Then we lift up our eyes again and see that weary struggle still going on (148-164), and perhaps feel an impatience with Achilles that he should sit mourning for his dead comrade while others fight for him. So again the natural sequence follows, and our dissatisfaction is immediately allayed. For the very thought comes to Achilles in the shape of Iris, who urges him to try the effect of his sudden appearance on the field.

The question has been raised (was ever a poem so minutely scrutinized?) as to why Hera should be represented as acting without the knowledge of Zeus (168). Well, she is still under interdict not to interfere, and she naturally thinks that Zeus is still aiding the Trojans, and is happy in the feeling that she is making a clever move against him. It is a gratuitous little bit of comedy that Homer touched in, hoping to amuse us. But the critics are not amused. They are deeply suspicious. They point out that Zeus does not desire the body of Patroclus to fall into the hands of the Trojans, and therefore there is no need for Hera to take this step secretly. Quite so, and that is why her careful secrecy is amusing. It amuses Zeus. He never does any more than he has to; he exerts himself as little as possible. Having at last, through a masterly, if intermittent, manipulation of circumstances and characters, brought about the fulfilment of his promise, he is content for the moment to let nature take its course, and when Achilles appears at the trench, Zeus recognizes, in this unexpected but wholly satisfactory addition to the programme, the hand of Hera, and ironically congratulates her on her success in stealing a march upon him (357-359).

The reappearance of Achilles is splendidly staged. It is a great moment in the poem, and the poet has risen triumphantly to it. Leaf calls the passage "one of the supreme pieces of poetical imagination which the world has brought forth".[1] αὐτὰρ Ἀχιλλεὺς ὦρτο (203),—"And Achilles arose". Can anyone who has read the poem through from the beginning with even a half-interest miss feeling a lifting of heart at the words? It is after all for this that we have waited and watched. And Homer does not let us down; he does not leave the reader's imagination to do his work for him. Again he takes his top note at full voice, expresses the greatness of the occasion. What he says is, as always, very simple, very concrete, but there is something in the sound and orchestration of the language that reproduces for the hearer the effect he is describing. First, a burst of stately music, rich and elaborate and tremendous in volume (203-214); a pause—a plain statement of fact (215-218); then the long-drawn ringing note of a trumpet-call (219-221). The reader's heart stands still too.

What Homer has expressed here by the metaphor or the miracle of Athena's aegis, and the cloud of fire blazing from his head, by the great simile of the beacon-fires, and the ringing voice, is the mysterious power of a great personality.

[1] *Companion*, p. 298.

"In Achilles", says Lascelles Abercrombie,[1] "chiefly lives Homer's sense of the goodness of life. It is personal ascendancy. Homer has no need to explain what this is, nor to say why it is good. There it is, for him; heroic virtue, the one thing in life good past all mistake, the unaccountable and irresistible *prowess* which men like Achilles announce by their mere presence before us." That is what he has sought to communicate here—the effect of Achilles' presence. The storm-cloud of the goddess about his body, the blazing golden cloud that she lit above his head—these things are not Homer's attempt to account for the splendour and the effect of his appearance, to explain them; they are "his sublime metaphor of inexplicable virtue."

And so under cover of his presence the body of Patroclus is brought into the camp (231-233). Then

'Ήέλιον δ' ἀκάμαντα βοῶπις πότνια Ήρη
πέμψεν ἐπ' Ὠκεανοῖο ῥοὰς ἀέκοντα νέεσθαι.

(239-240)

("Hera sent the unwearying sun to the streams of Ocean, being reluctant to depart.")

Leaf has prosaically seized upon this statement to support his theory of a shorter original poem:[2] "The supernatural shortening of the day seems to imply that this passage belongs to the early form of the Μῆνις, when the day which began with Bk. XI did not contain the same extraordinary number of events we have now seen forced into it." A feeble argument in itself, because even an hour can have an extraordinary number of events crowded into it, which would take more than an hour to describe. The day is obviously drawing

[1] *Idea of Great Poetry*, pp. 150-1.
[2] *Commentary, ad loc.*

to its close (it was late afternoon when Patroclus fell) and
the postponement of the sunset for a few minutes or even
an hour would not make the difference between the credi-
bility and incredibility of this crowded day. Nor, observe,
is it necessarily implied that the day is shortened; Homer does
not say so; it is quite as reasonable an interpretation of the
words to understand that the sun was lingering beyond its
proper time. All the poet says is that Hera sent the sun down
"being reluctant to depart". But the particular interpretation
of the words is not important. The point is that Homer wants
to make this sunset an event, he wants us to notice it, to
remind us that it marks a vital moment in the poem. He
forces us to dwell upon the setting of the sun by himself
thus dwelling upon it and emphasizing it; we remember with
a start what this sunset signifies. It is the end of Hector's
triumph. That was the promise of Zeus to Hector at the
beginning of the day, "I will give him might to slay, until
he reaches the ships, until the sun sets and the sacred darkness
comes on",

δύῃ τ' ἠέλιος καὶ ἐπὶ κνέφας ἱερὸν ἔλθῃ.

(XI, 267)

That is why the sun is reluctant to depart; it feels, and
therefore makes us feel, that it is signing Hector's death-
warrant. And that is why it is Hera who hastens it on its
way. For it is she, not Zeus, who is glad that for Hector the
sands have run out. And so, with that preparation, the simple
words ἠέλιος μὲν ἔδυ (241) come like a note of doom, and
our thoughts are full of Hector.

And accordingly at once we see Hector. The scene shifts
to the Trojan camp, but there is no shifting of our thoughts.

It is Hector we are thinking of, and to Hector the poet turns. We hear Polydamas advising him to withdraw the Trojan forces into the city, and Hector rejecting his advice—a motif we have heard before, the significance of which therefore is immediately obvious. The wise counsellor is again unheeded; Hector has not learned by his former experience, but we have, and we see that it is indeed, as Andromache foresaw, Hector's own courage that destroys him. For the proud words he here speaks actually in the sequel stand between him and safety. The poet leaves us in no doubt as to the purport of the scene; ἐκ γάρ σφεων φρένας εἵλετο Παλλάς Ἀθήνη (311) is his comment—"Whom the gods will destroy, they first make mad." The purpose of this incident with its menacing associations is plainly to stir in the auditors excitement and foreboding for the morrow. That is the way Homer holds his poem together; he makes the event he is recording bring up the past and point forward to the future. It is obviously an excellent method in a long poem composed for listeners. The full effect of an incident depends upon remembering some past event, and listeners cannot turn back to refresh their memories. He therefore shapes the incident so as to roll up the pertinent past along with it; he depicts the present as the past turning into the future, the growing significance of things past as the event to which they are moving becomes nearer and clearer.

We have seen how naturally, how necessarily, these last two scenes—the return of Achilles and the Trojan assembly—have followed upon the departure of Thetis, but in a sense they have been an interruption, and, as less careful artists would say, we must now return to Thetis and the errand on which she started. But Homer does not jerk the minds of his audience about in that fashion; he shifts his scene often, it is true, but that is because he has his eye on the emotional

continuity, not on the factual. Monro says:[1] "The interval
between the meeting of Thetis with Achilles and her arrival
at the house of Hephaestus is filled by incidents of a sub-
ordinate character. The changes of scene are frequent, and
there is little interdependence between the action that goes on
at different places. The Trojan assembly, the lament of
Achilles, the dialogue of Zeus and Hera, and the making
of the new armour are more or less contemporaneous.
Moreover, the transitions from one to another are not made
with the smoothness that belongs to the Homeric manner."
A critic should always be careful to stand back and look
at the whole picture. The point I have been making is that
the rapid shifting of scenes is directed to maintaining this
very smoothness of transition. I have already noted this in
the shift from Achilles to the Trojan assembly. The narrative
follows the flow of the thought. So now he does not turn
abruptly from Hector to Thetis; he keys us back through
Achilles to the mood in which we saw Thetis depart. As the
Trojans in the infatuated mood inspired by Hector's words
prepare their supper round the fires in the plain, we hear, as
they do, the sound of lamentation for the dead Patroclus rise
threateningly from Achilles' camp (314-315), and Achilles'
vow of vengeance (333-342) answers Hector's proud words.
The shifting of the scene is accomplished without any emo-
tional jerk by the splendid simile which points the juxtaposition
of the two opposing scenes:

ὥς τε λὶς ἠϋγένειος,
ᾧ ῥά θ' ὑπὸ σκύμνους ἐλαφηβόλος ἁρπάσῃ ἀνὴρ
ὕλης ἐκ πυκινῆς· ὁ δέ τ' ἄχνυται ὕστερος ἐλθών,
πολλὰ δέ τ' ἄγκε' ἐπῆλθε μετ' ἀνέρος ἴχνι' ἐρευνῶν,
εἴ ποθεν ἐξεύροι· μάλα γὰρ δριμὺς χόλος αἱρεῖ.

[1] Vol. II, p. 337.   (318-322)

("As a bearded lion, whose whelps a hunter has stolen out of a deep wood, mourns, when he comes, to find them gone, and follows his track across hill and dale, seeking him, for bitter wrath has hold of him.")

It should also be noted that the scene in Achilles' camp (343-353) picks up and carries on the theme of reverent care for the dead body which was dwelt upon in the case of Sarpedon, and which is to play so large a part in the horror and the beauty of the closing movement.

In these last three scenes too the poet is dropping the curtain on the events of the day, and for our satisfaction disposes of the various groups and characters with whom we have been concerned, so that we feel that a natural pause has come in the action. Of the tone of the brief scene between Zeus and Hera (356-367) I have already spoken. It is right and proper that we should hear Zeus comment on Hera's interference, to finish off the hint suggested about the secret coming of Iris, to confirm the smile with which the intelligent noted it. But the scene also helps effectively in making the transition to the next topic. With the re-introduction of the gods our thoughts naturally return to Thetis, and Hera's very words make us think of her errand.

Of the effect of the concluding passage of the book Miss Stawell has given a perfect appreciation[1]: "Then we pass, if Homer may lead us, from the strain of these sights, from the places of battle and death and agony, away to the peaceful home of the gods and the marvellous smithy of Hephaestus. The effect of the change can hardly be over-estimated. We have had a day of crowded emotion and excitement; we have

[1] op. cit., pp. 68-70.

felt the rush of conquest and the terror of defeat; our hearts
have been torn with sympathy for each side in turn, for the
doomed Troy, for Hector, for the Achaeans in their dread, for
Achilles in his punishment. We are at the very heart of the
tragedy. The evening has come, and there is a natural pause.

"The terrible day is over, and the sacred darkness has fallen,
and now with no undue abruptness, still united to the tragedy
by the mournful figure of Thetis, we are gently taken away to
the starry house of Hephaestus and the fairy world of handi-
craft and rest. Like the similes in the battle, the change at
once relieves and heightens the tragic impression of the whole.
And the effect gains in breadth and grandeur by the character
of the scenes that are inlaid upon the shield. Why are they
described in such fullness and with such exuberant delight?
Not merely because the poet wanted to make a magic piece
of workmanship in the fashion of his day, but because at
this moment his mind turned instinctively for rest and
strengthening to larger pictures of life, away from the passion
and turmoil of these individual sorrows to general views of
other lives in peace and war, to other battles and sieges, to
marriages and dances, and trials at law, to vintages, and
plowing, and all the work of the fields. Troy may fall and
Achilles' life be wrecked, but the world goes on as before.
The tragedy is at once more pathetic and more bearable when
seen in the larger setting."

That is in every particular a just estimate. The poet has
ingeniously seized on the opportunity afforded by the making
of the arms to put before us, just where it is most telling, a
picture of the larger life within which the tragedy of Troy
takes place. He lifts our eyes from their concentration upon
the battlefield to the contemplation of other scenes which

remind us of the fullness and variety of life; it is a breathing-space in the battle, in which we have time to look around us and remember that this is only an incident in the busy world of human activities, that "though Troy may fall and Achilles' life be wrecked, the world goes on as before", and in that remembrance there is at the same time relief of emotional tension and yet a heightening of expectation through the holding back of the long awaited crisis, and also a deepening of the poignancy of the tragedy by seeing it thus against the large, indifferent background of the wider life of the world.

There is no simpler or clearer illustration of "the art of amplification" as employed by Homer than this interlude. It would seem that there is no restriction, that anything that strikes his fancy at the moment is thrust there and then into his poem without regard for the requirements of his story. And yet this careless profusion of interests does not cause confusion. The Iliad is, in this respect, a triumph of artistic audacity. The poet has tried to include too much—and he has succeeded. The story is never lost, nor even disturbed, by these vagaries. The explanation is very simple. The poet's method, just considered as a piece of literary engineering, may be described as the device of the single plane. All the asides and "interpolations" of unnecessary matter he projects upon the single plane of these few days' action. This device enables him to wander without confusing his listeners; they always know where they are because they are always in the same place. Stories of other times and distant lands take their place on the scene of action as reminiscences of persons engaged in the action and with reference to it. As we have noted, the long past preliminaries of the story are worked into the first day's fighting. A series of raids carried out by

Achilles earlier in the war, by which his greatness as a warrior
is built into the background of our thoughts of him, is
described by incidental allusions. And of the world that
lies away from the battlefield, the world of nature and of
human life generally, he gives us vivid glimpses by means of
similes, which in their place are both pictorially and dra-
matically effective. Through such similes the poet unob-
trusively unfolds the background of his story, so that we feel
its action not as an isolated event played upon a specially
prepared stage, but as something taking place in the real
world of ordinary men and women. We can feel the whole
life of the Homeric world stirring and moving and going
on its way behind the events of the story, giving depth and
reality and colour to its action. The countryside with its
farms, vineyards and pasture lands, scenes of hunting and all
the homely crafts, nature in its beauty and calm, and in its
storms and terrors—we are thus enabled to see it all without
straying from the battlefield.

So here the poet pauses in his tale, turns aside from the
subject of his poem, to describe in a series of set pictures this
world behind the scenes. The way he does it illustrates almost
concretely what I mean by the device of the single plane.
He shows us the life of man outside the story of the poem,
but he puts it on the shield of Achilles, which is well within
the story.

BOOK XIX

NOW that we are on the verge of the promised meeting of Achilles and Hector, Homer proceeds to hold it off, and he actually manages to postpone it for more than 1500 lines. It is the same principle of construction as we saw at the end of Bk. XII. When the story has roused an excitement and expectation great enough to last for a considerable length of time, it is then that he judges it safe to make it wait while he crowds in his additional material; the impetus the story has got, he apparently thinks, will carry it unimpaired through a great mass of minor incident. Thus here, having cleared the stage for the culmination of the story—the meeting of Achilles and Hector—he proceeds to work in some of the extra material he has on hand. I do not mean to imply that the expansions are introduced just for the sake of the delay. Their main object may be to swell the poem to the desired length, so that instead of skill in condensation what was required of the poet was skill in amplification, skill, if you like, in padding. And as this portion of the Iliad—Bks. XIX to XXI—is perhaps the most striking instance of delayed action, it offers us an excellent opportunity to estimate his skill in padding, how, that is, these excrescences on the story, besides holding it back at the crises, are themselves shaped and moulded to form the giant limbs of the whole organism.

We must bear in mind also that the effect on us is different from what it would have been on Homer's original audience. They did not know, as we do, that the meeting of Achilles and Hector comes in Bk. XXII, and that we are only in Bk. XIX now. For them therefore he is holding off the crisis from moment to moment; he brings it near and then removes it again, blocking and re-blocking the action by more delay. Thus they would be carried through what follows by the constant excitement of what is to happen on the next page, as it were; we read without hope of getting to the point till Bk. XXII begins. And whereas to many of us it is perhaps the prolonging of a task, to his proper audience it is the prolonging of an entertainment, and their exasperation at the continual postponement would be the pleasant exasperation that comes from intense interest.

The subject of Bk. XIX—the renunciation of the wrath —is indeed integral in the story. It is only the length to which the description of it is carried that makes it retard the story. In fact this book constitutes a kind of picture of what the poet is doing at this stage—the story struggling to burst through and get going, and being blocked and quenched by some other material being flung upon it. That the poet is fully aware of what he is doing, fully realizes the exasperation he is causing by his long-windedness, is shown by his representing Achilles as exasperated almost beyond endurance by the very thing that is exasperating us. That is, he uses our feelings to make us understand Achilles' feelings, and dramatizes and hence relieves our impatience by giving it utterance, and so creates in us a better understanding of and sympathy with Achilles' mood when he drives out to the battle.

Achilles, having received the armour from his mother, summons the Achaeans to assembly, and formally renounces his wrath in a speech which voices his own and our impatience to get on with the action. Agamemnon's reply strikes the first note of delay in the long and curious story about the

birth of Heracles. Achilles in his brusque reply dismisses the
question of the gifts as unimportant now, and again presses
to get on with the story without all this talk: "But now let us
think of fighting at once; it is no time to be sitting here
spinning things out and delaying; there is a great deed yet
undone" (149-150). There can be no question who has the
sympathy of the audience here.

Odysseus now intervenes, and proceeds to lay before us
and the assembly a program of necessary delays. First, he
points out that the army has not breakfasted yet, and takes
some time arguing on the disadvantages of fighting on an
empty stomach. And he is not at all ready to accept Achilles'
view about the gifts; and quite rightly; there is a principle at
stake. He does not want an unfortunate precedent created.
All the formalities must be observed. The gifts are to be
brought to the assembly that all the Achaeans may see them;
Agamemnon is to restore Briseis and take oath that he has
treated her with the respect due to another man's property;
then he is to give Achilles a feast of reconciliation. His impli-
cation is that Achilles' personal desire in the matter has
nothing to do with the case. It is his duty to the community
to accept the full and formal atonement (155-183).

So Agamemnon bids Achilles and all the others wait
where they are until the gifts are brought and ceremoniously
presented, and the oath given with solemn sacrifice. At the
prospect Achilles bursts out: "Surely you should postpone all
this to a more suitable time when there is a natural pause in
the fighting and the fury in my heart is less fierce. But now
they lie mangled—those whom Hector slew—and you are
calling men to food. I say, let the sons of the Achaeans fight
fasting, and at the setting of the sun prepare a great meal,
when we shall have avenged the shame. Till then, down my

throat at least neither drink nor food shall go; my friend is
dead; in my tent, hacked with sharp bronze, he lies with feet
towards the door, and his comrades mourn around him.
Wherefore in my heart is no thought of these matters, but of
slaying and blood and the groans of dying men" (200-214).

But Achilles finds that the force of custom is too strong
even for him, and he, and we, have to submit to watching the
solemn, unhurried performance of all these threatened rites.
And when it is all over, and Briseis is restored, and has duly,
and very beautifully lamented Patroclus (Poor girl! the story
has left her far behind; she who had been the *casus belli* is of
no importance now; our feeling about her is covered by
Achilles' brutally indifferent "Would that Artemis had slain
her on that day when I took her at the destruction of
Lyrnessus!")—when all this is finished, and the Achaean
host begins to move out to the plain, and Achilles arms, and
drives forth to the battle, no doubt those first hearers mur-
mured "At last!" They did not know what was to come.

Thus, so far, the delay is intensely dramatic, and has
distinctly increased the feeling of excitement, just as the fury
of Achilles has grown by his enforced inaction. It makes, as
I have said, an excellent dramatic preparation for his entrance
to the battle. The very fact that he has been delayed increases
his eagerness, as the very fact that we have been delayed
increases ours. The delay does more than delay; it transmits
to us the impatience of Achilles.

This is the beginning of the last movement of the Iliad,
and it opens with the same action as the first: Achilles
summons the Achaeans to an assembly (*cf.* I, 53-54).

The speech of Achilles (56-73) is brief, straightforward,
and unadorned, in dramatic contrast with the designedly
laboured speech of Agamemnon which follows. These are

dramatic speeches, dramatically realized; I mean, not only is what each one says appropriate to the situation and the speaker, but also the way he says it, the manner of the speech, reveals the mood of the speaker. In the case of Achilles, one feels by the careless indifference with which he dismisses the subject how utterly insignificant the whole business of Briseis and his quarrel has become. Because of this "girl", of whom he speaks so contemptuously now, he has almost brought the whole Achaean cause to irreparable disaster. Hundreds of good men have perished who might be alive now, as he himself notes (61). What his tone shows, of course, is not that he is indifferent to these facts, but that he is indifferent to this tedious business of reconciliation. His mother has pointed out to him the necessity of formally renouncing his wrath, and he is going through with it as quickly as he can. The sublime arrogance of his attitude is brilliantly thrown into relief by the preceding picture of the wounded chieftains painfully limping into the assembly (47-53). It is to such men, Homer thus makes us realize, that these words are addressed—to men who in the peril caused by his action have valiantly been facing death, and bear on their bodies the marks of that desperate struggle. There is not a trace of shame or apology in his words—nor of the defiance in which a smaller man might try to cover up his sense of guilt. He has no sense of guilt; he speaks with the self-confidence, not of impudence, but of a man who is perfectly sure of his position and his importance. "Personal ascendancy—the unaccountable and irresistible prowess which such men announce by their mere presence." Because he feels this ascendancy himself, he speaks as he does, and so makes us feel it and realize that all the assembly feel it.

To my ear there is an individual note about almost everything Achilles says. In whatever mood he speaks the words seem to be his own, not the poet's. The full force of a unique personality is felt behind them, whether as in the great speech in Bk. IX he is pouring forth his indignation, or, as in Bk. XVI, struggling with conflicting emotions, or, as here, absorbed by a single determination. There is a vehemence and directness about them, a strange and indescribable ruthlessness of utterance that makes his voice unique, and so creates in us the sense of a real, living personality.

Even the dullest reader must be struck by the contrasting tone between Achilles' speech and Agamemnon's reply. "The disjointed character of all the exordium of Agamemnon's speech seems designedly to portray the embarrassment of his position, and indeed vividly expresses the peevish nervousness of a man who feels in the wrong and is under the disadvantage of following a speaker who by his frank admissions has won the sympathy of the audience. He makes various attempts to start his speech, but does not fairly see his way till line 86."[1]

But Agamemnon suffers under another disadvantage. It has been made a point against Bk. IX that in this speech, when Agamemnon is presumably trying to make the best of his case, he does not plead the strongest point in his favour, *viz* that he had spontaneously offered reparation and that Achilles had rejected it. The only possible excuse for introducing such a plea would have been to prove that Bk. IX belongs to the poem; dramatically it would have been entirely inappropriate. For Agamemnon's greatest difficulty is precisely that he must say nothing in his defence that would tend to offend the irascible Achilles. He must be careful not

---

[1] Leaf: *Commentary, ad loc.*

to impute any blame to him. It is the consciousness of that
which makes his speech so lame. He is, in consequence,
nervous. He must make a public apology to Achilles and
does not quite know what to say. And so after fumbling
about for an opening he falls back on the same plea he had
used in Bk. IX, that he was in the power of Ate when he
wronged Achilles, which is no more than saying that he
acknowledges now he was mad to behave as he did. It does
not excuse him, except in so far as it is an excuse to say that
all men are subject to these accesses of passion which blind
them to all considerations save the satisfaction of their passion;
and he desperately fills out his speech by relating the story of
how the spirit of Ate came among men. But, having thus
said nothing at impressive length, he cannot forbear at the end
hinting, with a kind of peevish irony, at what he might say
if he could:

ὡς καὶ ἐγών, ὅτε δὴ αὖτε μέγας κορυθαίολος Ἕκτωρ
Ἀργείους ὀλέκεσκεν ἐπὶ πρύμνῃσι νέεσσιν,
οὐ δυνάμην λελαθέσθ' Ἄτης, ᾗ πρῶτον ἀάσθην.

(134-136)

—"when again Hector was destroying Argives, I could not
forget the madness that possessed me"—, just not saying that
the first time Hector was successful, he had put aside his
anger and tried to make amends. And this indirect reminder
is immediately followed by a direct reference to the embassy:

δῶρα δ' ἐγὼν ὅδε πάντα παρασχέμεν, ὅσσα τοι ἐλθὼν
χθιζὸς ἐνὶ κλισίῃσιν ὑπέσχετο δῖος Ὀδυσσεύς.

(140-141)

("I am here to offer all the gifts which Odysseus yesterday
promised in your tent.")

Achilles' curt comment (146-153) admirably underlines, for the hearer, the nature of Agamemnon's speech, and shows us how he has been chafing at all this unnecessary elaboration of a simple point.

Then an attack upon his impatience comes from another quarter. Odysseus' interference and the rest of the business of the assembly bring out the point that on the original issue Achilles has been right and Agamemnon wrong. Odysseus' insistence is due to his anxiety to protect the rights of the subordinate chieftains. As he remarks, when he has listed the due formalities to be observed: "And you, son of Atreus, will be more righteous hereafter in the case of another; for it is quite right that a king should make amends when the fault of a quarrel lies with him" (181-183).

Nor is the lament of Briseis for Patroclus mere delay. It too creates its artistic justification. Her return to Achilles must be signalized in some way, for it puts the seal on the recon-ciliation, it marks the end of the quarrel begun in Bk. I. And how can it be better signalized than by showing its sig-nificance in relation to the present situation? The price Achilles has paid for her restoration is the life of his friend. The poet does not point this out to us; he makes us feel it by bringing the two—Briseis and the dead Patroclus—into relation with each other. And by this means too he makes the closing of the one set of events part of the forward move-ment of the poem. For, just as the taking of Briseis was the exciting cause of all the previous events, the death of Patroclus is the exciting cause of all that is to come. The poem takes on fresh life from the death of Patroclus, and so the passing of Briseis and the fading of the momentum given the poem at the outset is made to contribute to the fresh momentum it has received in the sorrow for Patroclus. For that Briseis should thus feel that she has lost a friend both indicates the attractiveness of his character, just when the realization of it is most effective (making *us* the more sorry for his death), and carries our thoughts to Achilles and the infinitely more that loss must mean to him. And so her lament leads naturally and effectively to the renewed picture of his grief (303-337), that we may see him set out to his revenge under the immediate impetus of his profound grief, the thought of which, so prominent in Bk. XVIII, has been somewhat obscured, of necessity, by the interruption of the assembly scene. The poet is doing all he can to increase the pathos of Patroclus's fate, so that we may give Achilles a good send-off as he drives into the battle.

The arming of Achilles (369-391) recalls verbally, point by point, the arming of Patroclus in Bk. XVI. That is the poet's way of making us realize the thoughts that are torturing Achilles as he puts the pieces on. Achilles arms, and behind we see in memory Patroclus arming. We know his thoughts not by being told what they were but by thinking them. By the repetition one set of words conveys two trains of thought at the same time. And Achilles' rebuke to his horses (400-403), which concludes the explicit description of his preparations, is that underlying thought, which has been haunting him (and us), coming to the surface. The two levels of thought join in this utterance and proceed together in the thought that Achilles too has been preparing his own death. It is in order to find means to make this point explicit that Homer endows Xanthus with speech. Thus we are reminded again as we watch Achilles drive triumphantly into battle that he is, as I have said, in his erroneous, unchristian way, consciously and gladly, laying down his life for his friend.

BOOK XX

ZEUS summons all the gods to Olympus, and gives them permission to take what part they like in the ensuing battle. His motive is, he says, to strengthen the resistance of the Trojans to Achilles, that he may be prevented from destroying Troy before the appointed time (26-30). This is really the poet making an excuse for holding back the meeting of Achilles and Hector until he is ready for it, and giving notice that the story is going to be diverted from its expected course.

"The plan of the book," says Monro,[1] "brings out one of the contradictions which are the stumbling-blocks of critics, but which really lie deep in the nature of epic poetry. Achilles is burning to avenge his friend; he ought therefore to seek out Hector and bring his quarrel to a speedy issue. Instead of this he is drawn away into a slaughter of Trojan rank and file, with incidents which occupy two books. The reason is that the poet has to fill his canvas. The death of Hector must not stand by itself in the picture, but form the climax of the last and greatest of the days of battle. The difficulty is met by the Olympian assembly at the beginning of the book. The gods that are friendly to Troy are again left free to act, and their interference brings about the due retardation in the course of events."

[1] p. 365, vol. II.

That is, when he says "the poet has to fill his canvas", he means not simply that he has to keep his poem from ending too soon but that the account of the slaying of Hector requires as its setting the rout of the Trojan army. That has to be depicted in some way, and it is the way chosen he refers to when he says that this book "brings out one of the contradictions which are the stumbling-blocks of critics but which lie deep in the nature of epic poetry". It is the way of epic poetry, he means, to elaborate even its minor points, because here some account of the preparatory exploits of Achilles is required, to use it as an excuse for including additional incidents in his poem. Having said so much justly and truly, Monro promptly himself falls over the stumbling-block he has warned others against, and proceeds to reject the passage describing the meeting of Achilles and Aeneas on the score of its being one of the contradictions which, as he has claimed, lie deep in the nature of epic poetry. But I am not concerned with the considerations he adduces as marking this incident as an interpolation. It is quite possible that the Iliad has been formed in part by the working together of many once separate poems, and the fact, if it is a fact, that in this instance the joining shows through is a matter of purely superficial interest. For the poem I am examining is just this conglomerate which is and has always been the Iliad and which was put before the world in this form with the intention of being understandable as one coherent story. My object is to consider the purpose of this insertion, and that must be measured by its effect coming where it does, always keeping in mind the nature of epic poetry as it has already been exhibited throughout the poem.

Where many of the searchers for the "original" poem run off the rails aesthetically is in assuming that by showing that a passage is unnecessary to the intelligibility of the story they have thereby shown that it is not necessary in the poem. For to say that it is not necessary to the intelligibility of the story is not the same as saying it is not necessary artistically. Of course the story must be intelligible and reasonably consistent, but the *art* of narrative does not lie there. A reasonable consistency is merely the preliminary condition within which the narrator must exercise his art. That is directed to making the reader see and feel the significance of the story as nearly as possible as he himself does. He aims to record and communicate the full quality of it as it affects his imagination, and the incidents and speeches he puts in and the way he arranges and develops them are the means by which he seeks to transmit these effects into the imagination of others. The appropriateness of a passage should be estimated primarily by reference to this purpose. Only when so doing are we studying the art of a story. We should look beneath surface effects of logic and necessity, and remember that, as Aristotle said, "faults" are right in a work of art if through them the end of the art is better attained. A narrative poem must be consistent up to the point that this is necessary to support the emotional effect; one thing must follow from another according to necessity or probability, not for the sake of the logic, but to supply a "frame of reference" for the emotional effects; and logical discrepancies may be even desirable if through them these effects are enhanced, and are allowable in so far as they do not disturb by intellectual doubts the imaginative response of the hearer.

Undoubtedly the temperature of the poem seems delib-
erately lowered in this book and the next, and at this critical
point we are asked to move on an inferior plane of interest.
Looking at the last movement as a whole, one can see in a
general way what the narrator's idea was in doing this. It is
not only that he wishes to lengthen his poem, to hold back
the crisis, or to get in as many incidents as he can without
breaking the continuity of his narrative; he wishes also to
variegate the tone of this last movement; for it is in its own
proper subject of a uniformly tragic and sorrowful cast, and
the strain of an unbroken series of tragic happenings and
lamentations is too great; the feelings tend to become
deadened; if the audience are fed too steadily with horrors,
direness may become familiar to their thoughts and fail to
start them; so that the purpose is not exactly to lighten the
gloom, but rather to ensure our not growing accustomed to
the gloom. I am sure that the tragedy of Bk. XXII is felt
more keenly because it is held well away from Bk. XVIII than
it would be if it followed immediately on the tragic scenes
of that book. We may acknowledge that in this respect the
plan is sound enough, though we may still question the fitness
of some of the incidents he has chosen to use for this purpose.

The battle begins magnificently with the gathering of the
gods upon the field (31-74). The passage is, in part, a pano-
ramic preview of interests to come, the gods being paired off
in preparation for the actual clash between them in Bk. XXI,
and ll. 73-74 foreshadowing the fight with the river. But
the tone of the two passages is quite different. Here he uses
the presence of the gods to fill the mind with images of
terror and grandeur as a suitable setting for the final battle.
Achilles has taken the field, and the scene is made appropriate
to the greatness of the occasion.

But after this thunderous introduction the tone changes. It flattens down to the slow-moving, comparatively spiritless account of Achilles' meeting with Aeneas. The faults of this incident are plain to see. It is in itself one of the least effective fights in the Iliad, and it stands out particularly glaringly here because the action has been moving at such high tension. Also, a futile fight would seem to be exactly the thing *not* to give Achilles at this time; it seems to slow him up, to blunt the keen edge of his wrath, and so to blunt the keenness of our expectations. If legend forbade Achilles to kill Aeneas, why make him meet Aeneas at all?

This is the last day of battle in the poem, and it is built on the model of the first battle. There Diomedes was the central figure, here it is Achilles. When Diomedes made his entrance upon the field, "Pallas Athena put strength and courage into him and made fire blaze from his helmet and shield"—δαῖέ οἱ ἐκ κόρυθός τε καὶ ἀσπίδος ἀκάματον πῦρ, Bk. V, 5. When in Bk. XVIII Achilles' appearance at the trench heralded his return to battle, Athena similarly "crowned his head with a golden cloud and lit a flame of fire from it"— ἐκ δ'αὐτοῦ δαῖε φλόγα παμφανόωσαν. The memories of Diomedes' exploits accompany those of Achilles now. The fight with Aeneas is a repetition of Diomedes' fight with Aeneas. It ends in a similar way; there Apollo rescues Aeneas, spiriting him away; here Poseidon. And this reminiscence continues; for, as in the Diomedes episode we have the light and laughable incidents of the wounding of Aphrodite and Ares, so the exploits of Achilles on this day are diversified by the farcical battle of the gods written in just the same spirit. Leaf puts the point in his own way when in his condemnation of that incident he says it owes "what little interest it has to the reminiscences of the wounding of Aphrodite in E, on which it is doubtless founded."[1]

Thus the poet, while driving ahead with entirely new matter, backs it with memories that colour what we are hearing. The shadow of Diomedes accompanies Achilles as he proceeds to his revenge. And why? Diomedes' exploits ended in the meeting with Glaucus, and the pleasant reminder that there are after all chivalrous feelings and ties that override the bitter relationship of foe with foe; Achilles' exploits on this day end in the dreadful meeting with Hector. The contrast points and underlines the tragedy.

I described the battle in Bk. V as a picture of a battle in the days before Achilles withdrew dramatically transferred to the time after his withdrawal, and with the role of Achilles played by Diomedes, and suggested that the character of Diomedes is drawn in direct contrast to that of Achilles that it may furnish a background against which we may measure the conduct of Achilles. This time Achilles appears in person, and that background unrolls again in the rhythm of the incidents that describe his actions, throwing into stronger prominence the tragic significance of what is happening. It is the great virtue of *sophrosyne*, of which Diomedes was the exemplar, that Achilles lacks or has lost. Blinded by his fury,

---

[1] *Commentary*, vol. II, p. 315. There are indeed a remarkable number of such reminiscences in that scene: in V, 355 *ff*. Aphrodite when wounded asks help from Ares; here (XXI, 416) she goes to his help. In XXI, 505 *ff*. Artemis after being roughly handled by Hera is comforted by the amused Zeus; in V, 370 *ff*. there is a longer but similar scene in which Aphrodite is comforted, first by her mother, and then by the smiling Zeus. Ares (XXI, 396) explicitly recalls the former occasion: "Don't you remember", he asks Athena, "when you incited Diomedes to wound me?" And even ll. 464-466 echo Glaucus's famous words in VI, 146 *ff*.

See also Nilsson: *Homer and Mycenae*, pp. 258-9.

blinded again by Ate, he is rushing to the destruction foretold
by Phoenix for men who will not listen to the suppliant
prayers of those who have wronged them:

ὃς δέ κ' ἀνήνηται καί τε στερεῶς ἀποείπῃ,
λίσσονται δ' ἄρα ταί γε Δία Κρονίωνα κιοῦσαι
τῷ Ἄτην ἅμ' ἕπεσθαι, ἵνα βλαφθεὶς ἀποτείσῃ.

(510-512)

("Whoever denies them and stubbornly refuses, they go and
entreat Zeus that Ate may now follow him that he may fall
and pay the price.")

Is that judgment to fall on Achilles? Or will the limping
prayers yet reach him and prevail? Perhaps the shape of the
Diomedes episode, recalled thus to the memory, hints at the
answer and keeps hope alive. For on its little scale that episode
began with Agamemnon's gratuitous insult to Diomedes and
ended with two enemies shaking hands as friends, as the great
span of the Iliad stretches from the insult to Achilles to Priam
kissing the hands of the man who had slain his son.

The fight with Aeneas is not developed as it is with this
one purpose in view. As usual the poet elaborates it for its
own sake on lines that go beyond this "context" purpose of
reminiscence, exactly as his similes beside their context value
of illustration or emphasis grow into pictures that exist in
their own right.

Aeneas's extended sketch of his ancestry (213-241) should
not surprise us by its apparent ineptitude at such a moment;
we have had this sort of thing before; it is indeed a duller
version of Glaucus's address to Diomedes in Bk. VI. Such
speeches before a fight are a literary development of the taunts
which apparently were really uttered in this kind of fighting.
And though it may seem to us surprising that the relation of
Aeneas's ancestry should have been regarded as interesting

either by the poet or his audience, it is a fact that early story everywhere shows that there was a deep interest in genealogies.[1]

There is one very minor point in the account of this battle which those who are offended with it for the reasons I have cited have distorted to do it still further discredit. They say that Achilles, who has come out to do battle in such blind fury, is represented as afraid of his first antagonist. Homer says nothing of the kind. He describes Achilles' instinctive throwing forward of his shield as Aeneas cast and struck it:

$$\Pi\eta\lambda\epsilon\dot{t}\delta\eta s \ \delta\dot{\epsilon} \ \sigma\acute{\alpha}\kappa os \ \mu\dot{\epsilon}\nu \ \dot{\alpha}\pi\grave{o} \ \ddot{\epsilon}o \ \chi\epsilon\iota\rho\grave{\iota} \ \pi\alpha\chi\epsilon\acute{\iota}\eta$$
$$\ddot{\epsilon}\sigma\chi\epsilon\tau o \ \tau\alpha\rho\beta\acute{\eta}\sigma\alpha s \cdot \ \phi\acute{\alpha}\tau o \ \gamma\grave{\alpha}\rho \ \delta o\lambda\iota\chi\acute{o}\sigma\kappa\iota o\nu \ \ddot{\epsilon}\gamma\chi os$$
$$\dot{\rho}\acute{\epsilon}\alpha \ \delta\iota\epsilon\lambda\epsilon\acute{\upsilon}\sigma\epsilon\sigma\theta\alpha\iota \ \mu\epsilon\gamma\alpha\lambda\acute{\eta}\tau o\rho os \ A\dot{\iota}\nu\epsilon\acute{\iota}\alpha o,$$
$$\nu\acute{\eta}\pi\iota os, \ o\dot{\upsilon}\delta' \ \dot{\epsilon}\nu\acute{o}\eta\sigma\epsilon \ \kappa\alpha\tau\grave{\alpha} \ \phi\rho\acute{\epsilon}\nu\alpha \ \kappa\alpha\grave{\iota} \ \kappa\alpha\tau\grave{\alpha} \ \theta\upsilon\mu\grave{o}\nu$$
$$\dot{\omega}s \ o\dot{\upsilon} \ \dot{\rho}\eta\dot{t}\delta\iota' \ \dot{\epsilon}\sigma\tau\grave{\iota} \ \theta\epsilon\hat{\omega}\nu \ \dot{\epsilon}\rho\iota\kappa\upsilon\delta\acute{\epsilon}\alpha \ \delta\hat{\omega}\rho\alpha$$
$$\dot{\alpha}\nu\delta\rho\acute{\alpha}\sigma\iota \ \gamma\epsilon \ \theta\nu\eta\tau o\hat{\iota}\sigma\iota \ \delta\alpha\mu\acute{\eta}\mu\epsilon\nu\alpha\iota \ o\dot{\upsilon}\delta' \ \dot{\upsilon}\pi o\epsilon\acute{\iota}\kappa\epsilon\iota\nu.$$

(261-266)

---

[1] cf. W. W. Lawrence on Beowulf: "There is plenty of stirring action, the proper business of Epic. But the audience obviously waited with no less eagerness for reminiscences of old historic tradition. Almost every page of Beowulf gives evidence of how completely this filled their minds . . . the poet's digressions often seem to us to clog the action and distract attention from it. But there was little suspense in the plot; the story was familiar, what was important was the detail. And no part of this detail, in days when there were few ways of learning about the past, was more absorbing than history, or what passed for history. Tastes have changed since then. One sometimes wonders at the fascination exercised by long genealogies. In the Icelandic sagas the luxuriant family trees, with every bough and twig duly pictured forth, seems to us to darken high adventure with their spreading branches. The same is true of Irish and Welsh. As for Beowulf, a modern story-teller would hardly have thought it worth while to give the entire royal lines of both the sovereigns at whose court the action takes place. But the earlier habit of mind is of great significance. If we are to read the epic, as it was meant to be understood, we must endeavour to recapture, so far as we may, its intense interest in early heroic tradition, and to gain familiarity with its complexities."

("The son of Peleus held his shield away from him in fear; for he thought that the spear of Aeneas would easily pierce it through, not realizing in his folly that the glorious gifts of the gods do not easily yield to the strength of mortal men.")

That is, he held it well away from him for fear that the spear would pass through it, forgetting it was made by a god. It is sheer perversity to interpret that as meaning Achilles was frightened of Aeneas. It is a vivid touch to recall the glory of the armour in which he was clad.

Aeneas is rescued, somewhat mysteriously, by Poseidon; some legend about Aeneas seems to be lurking behind these events. Achilles proceeds upon his victorious way, and at l. 375 we are reminded that Hector is being held back. Then begins the slaughter of the Trojans (381-489). Among the slain is Polydorus, son of Priam, and Hector advances against Achilles to avenge him (421). The poet is sharpening the excitement for the actual meeting, and I expect every listener leant forward when Achilles sprang to meet the long-sought Hector (423-427). But he is snatched away by Apollo. The time is not yet come. For it must be remembered that the poet has to describe not only the killing of Hector, but the rout of the Trojan army by Achilles. The combat with Hector is to be the climax of the battle. So at l. 490 comes the break-up and flight of the Trojans before the charge of Achilles, vividly depicted in two similes (490-497). The glory and resistless might of Achilles seem at their zenith; it sounds as if the poet were just going to stage the culmination of his fury and bring him face to face with Hector.

BOOK XXI

HALF of the Trojans make their escape across the plain to the city, but the rest Achilles cuts off and drives into the river Xanthus. In the midst of the slaughter that follows Homer pauses to dwell upon the slaying of Lycaon, a son of Priam. The incident is full of associations that carry us backwards, and of suggestions that carry us forward. It puts before us, in Homer's objective way, as an event, the true inwardness of the tragedy of Achilles. The Achilles that has been, the Achilles that is, and the Achilles that shall be are all united here. For the past history of Lycaon—how he was caught before by Achilles and his life spared—is given to emphasize the terribleness of Achilles' present mood. This pathetic figure, with his pitiable story and his childish plea that he is only half-brother to Hector "who slew your comrade, the gentle and strong" (96)—if he cannot win mercy from Achilles, we get a dreadful foretaste of what the meeting with Hector will be like. The poet is giving us a glimpse into the black hate that has filled Achilles' heart. But he gives us a glimpse of something more. The reply of Achilles to Lycaon's plea (99-113) is one of the masterstrokes of the Iliad:

"Poor fool, proffer me no ransom and no talk. Before Patroclus met his doom, in those days I found it more pleasing to my heart to spare Trojans, and many I took alive and sent across the sea. But now there is not one who shall escape death whomever before Ilios God shall throw into my hands, of all the Trojans, and, above all, children of Priam. Nay, friend, do you too die. Why do you sorrow so? Patroclus died, and he was a much better man than you. Look at me—am I not fair and great? The son of a princely father, and the mother who bore me, a goddess. Yet over me too is the shadow of death and overmastering fate. There will come a dawn or an evening or a noontide when someone shall take my life too in battle, in the hurling of a spear or an arrow from the bowstring."

In a stroke we have focused there the tragedy of Achilles, almost one might say the tragedy of human life, as Homer saw and embodied it in the figure of his hero. Here is the ruthless, terrible, hateful Achilles who is to slay Hector and outrage his body; here, as a half-troubled memory passing through his own mind, Achilles the generous enemy, whose *aidôs* time after time has stayed his triumphant hand; here too a hint of that Achilles who is to weep with Priam and find himself united in sorrow with his deadliest foe; and here Achilles the embodiment of the glory and pride of life, and of its brevity and futility.

The speech is all these things dramatized, synthesized. It shows us these various aspects of Achilles as a unity, by combining them in one complex of tortured feeling—his ruthlessness and brutality arising from his intense absorption in one over-mastering passion, his strange compassion that broadens into a vision of the ruthlessness of life itself and of the splendid, pitiable futility of the human adventure, which he recognizes with unflinching clarity and which he symbolizes. Thus in its setting it is a contemplation of the character of Achilles before we plunge into the full horror of the scene of Hector's slaying. The poet is accounting in terms of character for all that is to come by gathering up the various and contradictory aspects of his strange hero, which motivate, for the reader, his conduct in what follows. Here is his summary of the tragic character which the story, as he planned it, seemed to him to demand. He wishes us to see him clear before he enters the shadow, and by the flicker of his magnanimity which for a moment lights his conduct here to feel the more strongly its complete absence in the scene to which this is a prelude.

This which would be done in a novel, let us say, by analysis and description is made into an event. The pause of preparatory contemplation is achieved without stopping the action. It is part of the picture of the Trojan rout, one of the incidents to make the description of the rout vivid.

Also, it strikes the preparatory note of pity for the Trojans which is to be the predominant strain in Bk. XXII. The close of Bk. XVI turned our sympathies away from Hector, and sorrow for the death of Patroclus has since then been the prevailing emotional theme. Now, faint and far away, yet distinct, the theme of Troy's sorrow begins to obtrude itself again. Our minds are doubly prepared for the swing round of sympathy by the ruthless brutality of Achilles and the pathos of Lycaon's story.

The incident that succeeds this, the slaying of Asteropaeus, descendant of a river-god, serves to make the transition from reality to wonderland, from fights with opponents of flesh and blood to the fantastic fight with the river Xanthus. The first rumble of the river's discontent comes in ll. 136-8, with the dumping of Lycaon's body into it.

This famous scene, I confess, rather jars on me, and I wonder whether it may not have been meant to. I feel that

with l. 212 an alien atmosphere comes into the poem, that
in the fight with the river we are in a different artistic world
from that we have been moving in; the imagination is startled
by this sudden humanizing of a river. A river-*god* appearing
in human form and fighting like a man would be in keeping,
but here, though at first the poet says ἀνέρι εἰσάμενος (213),
in the fight the river is both a live conscious person and still
very much a river. There is nothing like this anywhere also
in the poem; we seem to have passed back to an earlier, more
primitive type of story, into the world of fairy- and folk-tale,
which has been, except for brief, casual touches, so far
excluded from the poem. There is, in consequence, an effect
of grotesqueness and weirdness, which is perhaps the inten-
tion. It may be that this is accidental, that it is only on modern
minds that it produces this effect, and that the folk-tale charac-
teristics would not be noticeably different from the rest to
Homer's audience. But, as this note of sheer marvel seems
to be deliberately kept out of the main stream of the poem,
I do not think it is far-fetched to conclude that its intrusion
here is deliberate and is meant to be felt. The difference is
one of artistic atmosphere within the poem, and therefore the
recognition of it does not seem to be just due to a difference
of taste. After all, fairy tales still have their appeal, and most
of us can accept their marvels with pleasure when we are
prepared for them. So that on that score there is no reason
why this account merely in itself should strike us as odd any
more than the original hearers. I suggest therefore that we
are justified in assuming that the rather surprising effect of
the passage on us is indeed in the poem and not just in our
minds.

The introduction of this marvellous element, this discord-
ant note (as I have called it) of grotesqueness, cannot fail to
affect the imagination. It is partly horrible and partly amus-
ing, as if the unreal things of a dream had broken through
into the real world; and as such it seems to symbolize for the
imagination the horror and confusion descending upon the
poem as the catastrophe draws near. The scene becomes
weirder and weirder as the book proceeds. The earth is filled
with strange sights and commotions. Nature seems con-
founded. It is as if a howling storm swept down upon the
battlefield, or rather as if some ghastly nightmare were abroad,
which breaks up finally in the grotesque foolery, the laughter
of the battle of the gods.

This scene (385-513) both sustains and releases the effect
of what has preceded. It is still grotesque, but its grotesque-
ness becomes harmless, *merely* funny. And being such, Homer
sets it here just before the closing in of the tragedy. That
statement should be sufficient to account for its character. He
is purposely giving his audience a complete holiday from all
serious emotion, as a refreshment and preparation for the
intense emotional strain of the coming event. There is no
question that it does not affect a reader in the same way as it
would a listener. A reader is always more detached; there is
less strain on his attention, and hence his emotional response
is less direct; it is surrounded by an atmosphere of reflection,
and therefore the poet cannot sway and control him to the
same extent by a succession of feelings. His appreciation is
more intellectual, and therefore to him things in a poem
meant for recitation, which depend for their whole effect on
their immediate and transient emotional contact, take on a
character they were not intended to have.

No doubt this is rather crude and clownish sort of fun,[1] and seems to us readers out of keeping with the terrible seriousness of the event we know is approaching, but no doubt also it was heartily appreciated by the comparatively naive minds of those listeners for whom it was composed, and excellently served its purpose of giving them the recreation of simple laughter, so that they might re-enter the solemn and darkening scene of human suffering with renewed zest for the pity and terror of it.

The rest of Bk. XXI really belongs to the next book, that is, the poet is here clearing the stage for the slaying of Hector. Priam, seeing the rout of the Trojans, gives orders that the warders stand by to fling open the gates for the fugitives, and to be ready, as soon as all are in, to close and bar them against the pursuer (531-536).

The little incident of Agenor's stand (544 to end) is part of the poet's setting of the stage. We can see, if we look ahead, why he introduced it. His plan for Hector's fight includes the wild pleas of his parents from the wall and Hector's debate with himself; these are both vital for the effects he aims at. But the situation at this point is—the Trojans are rushing for the open gate with Achilles at their heels. Obviously then, to allow for that projected scene Achilles must somehow be temporarily removed from the

---

[1] Leaf says of the Battle of the Gods that it is "one of the very few passages in the Iliad which can be pronounced poetically bad. In place of the imposing conflict of the divine powers which we were led to expect at the beginning of XX, we are presented with a ridiculous harlequinade." A good description, this last phrase, of its effect, but if Leaf was led to expect an imposing conflict, that is his own fault. For when you come down to actual details, how can a battle between immortal beings be anything but a farce?

gate. A god's aid is indicated—a god, because Hector alone of the Trojans is to remain outside the city, but obviously that god must take the form of some Trojan to lure Achilles away in pursuit. It is a makeshift arrangement, but it serves well enough. But why does Apollo not at once take the likeness of Agenor, instead of first inspiring him to await Achilles, and then, when the man is on the point of being killed, taking his place? The question is not really important; clearly it might just as well have been done the other way. But perhaps the method he has chosen has something to do with the soliloquy of Agenor (552-570) as a kind of preparatory attuning of the ear to the soliloquy of Hector a few lines further on.

BOOK XXII

THIS book is the culminating point of the Iliad,
that to which all that has gone before has been building, and
which creates the situation to which the termination of the
poem provides the solution. "Splendid though the book is in
its directness, speed, and pathos," says Leaf,[1] "the effect which
it produces on a modern reader is probably very different
from that which was aimed at by the original poet. For us
it is Hector who is throughout the object of our sympathy
and admiration. Fighting a hopeless fight for his country
against gods as well as the mightiest of heroes, he presents
himself in a far nobler light than Achilles, whose strength is
helped by divine aid denied to his enemy, and whose over-
mastering motive is not patriotism but the gratification of a
private revenge. It is in the last scene of all that we feel this
most keenly; first, in the treacherous interposition of Athena,
which seems so needless as well as so revolting; and secondly,
in the brutal ferocity with which Achilles refuses the offer
of Hector that the victor shall give the vanquished honourable
burial. One might think that the poet had purposely done all
in his power to exalt the Trojan hero at the expense of the
Greek."

That such is the effect on a modern reader there is no
question, and it is equally clear that this is the effect intended
—unless for the Greeks words meant almost the opposite of

[1] *Companion*, pp. 354-5.

what they seem to mean. Leaf, it must be remembered, is speaking not of the Iliad, but of a poem of his own imagination called the Μῆνις, which ends with l. 404 of this book. In the Iliad as we have it now, it is not necessary to wrest the plain meaning of Bk. XXII to make it fit. There may or may not have been an original poem on the Wrath such as Leaf has imagined, but if there was, certainly in this part it has been so rewritten and adapted to a new purpose that it is impossible to recover the original treatment of the story here. To end a poem of which Achilles is the hero on such a note is unthinkable, and accordingly Leaf finds an explanation for it which he admits is unthinkable for us because our ways of thinking are different from the Greeks'. But since the poem, as a matter of fact, does not stop here and since the conclusion to which we are brought fully explains and justifies, with no forced interpretations, the place of this book in the development of the tragedy of Achilles, we need have no hesitation in following our own natural response to its events. It is the climax of horror, and any attempt to reverse our instinctive judgment throws out the balance of the poem, and nullifies all the vast artistic effort that has gone to the preparation of this situation.

But while we are intended to condemn, and utterly condemn, Achilles' conduct here, it is not intended that he should lose all hold on our sympathy. He still remains an object of awed admiration. Every sensitive reader, watching his deed horrified, must feel the pity of it, and in that pity there is understanding. For we have been prepared to expect and dread such conduct as this and should even be disappointed with less. It was a grand idea not to let us see Achilles in action until he was moved by so profound a passion. De

Quincey has put this point with appropriate force[1]: "His friend perishes. Then we see him rise in his noontide wrath, before which no life could stand. The frenzy of his grief makes him for a time cruel and implacable. He sweeps the field of battle like a monsoon. His revenge descends, perfect, sudden, like a curse from heaven. We now recognize the goddess-born. This is his avatar—the incarnate descent of his wrath. Had he moved to battle under the ordinary impulses of Ajax, Diomed, and the other heroes, we could not have sympathized or gone along with so withering a course. We should have viewed him as a scourge of God or fiend, born for the tears of wives and the maledictions of mothers. But the poet, before he would let him loose upon men, creates for him a sufficient, or at least a palliating, motive. In the sternest of his acts we read only the anguish of his grief. This is surely the perfection of art."

Such is the mental reservation that acts as a check upon our condemnation; though we condemn his conduct, there is something that forbids our utterly condemning him. The very violence of his fury is aesthetically admirable and the emotion that causes it even morally admirable. This is the feeling that craves for satisfaction and finds it in the conclusion to which we are finally brought. Thus this book leaves the reader with a sense of incompleteness both with regard to Hector and with regard to Achilles.

At the beginning the poet sets himself to wake in us again our sympathies with Hector. For some time now our thoughts have been with Achilles, and the poet has been making us sorrow for the death of Patroclus so as to motivate in our

---

[1] *Homer and the Homeridae.* For this reference I am indebted to Professor E. E. Stoll's essay 'Art and Artifice in the Iliad'.

minds the wild fury of Achilles. But it is not in that emotional
atmosphere that Hector is to die. The preparatory note of
pity for the Trojans, for Priam and his sons, has been already
struck in the episode of the slaying of Lycaon; and for the
artistic purposes of the poem, Troy in its sympathetic aspect
means Hector. We love Troy, and sympathize with it, so far
as we do, for Hector's sake. Thus, in turning our hearts again
towards pity for the Trojans, he was turning them towards
Hector. Here that theme is gathered together and concen-
trated, and it is Hector surrounded by the memories of those
former scenes that endeared him to us whose death we are
made to see.

He is standing alone outside the walls of Troy, and we
know the time has come for him to die; the poet practically
tells us so (l. 5). Then we see death approaching him in the
baleful figure of Achilles swiftly bearing down upon him
across the plain, and the full significance of the coming event
is brought home to us dramatically in the appeal of Priam
(38-76). It is not just the doom of Hector we are witnessing; it
is the doom of Troy. Priam sees that Hector holds in his hand
the lives of all of them, and through his eyes we see as in a
vision the events that we know actually resulted from the death
of Hector. What is at stake here is shown to us by reminding
us, who know the end, of the sack of Troy and the slaying of
Priam (56-71). It is also at the same time an excellent and
well-judged appeal, putting before Hector the motive most
likely to affect him. The picture is vividly drawn, and serves
as a vivid reminder to us of that future scene, but it is impor-
tant here chiefly as increasing the stature of Hector, and our
sympathies must not be diverted from him to the wider issue.
Observe how we are brought back to him and his personal

tragedy. Priam sees Troy falling as a result of Hector's present
hardihood; Hecuba has no such thoughts. She thinks of no
one but Hector; he is to her just the little son she nursed at
her breast, and all her imagination pictures is the body of her
dead child being foully outraged far from her loving care
(82-89). Could there be a more fitting instrument to turn
our thoughts on the person Hector away from what he stands
for? That is the way she as a mother thinks; Troy means to
her her sons and her sons' lives. Hector is wholly and solely
Hector, not the defender of Troy. Thus, in the most natural
way conceivable, our thoughts, our feelings, are concentrated
on Hector the individual, as we watch the distant figure of
Achilles drawing nearer and looming larger and larger
(90-97).

Of Hector's soliloquy Leaf says:[1] "It is strange that Hector
should not make even a passing allusion to the moving appeals
of his parents, and still more strange that he should thus
entertain the thought of surrender after the vigorous descrip-
tion of his heroic attitude." This soliloquy stands among the
supreme dramatic utterances in the Iliad. The poet has tried
to make us see why Hector does not reply by showing us the
thoughts with which at this dreadful moment his mind is
occupied. Hector knows he is doomed; he knows it because
we know it. It is Hector facing death that we are seeing, and
not the least part of the horror of this, the most terrible book
in the Iliad, is that we should hear the secret thoughts of that
lonely, gallant figure. Hector is held there by his own past
words and as a result of his own folly. To the onlookers it
looks like splendid courage, and it is, but we are forced to
look beneath the surface and to realize that courageous acts

[1] *Commentary*, introduction to Bk. XXII.

often have strange motives behind them. What he is actually seeking, as he stands there with unquenchable courage (ἄσβεστον ἔχων μένος), is some way of escape, or at least he is exploring the possibilities of escape, wondering whether in some way this cup may not pass from him.

This speech brings back to the memory other scenes in which Hector figured and by which he became known to us. For this is the occasion to which they were pointed and for which they were developed as they were. It was in order that Hector might feel this bitter self-reproach which binds him here that the scenes with Polydamas in Bks. XII and XVIII were introduced. One can see how essential that is. Hector knows that if he waits he is almost sure to be killed; he also knows that Troy and all he holds dear will perish in his death. Some convincing motive then is required to justify his risking all, and that motive has been built up through the Polydamas scenes (99-110). We can call the motive moral cowardice if we like, but surely nothing could be more convincing and human and pathetic. But it is not just the dramatic appropriateness of his reflections that I am speaking of. My point is that the poet has planned those earlier scenes with a view to their effect on us now when Hector is going to his death. All these scenes make Hector for us, and his vital place in the poem is this, to die as he does die at the hands of Achilles. Therefore now that the occasion for which they exist has come, the poet is here bringing them back upon the stage in such dramatic fashion as the situation allows.

The thought of surrendering Helen and her wealth (111-117) takes us back to Bk. III, and the circumstances surrounding the duel between Paris and Menelaus. The poet is reminding us of the broken faith on which the cause of Troy

rests, and, just where it is most telling, of Hector's own con-
demnation of it. "The greatness and the sadness of the course
followed by Hector lay in this: that he was the champion of
a cause which was distasteful to him, fighting a foe whom
he regarded as his superior, and, most pathetic of all, he
could not hope for the sympathy of the gods in a cause which
he himself condemned. He was in the war solely as a de-
fender of his family and his state. For these he urged others
to die and for these he himself gave his life. No other charac-
ter in Homer resembles Hector in the motives which led him
to action."[1] I should add to that the pathos of his realization
that all such avenues are now closed, that it is too late to right
the wrong. Not only does he know that Troy is hopelessly
doomed, but he knows that there is no hope of mercy or
consideration for himself; he knows as well as we do that
the death of Patroclus has settled all such questions.

As for the most memorable scene of all, who can fail to be
thinking of it? The very place is reminiscent of it, both for
us and for Hector. He is standing outside the Scaean Gate,
and it was at the Scaean Gate that he parted from Andro-
mache—ὅθι ᾗ ὀάριζε γυναικί (VI, 516). And it is the very
situation she feared:

> δαιμόνιε, φθίσει σε τὸ σὸν μένος, . . .
> . . . τάχα γάρ σε κατακτανέουσιν Ἀχαιοὶ
> πάντες ἐφορμηθέντες.
>
> (VI, 407-410)

("Your courage will be your death . . . for soon the Achaeans
will slay you, all setting upon you.")

That is just what it looks like; the whole Achaean army is
advancing towards the city (ll. 3 and 4), and one figure

---

[1] Scott: *Unity of Homer*, p. 217.

stands before the gate alone. But there is no need to stress the reminiscence; every sympathetic reader's thoughts must be full of that scene. And so are Hector's, but he does not mention her nor make any explicit reference to that sacred hour. "Hector has his death before his eyes; he knows that Achilles is a better man than he; he dares not let himself think of Andromache by name, but, unbidden and half veiled, a symbol of their love rises and lingers in his heart."[1] Hector is resolutely *not* thinking of Andromache, and, as he makes up his mind to stand his ground, he dismisses his irresolution with a half-jest at himself—"This is no lovers' meeting this time; there won't be any opportunity for the pleasant chat I have been picturing."

> οὐ μέν πως νῦν ἔστιν ἀπὸ δρυὸς οὐδ' ἀπὸ πέτρης
> τῷ ὀαριζέμεναι, ἅ τε παρθένος ἠΐθεός τε,
> παρθένος ἠΐθεός τ' ὀαρίζετον ἀλλήλοιιν.

(126-128)

("This is no time to meet and talk to him, as youth and maiden meet by oak or rock, as youth and maiden meet and talk together.")

In the wistful insistence with which he repeats παρθένος ἠΐθεός τε you can see him trying to protect himself from the precise memory and struggling to keep it generalized.

Hector has put aside his hesitation, and resolved to fight it out. Then comes one of the great shocks of the poem. As Achilles draws near, Hector's nerve gives way and he runs (136-137). Now why does the poet do this? Gilbert Murray pronounces this flight of Hector "one of the greatest feats of skill in imaginative literature. It is simple fear, undisguised; yet you feel that the man who flies is a brave man.

[1] Stawell, *op. cit.*, p. 77.

The act of staying alone outside the gate is much; you can just nerve yourself to it. But the sickening dread of Achilles' distant oncoming grows as you wait, till it simply cannot be borne. The man must fly; no one can blame him."[1]

We are witnessing for the first time Achilles on the field of battle, and this meeting with Hector is the climax of his dreadful exploits; the terror of his coming is mounting ever higher and higher, and with the climax of his exploits must come the climax of our terror. For, as Murray has seen, the poet is conveying to *us* the sense of the terror of his coming. From the beginning of the poem we have been waiting for Achilles to take the field, Achilles who has been held before us as the unequalled warrior, acknowledged by the greatest as the greatest beyond compare; all this immense preparation demands something tremendous to satisfy the expectation. The feeling of terror is rising and rising, and as we approach the climax, it must rise still more. And so we are made to stand by Hector's side, and watch the figure of Achilles drawing gradually nearer. "The sickening dread of Achilles' distant oncoming grows as you wait, till it cannot be borne. The man must fly; no one can blame him." The poet reaches, triumphantly expresses, the culmination of our terror (and our hope). We cannot bear it, and so Hector flees. In taking his stand Hector has not overestimated his courage; he has underestimated what it was to meet.[2] The flight of Hector is the final satisfaction of what we expect of Achilles the warrior.

Secondly, it is a device for holding the great climax. This, the event for which the whole poem waits, must be dwelt

---

[1] *Ancient Greek Literature*, p. 42.
[2] See E. E. Stoll: *Art and Artifice in the Iliad.*

upon, made adequate emotionally to its importance. By this
flight and pursuit it is not only held and dwelt upon, but the
holding is made intensely exciting. The excitement grows
and grows until it becomes almost intolerable. The drawing
of it out is done with great but unobtrusive skill. The poet
must make the chase seem long, and yet must avoid monotony.
First he pictures the course by details; we follow them point
by point all round the city (145-161). He measures, as it
were, the length of it, so that we can henceforth follow
with the mind's eye.

"The pursuit must not be too brief," says Jebb;[1] "that
would rob both the heroes of glory. And, in fact, they make
three rounds of the city walls. But how is the poet to main-
tain, and gradually raise, the excitement of so prolonged a
race? How is he to provide that his hearer or reader shall
follow that race to the very end, with an interest which not
only shall not flag, but shall increase from moment to
moment? He has recourse to one of the greatest but most
difficult secrets of Homeric epos—the blending of divine with
human action. They have completed two circuits and the
third is in progress; the intense excitement of the pursuit,
watched by Trojans from the ramparts and by Greeks from
the plain, is marked by the crowning words—'and all the gods
beheld'. The poet then immediately proceeds: '*And to them*
spake the father of gods and men'. In an instant we have been
wafted from the plain of Troy to Olympus, and are listening
to a debate among the gods, which ends in Athena obtaining
leave to help Achilles, and darting down to earth." That is
right; it is a device for expressing the growing excitement,
and helping it to grow. The simple but grand phrase

[1] *Growth and Influence of Classical Greek Poetry*, p. 66.

θεοὶ δ'ἐς πάντες ὁρῶντο ("And all the gods looked on") makes
such a natural transition that we do not feel any inter-
ruption. The scene is one that deserves an audience of gods.
Also, the story is reaching its crisis, and the poet thus calls
attention to the fact. He is noting the progress of his plot,
and as ever does so through the mouth of Zeus and the other
gods. The great moment is coming, and it is as if he said
"Now give your closest attention; we are on the verge of the
death scene of Hector."

But it has greater artistic merits than these. The scene on
Olympus echoes that in Bk. XVI when Zeus in his regret for
Sarpedon had thoughts of revising his plan:

> διχθὰ δέ μοι κραδίη μέμονε φρεσὶν ὁρμαίνοντι,
> ἤ μιν ζωὸν ἐόντα μάχης ἄπο δακρυοέσσης
> θείω ἀναρπάξας Λυκίης ἐν πίονι δήμω,
> ἤ ἤδη ὑπὸ χερσί Μενοιτιάδαο δαμάσσω.

(XVI, 435-438)

("My heart is divided, and I am considering whether I shall
catch him up out of the fight and set him down safe and
sound in the rich land of Lycia, or let him fall now beneath
the hands of Patroclus.")

Here he says:

> ὦ πόποι, ἦ φίλον ἄνδρα διωκόμενον περὶ τεῖχος
> ὀφθαλμοῖσιν ὁρῶμαι· ἐμὸν δ' ὀλοφύρεται ἦτορ
> Ἕκτορος, . . .
> ἀλλ' ἄγετε φράζεσθε, θεοί, καὶ μητιάασθε
> ἠέ μιν ἐκ θανάτοιο σαώσομεν, ἠέ μιν ἤδη
> Πηλείδη Ἀχιλῆϊ δαμάσσομεν ἐσθλὸν ἐόντα.

(168-176)

("Alas, it is a man I love my eyes behold pursued around the
wall; my heart mourns for Hector. . . . But come, ye gods,
consider and decide: shall we save him from death or, for

all his goodness, let him fall now beneath the hands of Achilles?")

And Athena here answers in the very words of Hera there (see p. 159):

> ἄνδρα θνητὸν ἐόντα, πάλαι πεπρωμένον αἴσῃ,
> ἂψ ἐθέλεις θανάτοιο δυσηχέος ἐξαναλῦσαι;

(179-180)

Again as in the former scene the poet is perhaps expressing his own feelings, his momentary shrinking from the cruel necessities of his plot, and certainly giving some relief, some outlet to the feelings of his auditors; if someone did not express the pity and horror of what is happening, of what is going to happen, the pain would be intolerable. Surely this justifies that earlier scene in Bk. XVI as something more than a lovely decoration. It is part of the deepest fabric of the poem. For in repeating here the opening notes of the Sarpedon theme, he sets the ear waiting for its completion. The soothing strain begins again, and, though it is as before immediately interrupted by a return of the fierce battle music, the memory of its close lies in the background of the mind, an undercurrent of hope and comfort that softens a little the horrors that follow.

Zeus dismisses Athena to direct the slaying with the words ἔρξον ὅπῃ δή τοι νόος ἔπλετο, μηδ' ἔτ' ἐρώει (185)—"what thou doest, do quickly"—, and we return with her to the battlefield to find the chase still continuing. This time it is described by two similes, one showing the relentlessness of the pursuit (189-192), the other recognizing and crystallizing the feeling of fascinated horror which makes it seem to last for ever (199-201). That has been the character of the book from the beginning. It is like a slow-motion picture without its grotesqueness. Everything is rushing to a climax, and yet it all stands still—as when we watched Achilles coming swiftly across the plain, the time seemed endless.

The poet now gives warning that the crisis has been reached:

> ἀλλ' ὅτε δὴ τὸ τέταρτον ἐπὶ κρουνοὺς ἀφίκοντο,
> καὶ τότε δὴ χρύσεια πατὴρ ἐτίταινε τάλαντα,
> ἐν δ' ἐτίθει δύο κῆρε τανηλεγέος θανάτοιο,
> τὴν μὲν Ἀχιλλῆος, τὴν δ' Ἕκτορος ἱπποδάμοιο,
> ἕλκε δὲ μέσσα λαβών· ῥέπε δ' Ἕκτορος αἴσιμον ἦμαρ,
> ᾤχετο δ' εἰς Ἀΐδαο, λίπεν δέ ἑ Φοῖβος Ἀπόλλων.

(208-213)

("But the fourth time they reached the springs, then the Father swung out his golden scales and set therein two lots of grievous death, one of Achilles, and one of horse-taming Hector; and holding them in the middle he lifted them; and down sank Hector's day of doom, and was gone to Hades; and Phoebus Apollo left him.")

The preliminaries are over. The end has come. We must brace ourselves for the final scene.

Now, what of the intervention of Athena? How does it affect us, and was that the effect intended? "Needless" and "revolting" Leaf called it; and in another place[1] he says "Why should Athena be invoked to turn against Hector at the last, and, worst of all, to delude him by treachery at the moment when all help was gone? The aesthetic answer to these questions is not easy to find—at least I have never been able to satisfy myself." The answer, I think, is very simple if only we allow ourselves to be affected by it as we are

[1] *Homer and History*, p. 17.

affected. The effect it has on me is to increase enormously my sympathy with Hector at the moment of his slaying, and the whole tone of the rest of the book convinces me that this is exactly the effect intended. The poet has in this book run a great risk. Through the opening portion he has been building up our sympathy with Hector by making us see the coming event through his eyes, and by gathering together all the touching and attractive memories associated with him; and then when the supreme moment comes, he dares to let him run away. It is terrible and life-like and a marvellously ingenious way of holding his crisis, and in the end perhaps it increases the pathos of his slaying, but, for the time being, it does to some extent mar our sympathy for him. *This* is the emotional compensation for that. Let me remind you once again that the poet was composing for listeners, whom he could sway and control by a succession of emotions, and that he could therefore trust much more to momentary and transient effects. So, just before the final scene he swings the audience back to whole-hearted sympathy with Hector; he wipes out, for the moment of the slaying, the emotional effect of the flight, by filling his hearers with indignation at the trick Athena plays on him.

The actual moment of the slaying is heralded by that fearful but perfect expression of utter desolation by Hector— ὦ πόποι, ἦ μάλα δή με θεοὶ θάνατόνδε κάλεσσαν (297)—"the gods have summoned me to death". He knows that he is really alone, that his god has forsaken him (301-303). And so with no other hope but to make a good end, he rushes desperately upon Achilles, and just before the blow falls, just before Achilles, with carefully calculated judgment, stabs with his spear, the poet in his odd way flashes a simile upon us—

οἷος δ' ἀστὴρ εἶσι μετ' ἀστράσι νυκτὸς ἀμολγῷ
ἕσπερος, ὃ, κάλλιστος ἐν οὐρανῷ ἵσταται ἀστήρ.

(317-318)

("Like the evening star, the fairest star in heaven, shining amid its fellows in the glooming of the night.")

What a time to remember the quiet evening sky!

In the words that pass between Achilles and the dying Hector nothing can be clearer than the poet's intention. There is not a trace here of anything noble in Achilles, nothing of the feeling that glimmered through the brutality of Lycaon's slaying (ἀλλά, φίλος, θάνε καὶ σύ). This is sheer unrelieved revenge without a spark of any other feeling to lighten it. All other feelings seem dead. But at the same time it is artistically right; we should be aesthetically disappointed if Achilles had shown the slightest relenting here; because the poet has been building to this point, anything less than this would leave us unsatisfied.

Bk. XXII shows us the wrath of Achilles at its blackest. That is one of the reasons why Hector has been made a sympathetic figure from the beginning; the poet had Achilles in his mind when he composed the parting scene of Hector and Andromache in the sixth book; Hector with his pathos and his beauty and nobility was designed to plumb for us Achilles' passion, to enable us to measure and see into its black deeps. For the heart of the Iliad is the tragedy of Achilles. So he gives us without flinching and without qualification the full horror of hatred working in a soul capable of the extremes of passion. He does this by putting his hero unmistakably and frightfully in the wrong, by heaping up the circumstances which will increase our horror of his conduct and our sympathies with the fallen Hector. He has shown us the chivalry that can exist between two noble enemies, to emphasize the inexorableness of Achilles to the pathetic prayers of Hector; he has shown us, too, that Achilles has been distinguished in the past for generosity to enemies, for his *aidôs*. Think of the Achilles whom Andromache remembered:

ἦτοι γὰρ πατέρ' ἀμὸν ἀπέκτανε δῖος 'Αχιλλεύς, . . .
οὐδὲ μιν ἐξενάριξε, σεβάσσατο γὰρ τό γε θυμῷ,
ἀλλ' ἄρα μιν κατέκηε σὺν ἔντεσι δαιδαλέοισιν
ἠδ' ἐπὶ σῆμ' ἔχεεν.

(VI, 414-419)

("My father glorious Achilles slew . . . but he did not despoil him—the reverence in his heart kept him from that—but he burnt his body with his splendid arms and raised a mound over him.")

And compare him with the Achilles we see now:

ἀμφοτέρων μετόπισθε ποδῶν τέτρηνε τένοντε
ἐς σφυρὸν ἐκ πτέρνης, βοέους δ' ἐξῆπτεν ἱμάντας,
ἐκ δίφροιο δ' ἔδησε, κάρη δ' ἕλκεσθαι ἔασεν
ἐς δίφρον δ' ἀναβὰς ἀνά τε κλυτὰ τεύχε' ἀείρας
μάστιξέν ῥ' ἐλάαν.

(396-400)

("He pierced the tendons of both his feet behind from heel to ankle and bound him with leathern thongs to the chariot, leaving his head to drag; and mounting his chariot and lifting in the glorious arms he lashed his horses forward.")

The poet underlines the pathos of this outrage by his own explicit comment on it:

τότε δὲ Ζεὺς δυσμενέεσσι
δῶκεν ἀεικίσσασθαι ἑῇ ἐν πατρίδι γαίῃ.

(403)

("So Zeus gave him over to his foes to be foully treated in his own fatherland.")

And he follows up Achilles' simple expression of his triumph —"We have won great glory, we have killed the splendid Hector to whom the Trojans prayed as to a god"—with the lamentations of Priam, and Hecuba, and Andromache; that is, sorrow for Hector and Troy occupies the rest of the book and drowns out all other feeling. The voice of lamentation fills the poem.

It is no wonder that Leaf, believing that our sympathies are expected to be with Achilles, not with Hector, is forced to drop the end of the book. It is so obvious that the poet who composed and set here the laments of Priam and Hecuba, and above all the picture of the unconscious Andromache going about her daily routine and preparing as usual for Hector's comfort on his return, meant to fill us with pity. Surely this at least is clearly intended not just to tell us what happened next but to give satisfying expression and hence relief to the feelings of the hearer or reader. Certainly this poet had no doubt where the sympathies of his listeners lay.

BOOKS XXIII AND XXIV

"THE two last books have been regarded by many scholars as additions to the original Iliad. . . . The grounds for this opinion are to be found, in the first instance, in the relation of the two books to the general structure of the poem, and to each other. The following points are worth notice:

"1. Neither of the books in question can be said to be necessary to the poetical completeness of the Iliad. The events of the twenty-second book bring the story to a conclusion, which—to a modern reader at least—leaves nothing to be desired. The anger of Achilles is appeased, his vengeance is satisfied, the danger to the Greeks has passed away. Hence, as Mr. Grote argued, 'the death of Hector satisfies the exigencies of a coherent scheme, and we are not entitled to extend the oldest poem beyond the limit which necessity prescribes.'

"2. The two books do not stand well together. They seem to represent two different ways of bringing the poem to an end. . . . While there might have been room (artistically speaking) for one last book—either the Funeral Games or the Ransoming of Hector—there is not room for both. A second episode, which fills nearly the same space on the poetical canvas, tends to disturb the effect of the first.

"3. This want of unity is accentuated by difference of style and tone. The narrative of the Funeral Games is cheerful and animated, the incidents in more than one place approaching the character of comedy. The twenty-fourth book is pathetic, and full of solemn and touching eloquence. The sudden return from the lighter vein to the gravest manner of the Iliad is certainly awkward, and unlike the art of Homer."[1]

I have quoted this passage from Monro in full because it calls attention to the very points in these two books which make them together form a perfect close to the story of the poem. On this showing we have every reason to be thankful that we have not got the original poem. And indeed that is true throughout; nothing can be plainer, as passage after passage is rejected by this or that scholar, than that the effectiveness of the whole is somehow subtly injured by the omission. The interpolators have done their work well. The Iliad turns out to be better as it is; and certainly nowhere more so than in the addition of the last two books. Bk. XXII so distinctly does not bring the story to a conclusion satisfactory to the modern reader. It leaves us with a feeling of incompleteness in regard to both Achilles and Hector. So much so that those who would stop the poem here have to postulate an ethical outlook on the part of the original audience admittedly unintelligible to us. Of course the story of the Wrath of Achilles might have been so composed as to make the death of Hector a satisfactory end, and it may be there was such a poem; but if so, Bk. XXII as we have it was not part of it. The present book was plainly written for an audience who thought and felt fundamentally like ourselves, was written with the present conclusion of the poem in view.

[1] Monro: vol. II, p. 397.

The base upon which this conclusion is built is the burial motif. Through this the poet sets the imagination looking for and unconsciously demanding the conclusion which, therefore, when it comes, comes as the satisfaction of an imaginative need. First the theme was given out complete. Patroclus killed Sarpedon, and there was a struggle for the possession of the body; it was stripped of its armour and seemed abandoned to the enemy; but the gods stooped down in pity and carried the body to his native Lycia for burial. Then, Hector killed Patroclus, and there was a greater struggle for the body; it too was stripped of its armour, but at last, with the intervention of the gods again, brought home and is now given honoured burial.

Achilles kills Hector, and the body is stripped of its armour. It is lying at the mercy of its enemies, as Sarpedon's did for a little, and Patroclus's for a longer time, and then—what do we wait for? No one who has been reading these books in order can fail to be expecting the coming of Bk. XXIV, or, rather, realizing when it comes that this was what the ear and the mind and the heart were unconsciously listening for. When the funeral of Patroclus in Bk. XXIII repeats the closing cadence of the Sarpedon episode, it confirms the need and creates the assurance of Bk. XXIV.

In Bk. XXII the poet gave us without palliation the full horror of Achilles' fury, and filled the end of the book with sorrow for Hector's death. Now (in Bk. XXIII) he attempts to restore the balance, to carry us back to sympathy with Achilles, and I think that if we surrender ourselves to the poet's guidance, he succeeds. The whole book does something towards softening that harsh figure; but this effect is, in the main, the result of the opening scenes—the picture of Achilles' agony of grief, the formal lamentation of the Myrmidons, and, above all, the vision of the phantom of Patroclus. That is, the figure of Achilles during the games, despite the fact that he is calm, self-possessed, even genial, is a mournful figure throughout because of this well-judged elaboration of his grief at the beginning. It is strong enough and impressive enough to colour his conduct for us through the trivial excitement of the games, so that we feel in his behaviour the changing and chastened mood of Achilles, and that chastened mood as the visible presence of his grief. Just after the lament and vision comes the final outburst of his ferocity in the slaying of the twelve Trojans upon the pyre of Patroclus, an action explicitly condemned by the poet (176). But from there on he is presented in a more congenial light, tactfully allaying quarrels, smoothing over difficulties, alleviating disappointment, considerate of Nestor's touching, and Agamemnon's touchy, pride, in order to make the transition from the Achilles of Bk. XXII to the Achilles of Bk. XXIV. Not that Achilles really changes, but our attitude towards him gets the necessary adjustment, so that we are more ready for the new mood of the last book.

The full and elaborate account of the funeral games just at this point performs a double function. It brings before us again all the chief persons with whom we have been concerned. We bid farewell to them before the poem closes. They are all brought back upon the stage—Menelaus and Agamemnon, Ajax and Odysseus, Diomedes, Nestor, Idomeneus, Antilochus. We see them for the last time among their comrades, and leave them in an atmosphere of kindliness and good fellowship. Secondly, the funeral games gave the poet the opportunity to lighten the mournfulness of the close, and hence to enhance and deepen the effect of its mournfulness. Just as the lower tone of Bks. XX and XXI separated Bk. XVIII from Bk. XXII, so this holds apart the sorrow of Bk. XXII and that of Bk. XXIV, and for the same reason. We have time to get our breath again before our sorrow is renewed.

And yet though the games thus broaden and refresh the solemn close by letting in the light and air of the more trivial interests of men, they do not constitute an interruption. For while the account is largely humorous and naturally in lighter vein, and the contests are described with the full, single-hearted gusto characteristic of Homer, the thread of tragedy runs unobtrusively but unmistakably through it all and keeps the story firm and steady to its mark. This is indicated by the very obvious fact that these are the games in honour of Patroclus; but it is the figure of Achilles that keeps our minds fixed on that mound, and makes our very interest in the contests the symbol of the pathos of the world's forgetfulness of the dead, which thought leads straight to the opening scene of Bk. XXIV, where Achilles is left alone with his unappeasable sorrow (3-18). That is the fact this description is recording; such grief as his is unappeasable. Achilles is seeking rest from his grief, and seeking it in vain. All he can do is to try to still his sorrow by repeating over and over the savage expression of his wrath, and he is finding that revenge has not brought, and can never bring, rest to his grief.

A tale of revenge is a difficult type of story to end satisfactorily. The achievement of the revenge forms its natural close, but is apt to leave the reader or listener dissatisfied, unless it is kept on the simplest lines. It is hard, for one thing, to prevent an undue amount of sympathy going out to the victim, and that creates a discord, and still harder to know in what mood to leave the avenger; he has been moving on such a high level of passion that the sudden cessation of his purpose leaves him imaginatively stranded, as it were.

Now, in Achilles Homer has created a character too big for the simple revenge-story. We have seen too much of the terrific intensity of his feeling to be ready to imagine that his grief could be allayed by revenge. Certainly it would have been much easier if the poet had so constructed his poem that we should have felt the story had its satisfactory conclusion with the slaying of Hector, and there may be so much truth in the theory that the poem should end there—that is, it may be that the simple revenge-story was what the poet began with, and as the character of Achilles grew in his imagination the poem grew to contain it. There can be no end to the grief of such a man. He may repeat, as the poet here shows, for ever and for ever the formal termination, and every day drag the corpse of his enemy round the tomb of his friend, but it will not bring peace to him nor will it convince or satisfy us. What then can the poet do? Achilles' grief can have no ending, but the poem must. The simplest way out of the difficulty would have been to get Achilles killed, and that way lay wide open to him in the recurrent and increasing warning that Achilles' death is near. But his subject is the wrath of Achilles, and he achieves his resolution of that subject without going beyond its limits. The poem ends with the funeral rites of Hector, and it is planned so to end. All through the poet has been building up our sympathy with Hector, so that after his death our chief feeling may be longing for the restoration of his body both for its own sake and for the sake of what it would signify in regard to Achilles. Homer has led us to love Hector and mourn for his death in order to make room for his Achilles.

Let us now consider in more detail the structure of Bk. XXIV. It deserves examination, for even those who choose to regard it as a later addition agree that it forms a perfect ending to the poem.[1]

To begin with one might note that there is no sense of hurry. One often has the feeling when a writer is coming to the end of his story that he has lost interest, and is perfunctorily winding it up as quickly as he can. Here there is no sign of flagging interest, no rushing to his conclusion. With unabated zest the poet sets himself again to fashion another incident with its own little plot and its own climax—the

[1] *e.g.* Leaf, *Companion*, p. 388: "The supreme beauty of the last book of the Iliad, and the divine pathos of the dying fall in which the tale of strife and blood passes away, are above all words of praise. The meeting of Priam and Achilles, the kissing of the deadly hands, and the simplicity of infinite sadness over man's fate in Achilles' reply, mark the high-tide of a great epoch of poetry. In them we feel that the whole range of suffering has been added to the unsurpassed presentation of action which, without this book, might seem to be the crowning glory of the Iliad."

Monro, *op. cit.*, p. 417: "The incidents of the book, especially the meeting in the tent of Achilles, and the reconciliation brought about between Achilles and Priam, are preeminently fitted for the closing scene of the Iliad. On this point we may quote the judgement of a great poet. Writing to a friend, Shelley says: 'I congratulate you on your conquest of the Iliad. You must have been astonished at the perpetually increasing magnificence of the last seven books. Homer there truly begins to be himself. The battle of the Scamander, the funeral of Patroclus, and the high and solemn close of the whole bloody tale in tenderness and inexpiable sorrow, are wrought in a manner incomparable with anything of the same kind.' In the face of such testimony can we say that the book in which this climax is reached—in which the last remaining discords of the Iliad are dissolved in chivalrous pity and respect—is not the work of the original poet, but of some Homerid or rhapsodist?"

journey of Priam—, so that it seems as if what happens merely turned out to be the conclusion of the action. The end of a story is generally artificial, because in real life things do not end, and the concealment of it as an artifice is also an artifice, depending for its success on the amount of emotional satisfaction the artifice gives.

The gods resolve to interfere and bring the thing to an end (23-76). We should not look for any allegorical significance in this. It is an artistic device and has no metaphysical bearing beyond magnifying the importance of the human action by making it so intimate a concern of gods. This has been the poet's regular method of announcing a new turn in his story. The will of Zeus has accompanied us throughout as the dramatized picture of the plan of the poem, and the ending therefore must be somehow represented within that picture too, must be expressed in terms of the divine action. In other words, the gods' part in the poem must be wound up also, and brought into accord with the events of the human story, so that gods and men arrive at the same terminus together.[1] The two strands are accordingly woven together in a repetition of the pitying gods motif which is an integral part of the burial theme. Also it serves as the valedictory of the gods; just as the games brought the mortals before us for the last time, so here we close the scenes on Olympus, and they

---

[1] We, who are not used to gods as an artistic means of externalizing a man's motives or thoughts, perhaps feel that this scene weakens the effectiveness of Achilles' surrender. The intention may have been the reverse, to leave the impression of him unimpaired. As in Bk. I his submission to Agamemnon's taking of Briseis was covered by Athena's command, so here the final responsibility for his swallowing his pride and wrath seems shifted from him sufficiently to disguise artistically his consent (in the interests of the poem) to end an impossible situation.

close too on a note of peace and reconciliation. But its immediate purpose is to set before us a new goal of expectation, to concentrate our interest on a new incident, and, although its outcome is indicated at the beginning, the poet manages to create suspense, to provoke excitement in the telling.

Apollo sets forth in no uncertain terms the dreadful savagery of Achilles' mood (39-54), and Zeus by his careful planning creates the impression that the situation is difficult to handle, and the issue doubtful. He distinctly feels that Achilles has to be managed. He sends Iris to summon Thetis —not simply on the poet's part, because Thetis is the natural person to act as mediator, but as always she brings with her the thought of Achilles' approaching death. The poet impresses the point upon us. When Iris finds her in her hollow cave with the sea-nymphs gathered round her,

> ἡ δ' ἐνὶ μέσσης
> κλαῖε μόρον οὗ παιδὸς ἀμύμονος, ὅς οἱ ἔμελλε
> φθίσεσθ' ἐν Τροίῃ ἐριβώλακι, τηλόθι πάτρης.
>
> (84-86)

("she in their midst was bewailing the doom of her gallant son, who was to die at Troy, far from his fatherland.")

And she herself, urging her son to put away his grief, warns him:

> οὐ γάρ μοι δηρὸν βέῃ, ἀλλά τοι ἤδη
> ἄγχι παρέστηκεν θάνατος καὶ μοῖρα κραταιή.
>
> (131-132)

("You have not long to live; already death stands near you.")

It is essential for the effect of the coming scene that we should be thinking of Achilles as on the verge of death.

Once more, as in Bk. I, we see Thetis on Olympus (93-120). Then she was sent there by Achilles to Zeus; now it is Zeus

who sends her to Achilles. The threads woven at the outset
are beginning to unwind. She gives her message, and receives
a terse and somewhat enigmatic reply[1]:

τῇδ' εἴη ὃς ἄποινα φέροι καὶ νεκρὸν ἄγοιτο,
εἰ δὴ πρόφρονι θυμῷ 'Ολύμπιος αὐτὸς ἀνώγει.

(139-140)

And in the elaboration of the account of Priam's mission
everything is done to surround it for us, despite the assurance
of Zeus, with a sense of danger. Indeed Zeus's preparation
to ensure his safety itself emphasizes it, and Hecuba's desperate
protest when she hears of his resolution, in showing her fear,
serves to remind us of the extreme apparent peril of such a
journey, and brings out Priam's own misgiving (218-227). His
outburst of unreasoning wrath against his friends and his
sons is a vividly human touch, as showing the tenseness of the
strain he is under, the greatness of the fear that underlies his
resolution. He has nerved himself to it, and his own belief
that he is going on something worse than a fool's errand
expresses itself in this sudden fury.

The very fact that we are made to watch every detail of
the preparations (the gathering together of the gifts, the
harnessing of the mule-wagon) increases the feeling of
tension. Hecuba makes one last attempt to shake his reso-
lution by suggesting that he should seek reassurance from
Zeus, and if that fails he should not go. Despite the omen,
and the momentary encouragement it gives them, as he drives

[1] Enigmatic enough for different interpretations to be put on it.
Some, placing a colon after εἴη, understand "So be it; let him that
brings the ransom take the body." Others, regarding ἄγοιτο as co-
ordinate with φέροι, which seems more natural, "He who may bring
ransom and take the body, may be here", which means "Let him come,
the man who would bring the ransom and take the body."

forth, "all his friends followed him with loud lamentations as if he were going to his death" (327-328).

Hermes' part too is well managed from the point of view of story interest. He comes to Priam and Idaeus as an unknown man, increasing their terror (354-360), and Priam's relief at his courtesy is again alarmed by the stranger's recognition of him (387-389).

Hermes' protection is necessary to account for Priam's getting to Achilles undetected. The thing could have been managed otherwise, no doubt, by slower and more prosaic means, but the poet's aim is not historical verisimilitude but dramatic effect. He has constructed his account of the journey solely with a view to bringing Priam and Achilles face to face and giving the drama of their meeting time to establish itself in our minds.

I have noted how Homer marks for the ear the closing of an incident or a part by bringing back in a new form the theme or themes with which it began. So here, in the last book of the Iliad, incidents of the first book recur. The scene on Olympus where Zeus sends Thetis to Achilles, the visit of Thetis to her son, bidding him put away his vengeance, and Achilles' acceptance of Priam's supplication repeat in reverse order the events of Bk. I, and each undoes what had there been done. It is like a gigantic rhyme with Bk. I, bringing to ear and mind the feeling of a close, of things rounded off and completed. The culmination of this returning movement is the meeting of Priam and Achilles. It repeats on a grand scale the scene with which the action began. (Notice the effective verbal echo in Priam's λυσόμενος παρὰ σεῖο, φέρω δ' ἀπερείσι' ἄποινα—"I have come to redeem him from you and I bring unmeasured ransom"—of I, 13 λυσόμενός τε θύγατρα φέρων τ' ἀπερείσι' ἄποινα—"who came to redeem his daughter bringing unmeasured ransom.") "It was no accident," says Sheppard,[1] "but a masterstroke of composition that made the Iliad begin with the wrong done by King Agamemnon to a suppliant father, and end with the right done by Achilles to the helpless Priam." That deed started the long series of tragic happenings, which is the poem; this reversal of it fitly marks its close. The theme is heard again with the discord in it resolved.

For it is more than a formal device. A good poet's rhymes fill and satisfy the mind as well as the ear. And here comes what we have been unconsciously waiting for and desiring. The wrath of Achilles has run its dreadful course, and there is not only an end, but satisfaction and a great peace. It is no tacked-on ending, for the solution it offers comes out of the poem itself; it resolves the discord in our thoughts and in the character of Achilles. The Achilles we see here is not a new Achilles. One immediately recognizes, not his acceptance of the suppliant merely, but his beautiful compassion for him as having been involved from the beginning. Though it comes with all the quality of a glorious surprise, it at the same time reveals and consummates a long-waiting expectation. By a few strong strokes here and there we have been imaginatively prepared for just this moment; Andromache read aright the heart of her foe.

But we have not been wrong to fear for Priam. We have lost nothing of Achilles; he is not changed; all of him is here. He is as fierce and dangerous as ever. Just as we are feeling at peace with him, we are suddenly made aware of the struggle that is going on within him against the terrific

[1] *Pattern*, p. 208.

passion of his grief. The way the sense of this struggle is communicated is a triumph of dramatic imagination. There is not a word of analytic comment; perhaps the poet was incapable of such reflective analysis; he just saw in his mind's eye what Achilles did, and reproduced it for us to see. Achilles' innermost feelings are revealed in his actions. That is imagination communicating to imagination.

Achilles has raised up the kneeling Priam, the gesture which signified the acceptance of a suppliant, and has spoken to him words of the profoundest sympathy and understanding. Priam presses him to confirm instantly what is implied in this action:

> μή πώ μ' ἐς θρόνον ἷζε, διοτρεφές, ὄφρα κεν Ἕκτωρ
> κεῖται ἐνὶ κλισίῃσιν ἀκηδής, ἀλλὰ τάχιστα
> λῦσον, ἵν' ὀφθαλμοῖσιν ἴδω.
>
> (553-555)

("Bid me not yet sit down while Hector lies here uncared for, but quickly release him that I may see him with my eyes.")

His insistence, besides irritating Achilles, brings home to him the full significance of what he is doing, and he finds it is going to be almost beyond what he can bear; his wrath wells up again and threatens to overwhelm him:

> μηκέτι νῦν μ' ἐρέθιζε, γέρον· νοέω δὲ καὶ αὐτὸς
> Ἕκτορά τοι λῦσαι, . . .
> τῶ νῦν μή μοι μᾶλλον ἐν ἄλγεσι θυμὸν ὀρίνῃς,
> μή σε, γέρον, οὐδ' αὐτὸν ἐνὶ κλισίῃσιν ἐάσω
> καὶ ἱκέτην περ ἐόντα.
>
> (560-570)

("Provoke me no further, old man; it is my purpose to release Hector to you. . . . So wake not my wrath again in my sorrows, lest even within my walls I keep not my hands from you, suppliant though you be.")

In his agony of mind and fear of himself he bursts from the room, but goes to comply with the very demand that has so enraged him, *viz.*, to arrange for the instant release of Hector's body. Hastily and with complete understanding of Priam's feelings (584), he prepares the body so that it may not seem "uncared for" (ἀκηδής) and places it with all marks of honour upon the cart for its return. Then, with a passionate prayer to Patroclus to forgive him for what he is doing, which reveals the agony the effort costs him, he puts away his wrath and returns to Priam.

> υἱὸς μὲν δή τοι λέλυται, γέρον, ὡς ἐκέλευες,
> κεῖται δ' ἐν λεχέεσσι.

(599-600)

("Your son is released, sir, as you asked, and lies on his bier.")

In another way, too, we have been imaginatively prepared for this scene. The range of the story was set for us long ago, and its end foreshadowed. In that earlier supplication when he rejected the suppliants in his obstinate pride and bitterness, the old Phoenix said: "Prayers are the daughters of Zeus, halting and wrinkled and furtive-eyed, whose task it is to follow in the steps of Ate. But Ate is strong and sound of foot, and easily outruns the prayers, and goes before them over all the earth, making men fall, and the prayers come afterwards to heal the hurt." Such has indeed been Achilles' experience, and the prayers have arrived at last, and so far as it may be the hurt is healed. And for us too, so far as may be, the hurt is healed; for this is the end of a tragedy; we cannot expect or even desire a happy ending. Hector is dead; Achilles, Priam, and all Troy are going forward to their death. Nor are we to feel that Achilles' grief is allayed; that can never be as long as he lives, or, according

to himself,[1] even longer. Here is indeed on all sides "inex-
piable sorrow". The poem lifts to its close, instead of, as so
often happens, sinking to it. Achilles' grief and our regret and
sympathy become here something larger. They expand into
a universal sorrow and a universal sympathy for the doom of
humankind. As the young Achilles, already within the
shadow of death, looks upon the old, bereaved, ruined Priam
kneeling before him and lifting to his lips the hand that slew
his son, "he wept", thinking of the young Patroclus now dead,
and "Priam wept", thinking of Hector, "and Achilles pitied
the grey head and the grey beard, and sprang from his seat,
and raised the old man by the hand" (509-516). And then he
speaks the words that seem the only adequate commentary on
the scene, words in which, as Butcher says,[1] "he rises above
the personal sorrow to the height of human pity, and draws
a picture never yet surpassed of 'the lot the gods have spun
for miserable men.'" And though the scene is one of almost
unendurable pathos, and though the picture Achilles draws is
a grim one, the words he speaks are strong, wholesome, and
strangely healing words. They bring out the fact that, as these
two enemies, with the deadliest causes of hatred between
them, meet face to face in the shadow of death, they recognize
that they are united in the sorrow and the splendour of their
common humanity.

Thus does the poet bring the story of the Wrath of
Achilles to a triumphant artistic conclusion in the expression

[1] εἰ δὲ θανόντων περ καταλήθοντ' εἰν 'Αΐδαο   ,
αὐτὰρ ἐγὼ καὶ κεῖθι φίλου μεμνήσομ' ἑταίρου.

(XXII, 389-390).
("if in Hades the dead are forgotten, yet even there will I
remember my dear comrade.")
Aspects of the Greek Genius, p. 139.

by Achilles not simply of his sorrow nor of Priam's sorrow, but of the tragedy inherent in the conditions of human life. "With the atonement offered to a noble enemy our thoughts are raised above the fierce passions of the moment, and even above the strife of Greek and Trojan. The bereavement of Priam, the loss of Patroclus, the impending fate of Achilles himself, are seen in their profound tragic meaning as examples of the infinite sadness of human things."[1] I say a triumphant artistic conclusion because it thus crystallizes the feelings that have been accumulating throughout the poem. In incident after incident the mind has been haunted with a sense of the greatness of the human spirit that rises above the misery and futility of the conditions in which it finds itself. Here that feeling is given explicit expression, and the mind rests on it as at a goal attained. The poem seems to gather itself together, to compass the utterance to which it has been striving. The poet's vision of life receives its seal and consummation.

It is the story of Achilles and the figure of Achilles—the dominating story and the dominating figure—that embody and focus this vision. Individual and unique as he is, Achilles typifies humanity in its greatness and in its sorrow and feebleness. His is an extreme case of the case of every man. Man as such is ὠκύμορος—of swift doom; Achilles is ὠκυμορώτατος —of swiftest doom; and he is all on that scale; he is superlatively heroic man. The glory and the brevity of human life— that is the double theme that keeps sounding through the entire Iliad; and glory and foreknowledge of early death are the things that control and shape the outlook and conduct of Achilles. Thus this arresting figure conveys immediately into the imagination the sense of the doom and salvation of humankind, as one age of the world saw them. Achilles

[1] Monro, *op. cit.*, p. 418.

measures the height of human splendour as that age conceived it, and sounds the depths of human sorrow. The poem as a whole pictures heroic human life, but the meaning of that life is embodied, symbolized in the story of Achilles. This is what makes his story something more than a moral tragedy, more than a tragedy of character. It is that, certainly, and the scene of the meeting of Achilles and Priam ends this tragedy satisfactorily in that it restores the character of the hero to harmony with itself and us to sympathy with him. But it does more. The splendour of humanity and the sorrow of humanity here meet under the shadow of death and are reconciled in a noble and universal compassion that has no touch of resignation but is exhilarating, making the sorrow part of the splendour, plucking the splendour out of the sorrow.

On that note the story as such ends. The storms of passion and hatred have ceased, and with the mind thus uplifted by a realization of the greatness of the events we have witnessed, there comes a sense of peace, which the poet holds in the high and solemn close. The story is over, and the return of Hector to Troy is the symbol of the content with which we watch the action die away. The poet thus expresses, and so ingeniously confirms, the emotional satisfaction in its close.